W0259484

PAKISTAN'S TERROR CONUNDRUM

PAKISTAN'S TERROR CONUNDRUM

KHALED AHMED

PENGUIN
VIKING
An imprint of Penguin Random House

VIKING

USA | Canada | UK | Ireland | Australia
New Zealand | India | South Africa | China | Singapore

Viking is part of the Penguin Random House group of companies whose addresses can be found at global.penguinrandomhouse.com

Published by Penguin Random House India Pvt. Ltd
4th Floor, Capital Tower 1, MG Road,
Gurugram 122 002, Haryana, India

First published in Viking by Penguin Random House India 2020

Portions of this book appeared originally in the *Indian Express, Newsweek Pakistan, Friday Times* and *Dawn*
Pages 255-60 are an extension of the copyright page

10 9 8 7 6 5 4 3 2 1

ISBN 9780670095087

Typeset in Adobe Garamond Pro by Manipal Technologies Limited, Manipal
Printed at Replika Press Pvt. Ltd, India

www.penguin.co.in

For Iqbal Z. Ahmed,
chairman of the Associated Group and
founder of Newsweek Pakistan,
where most of the content of this book was first published

Contents

Preface

As the Twig Is Bent

Most of the chapters in this book have been published in *Newsweek Pakistan*, *Indian Express*, *Friday Times* and *Dawn* over the years. I am grateful to the editors of these publications for their cooperation and support. The concerns raised in this book are as relevant today as they were when they were originally published.

This book describes the pain the people of Pakistan went through after the establishment of the state amid communal violence and a collective consciousness of danger. Conflict began soon after the creation of the state, with military action establishing the primacy of the army in Pakistan. Democracy was disputed from the outset between politicians nurtured by the British Raj and the clergy that advocated a utopia in which Islam was to be the ideological guide.

An unstable Pakistan, at war with neighbouring India, came to be dominated by the generals who wished to 'guide' the new state to security, but whose interference in governance inaugurated what is called the era of dictatorships. Pakistan was dismembered in 1971. The memory of this dismemberment permanently changed the way the country thought of itself. The present volume accounts for the events after the Soviet–Afghan War in 1979, when the global superpowers clashed in Pakistan's neighbourhood and encouraged it to take part in the conflict through its 'non-state actors', with whom the country soon learned to share sovereignty. The book describes the survival of the state in the midst of these non-state actors armed with superior ideology and immunity from law.

The state of Pakistan was founded on the 'consensus' that it has to be Islamic. As a religious state, it seeks sharia as an ideal. All states must seek an ideal as their foundational teleology. There is muted disagreement between ideologues and pragmatists over this ideal. It is muted because of intimidation, but it is definitely there, especially after the Talibanization of the country through illegal action by the Islamists. It is the threat of religion as an extra-legal force that is causing many Pakistanis to wonder if the state can move forward into the future with Islam as its credo.

The founding party, the All-India Muslim League (popularly called Muslim League), was apparently open only to Muslims because of its name. It challenged unsuccessfully the right of the Indian National Congress (INC) to represent Muslims too. The politics of the Muslim League unfolded in the midst of communal disharmony. Its 'separatist' electoral pitch compelled it to use Islam as a slogan. Muhammad Ali Jinnah used it too. He used the word 'sharia', but it is doubtful that he knew sharia the way Allama Iqbal did, which led the Allama to reject the Quranic Hudood laws, which later compelled General Zia-ul-Haq to reject Allama Iqbal. Jinnah more likely knew it through his legal practice in Muslim family law.

It is interesting to note that when in 1949 the Constituent Assembly of Pakistan adopted the Objectives Resolution, it used the less-threatening terms 'Quran' and 'Sunnah' rather than sharia, which later came to be embedded in Article 203(C) of the Constitution and is related to the Federal Shariat Court. The politicians who signed the resolution knew nothing about what the 'guiding code' meant, as they reassured the non-Muslim members that they would be equal citizens. The non-Muslims, not easily consoled, came down to Lahore only to learn from the clerics that they would be *zimmi*s (non-Muslim subjects of a state governed according to the sharia) who would have to pay a special tax. When General Zia shoved the Objectives Resolution into the Constitution through the 8th Amendment, he removed the word 'freely' from the sentence, which assured the non-Muslims that they would be able to practise their religion freely. No notation was made in regard to the change of text. In 1949, the resolution had 'God Almighty' in its first paragraph; it was changed to 'Almighty Allah' in 1953 without any reference to the assembly that had passed it. The guiding principles, passed off as harmless in 1949, became menacing for both Muslims and non-Muslims with the passage of time.

Pakistan became less and less viable as it converged on sharia. Jihad used to be the grand Islamic subterfuge, confusing the world about war and 'peaceful effort'; now it is straightforward *qital* (killing). It used to be accepted that jihad could only be declared by the state. Now it is consensually privatized and internationalized, thus undermining a fundamental function of the state. On the law of evidence, if a scholar leans on the Quranic text to challenge the clergy on the half testimony of a Muslim woman, he is told to shut up because sharia has already decided the matter. Sharia is what *fiqh* (Islamic jurisprudence) makes of the Quran and Sunnah. An Egyptian professor at the Saudi-funded International Islamic University of Islamabad contended that infibulation (female circumcision) was sharia in Egypt, under the practiced Shafi'i fiqh, but banned 'wrongly' under the official Hanafi fiqh.

It is the doctrine of *amr bil maruf wa nahi an al-munkir* (approving the good and stopping that which is banned) with which began the dismantlement of the state of Pakistan. It consists of taking vigilante action against *munkiraat* (banned practices), implying a rejection of state authority that is purported to be replaced by vigilantes. With jihad representing the external face of the Islamic state and *amr-nahi* (where 'amr' means command and 'nahi' means 'no') representing the internal face, the state is converted into a destructive black hole on the world map. An internally failed state because of 'amr' and 'nahi' is seen attacking other states through its armed citizens, that too without legal cover. The state is committed to ban modern banking, insurance and lotteries, etc., under sharia.

An Islamic state intent on a sharia-based revolution embraces isolationism as its programme, almost like the Stalinist slogan of 'socialism in one country'. After 1947, the state misunderstood itself as a castle of Islam. It fondly thought of itself as a society cut-off—that is what the word 'castle' means—from the rest of the world, with an ability to stand up to hostile sieges. It also presaged the totalitarianism of the clergy after the 'modern' state was overthrown. Pakistan also allowed the transnational concept of the umma to inform its ideology. It acknowledged that the concept of the nation state was not compatible with its teleology because of the concept of umma.

When it tested its first atom bomb, the state of Pakistan could not for long keep up the pretended doctrine that it was India-specific. It was soon acclaimed as an Islamic bomb, a transnational weapon that would threaten not only India but many other states across the globe. The moment it became a religious bomb, its transformation into a sectarian one was inevitable. Many respectable scholars believe that Pakistan's Sunni bomb caused Iran's Shia bomb to be produced. Just as a religious state Pakistan cannot avoid becoming a sectarian one, conceptually, its bomb too threatens Iran, in addition to threatening the entire non-Muslim world.

The terrorist outreach of political Islam is being opposed by strong powers that have the capacity to strike at its incubation grounds. If this polarity is interpreted as Christianity versus Islam, then Islam doesn't benefit from the neutrality of the non-Christian world either. In fact, the non-Christian world feels equally threatened and is inclined to forget its contradictions with the dominant Christian powers, seeking to form an alliance with it to confront Islam. Given this near-total opposition of the world, political Islam, thriving on lack of secular education, has little chance of surviving as a winning force. Political Islam can only eat its own children.

The Islamic state is not viable in modern times unless Islam is reinterpreted. This is not the project of Islam today; this inclination to change the world by force to fit sharia. This springs from the intellectual attitude of not rejecting the premise when it fails to encompass reality. The suicide bomber of today is an agent of forcible change of reality to the premise of Islam. When not democratic, the Muslim state begins its process of decline as a state denying rights; when Islamic, it begins its process of decline under challenge from the clergy; when theocratic, it achieves stability by suppressing demands for rights under the doctrine of *fasad fil ard* (corruption on earth). The theocratic stage is the terminal stage, after which the state is either undone or finds refuge in reverting to the identity of the modern state with economic imperatives overriding religious passions. Pakistan is in the process of entering the terminal phase and is looking at itself once again in 2020, hesitating in the face of a possible negative reaction from a scared world.

Introduction

Facing the Fallout

In September 2019, the Paris-based thirty-nine-member Financial Action Task Force (FATF), founded to combat money laundering and terror-funding, strongly urged Pakistan to comply with its demands by February 2020 or face being included in the FATF 'blacklist'—meaning sanctions. It said: 'To date, Pakistan has only largely addressed five of the 27 action items, with varying levels of progress made on the rest of the action plan.'[1]

Pakistan has been on the 'grey list' of the FATF because many of its 'non-state actors' used in proxy wars supposedly belonged to other states, such as Afghanistan, Uzbekistan and China. China was earlier heading the FATF through Xiangmin Liu of the People's Bank of China, when he was the president of the force. It's not only Afghanistan and Uzbekistan that complain about Pakistan keeping their terrorists on its territory; China, too, is a complainant. In 2017, it got together with Brazil, Russia, India and South Africa, as part of the trading bloc called BRICS, to express 'joint concern' about Pakistan-based terrorists listed as 'Eastern Turkistan Islamic Movement, Islamic Movement of Uzbekistan, Haqqani network, Lashkar-e-Taiba (LeT), Jaish-e-Mohammed (JeM), Tehrik-i-Taliban Pakistan and Hizb ut-Tahrir'.

Pakistan has had to act on the FATF's directions because of China. It can't afford to offend China and knows that it has not been very mindful of the Uighur Muslims from Chinese Xinjiang on its soil, allegedly engaging in cross-border terrorism. Pakistan has therefore put the leaders of major terrorist organizations under house arrest and taken over their madrasas, where hundreds of thousands of young men learn how to become 'pious warriors' in the service of Islam. Much of this takeover is credible, but a lot more remains to be done, as the FATF has observed. It does remain doubtful though whether or not Pakistan can run the madrasas competently when its own schools are in a bad shape.

Andrew Small, in *The China–Pakistan Axis: Asia's New Geopolitics*, revealed that Lal Masjid, or the Red Mosque, of Islamabad was attacked by Pakistani commandos in 2007 after China warned that the mosque, a watering hole for al-Qaeda and its affiliated terrorists, right in the heart of the capital city Islamabad, was sheltering Uighurs from China who had attacked and captured some Chinese working in a massage parlour in the city.[2] When the assault on the mosque was over, fourteen Uighur terrorists were found among the dead. No one in Pakistan got to know that the attack on the mosque was triggered by a Chinese protest.

Ahmed Rashid, in *Pakistan on the Brink*, the third book in his trilogy on the same subject, observed:

> China now faces the threat of Islamic militancy. Chinese Muslims, or Uighurs, from Xingjian have long journeyed to Pakistan to trade and to perform hajj in Saudi Arabia along a route that was part of the ancient Silk Road. But in the 1980s,

> Uighurs went to study in Pakistani madrasas and then went on to fight the Soviets Afghanistan. Now some are fighting along with the Taliban. Uighur nationalism is becoming much stronger in Chinese Xinjiang, but the greater fear is that Uighur Islamic extremism will grow; it is still a minor threat, but China blames Islamic groups for unrest in its eastern province.[3]

China is most upset over the East Turkestan Islamic Movement (ETIM), which was declared a terrorist organization in 2002 by the United Nations (UN). In October 2003, the Pakistan Army claimed to have killed ETIM leader Hasan Mahsum. In January 2010, his successor, Abdul Haq Turkistani, was reportedly killed in a US drone attack. Both of them were in Pakistan's Federally Administered Tribal Areas (FATA), which was merged with Khyber Pakhtunkhwa in 2018. An earlier outfit not ousted by Pakistan is the Islamic Movement of Uzbekistan that grew into a pan-Central Asian group and was ensconced in FATA recruiting Uighurs into terrorism. Yet another group upset China. This was the Turkistan Islamic Party which, in September 2011, claimed responsibility for some attacks in Xinjiang.

In 2009, al-Qaeda in Pakistan, too, launched attacks within China. It called for attacks on Chinese interests after riots in Xinjiang's Ürümqi left 200 Han Chinese Uighurs dead. After that, one could not blame China for getting alarmed by the shadowy Uighur warriors taking refuge in FATA. The Pakistani military intelligence, the Inter-Services Intelligence (ISI), has regularly informed the Chinese about Uighurs operating out of Pakistan, which has helped the Chinese pre-empt attacks. The ISI finally captured and extradited fourteen Uighurs to China in 1997, seven in 2002, nine in 2009 and five in 2011, 'including a woman and two children'.

In July 2011, the Uighurs attacked a police station in Hotan—or Khotan—in China, killing twenty, thus leading *China Daily*, on 2 August 2011, to reveal that the attackers had undergone training at some ETIM camps in Pakistan. Rashid writes: 'This prompted ISI chief General Pasha to rush to Beijing, where he reassured the Chinese that Pakistan would counter the ETIM.' In 2011, China also demanded the return of Uighurs settled in Malaysia, Thailand, Cambodia, Nepal and Kazakhstan.

Islamic State of Iraq and Syria (ISIS) in Pakistan

United States (US) President Donald Trump declared that on 27 October 2019, Abu Bakr Al-Baghdadi, the 'caliph' of the terrorist organization ISIS, also called IS, killed himself in a hideout with a suicide jacket when approached by a team of American commandos in the Idlib province of north-eastern Syria, next to the Turkish border. His bodily remains were collected and thrown into the sea, a repeat of what was done to Osama bin Laden after he was killed by American commandos in Pakistan in 2011.

Al-Baghdadi created a caliphate in Syria–Iraq in 2014, under an interpretation of Islam that the Muslims had been nursing off and on as a rejectionist–nihilistic world view: Kill the infidel, enslave their women and carry out permanent jihad against whatever world order holds sway. He actually believed that Prophet Muhammad himself practised this evil way of life and got non-Muslims to be looted and raped by his warriors. Al-Baghdadi killed Shias, a majority in his native Iraq, and enslaved an ancient Kurdish sect called the Yazidi, using its women as sex slaves. Around 5000 'warriors', mostly interested in copulation, arrived from foreign lands to join the caliphate, including girls from Europe to offer sex to the Muslim warriors as war-wives. This was the most shameful phase of Islam known in history: 143 attacks in 29 countries killing 2043, mostly Muslims.

Look at this sex fatwa:

> Yazidi women and children [are to be] divided according to the Shariah amongst the fighters of the Islamic State who participated in the Sinjar operations [in northern Iraq] . . .

> Enslaving the families of the *kuffar* [infidels] and taking their women as concubines is a firmly established aspect of the Shariah that if one were to deny or mock, he would be denying or mocking the verses of the Koran and the narrations of the Prophet . . . and thereby apostatizing from Islam.[4]

Many were attracted to the caliphate, including one 'commander' from India, who was recently killed in Afghanistan. In September 2015, in Pakistan, Khalid Cheema went to the police after his wife, Bushra, and their four children went missing from their home in Lahore's Johar Town. In October, Cheema finally heard from her. 'I love God and his religion, and I want to die a martyr's death,' she said in a voice message. 'If you can't join us, then at least pray your wife and children die in jihad.'

A minister in Lahore proudly asserted: 'She is one of the fifty Pakistanis who left for Syria. France has admitted that 1000 of its citizens have joined the ISIS, yet no one is accusing France of allowing the ISIS to establish a network there.' Many Pakistani cities boasted graffiti and banners from 'inspired' citizens ready to participate in the exciting movement called jihad. A number of militant groups and radical organizations, including Islamabad's infamous Lal Masjid, pledged their support to the caliphate and its self-proclaimed caliph. The police in Karachi detained six women thought to be recruiting other women on behalf of the IS; and the police in Sialkot detained eight young men, previously affiliated with Hafiz Saeed's Jamaat-ud-Dawah (JuD), who were recruiting for the ISIS. The police found weapons, explosives and discs with ISIS literature from these men.

A PEW Research Centre survey in 2015 found that only 14 per cent Pakistanis thought the ISIS was a threat. Around 62 per cent wouldn't give a clear opinion. The women who defected to the caliphate, or the ISIS, were formerly members of Al-Huda International, a women's Islamic organization then much favoured by the upper-class ladies of Pakistan. (Tashfeen Malik, the co-accused in the December 2015 shooting in San Bernardino,

California, that left fourteen dead and twenty-two wounded, was also once an Al-Huda member.)

Akbar S. Ahmed, in *Journey into Europe*, reports about a Pakistani girl in Scotland who became part of the caliphate. Aqsa was raised in an affluent Glasgow neighbourhood and attended a prestigious private school before enrolling in university.[5] Ahmed writes that according to Aqsa, 'the greatest threat to Islam and the Islamic State was the Shia, whom she blamed for the deaths of so many Syrians.'

Abu Bakr al-Baghdadi is dead. And Islam as a religion has taken a beating unless Muslims sit back and rethink their faith after rejecting the exegetes interpreting their faith as a jihad of savage cruelty.

Pakistan's 'Blunder'?

Imran Khan, during his September 2019 visit to the US, said, 'Pakistan, by joining the US after 9/11', committed one of the biggest blunders. As many as 70,000 Pakistanis died in this. Some economists say we lost $150 billion, some say $200 billion. On top of it, we were blamed by the US for not winning in Afghanistan.'[6]

A more objective economist summed up the plight of Pakistan thus:

> Pakistan faces a vicious debt trap and the balance-of-payments situation remains precarious. Foreign reserves plunged to just over US$8 billion in October 2018. It met its debt-servicing requirements only by borrowing more. Its current account deficit widened by 43 per cent to $18 billion in 2018, while the fiscal deficit ballooned to 6.8 per cent of gross domestic product. The country's central bank has devalued the rupee four times since December 2017, weakening it by more than 20 per cent.
>
> The government's financial administrators realized that they required a bailout of roughly $10 billion to $15 billion.

> Though a fresh bailout package from the International Monetary Fund was negotiated after serious hiccups, a new set of military-approved bureaucrats had to be brought in. Difficult tax burdens and resource-mobilization parameters have been imposed. Much will depend on this straitjacket. In the short term, it could involve a further devaluation of the rupee and increases in gas and electricity prices, which will add to inflationary pressures hurting not only the poor but also the business classes.[7]

Khan, replying to former US secretary of defence James Mattis' statement that Pakistan was the most dangerous country in the world, said, 'They [the insurgent groups] were indoctrinated into fighting foreign occupation [by the Soviet Union] as jihad. But now, when the US arrived in Afghanistan, it was supposed to be terrorism.'[8]

After the Soviet invasion, the US thought it could end the rule of the Communist Party in the Union of Soviet Socialist Republics (USSR) by cornering the Soviet army in Afghanistan and forcing it to surrender. Muslim 'warriors' arrived from all over the Islamic world, funded by the US and Saudi Arabia jointly. And Pakistan was dishing out hospitality and raking in 'assistance' for its wobbly economy then.

Prime Minister Khan said he was opposed to Pakistan joining the international war in Afghanistan 'from day one'. Yet, for General Musharraf who ruled Pakistan earlier, the Soviets were from 'the other side'—against the US and its allies, which included Pakistan. For him, the Soviet invasion meant the entry of India next door as a part of its 'encirclement' strategy. Pakistan had tasted its last defeat at the hands of India in 1971.

Pakistan was bothered by the Moscow-supported Kabul government that leaned on India to complete the 'strategic nutcracker' that would make Pakistan forget Kashmir. The Durand Line was challenged, and propaganda was unleashed to indoctrinate 'unhappy' Pakistani elements in Balochistan and the tribal areas. The warriors arriving in Pakistan carried an Islamic consensus of jihad against 'godless' Soviet Union. There was no way an 'Islamic' Pakistan could avoid joining the American war against the Soviet Union in Afghanistan.

Khan added, with hindsight: 'While fighting the Soviets, jihad was glorified. Jihadis were heroes. Their war against the Soviets was "organized by Pakistan's ISI that trained these militants who were invited from all over the Muslim world to do jihad".'[9]

On 11 September 2001, the 'Islamic warriors', headed by Osama bin Laden, thought they could also liberate the world from the US hegemony that raised Israel above the entire Islamic world through wars that the Arabs kept losing. The plot to attack New York was conceived in Karachi by al-Qaeda's Khalid Sheikh Mohammed; the nineteen warriors chosen for the 9/11 attack were made to meet bin Laden, for which they had to travel through Pakistan. But al-Qaeda, in the long run, was not comprised of foreign warriors alone. Later, a majority of them were Afghans and Pakhtuns, many trained by the ISI's Colonel Imam inside Afghanistan. He was killed by the Pakistani Taliban in 2010.

Pakistan could not have wanted it, but it was the 'host' country which served as the headquarters of the 'warriors' serving the US. Of course, Pakistan should have stayed out of what happened after 9/11, as Imran Khan said. But could it really?

The UN Security Council Resolution 1373, which made it possible to attack the Taliban government in Kabul, was adopted on 28 September 2001. It was adopted by the Security Council under Chapter 7 of the UN Charter, making it compulsory for all member states under the pain of sanctions. Pakistan saw India readying to offer a base for the US warplanes on its territory and had to pre-empt it by offering bases of its own in Balochistan.

General Musharraf knew what a Chapter 7 resolution meant; it was not like the Security Council resolution on Kashmir that was merely 'advisory', because it was under Chapter 6. Had Imran Khan been in power, he couldn't have defied it. However, there was another 'unavoidable' reason.

For an Islamic, worry-beads-in-hand Imran Khan, the Islamization of Pakistan would have been irresistible. Pakistan's jihad was inspired by the co-founder of al-Qaeda, Abdullah Azzam, who also founded the Islamic University of Islamabad and brought the concept of 'terrorist' jihad into the heart of the Pakistani state. He was himself killed in Peshawar because of al-Qaeda's internal struggle for leadership. But when, as an act of expiation, the university was given to a clearly non-jihadi vice chancellor, it was resisted by the staff and subjected to violence by al-Qaeda.

Sectarianism also came with jihad. Shia leader Allama Arif Hussaini was murdered in August 1988. Within a fortnight of Hussaini's murder, ruling President General Zia-ul-Haq died in an air crash in Bahawalpur amid rumours of Shia involvement in his assassination, although no solid evidence supporting this speculation was ever found. The then North-West Frontier Province (NWFP) governor, General Fazle Haq, whom the Shia accused of complicity in the murder of Hussaini, was ambushed and killed in 1991.

Sectarianism also affected relations with Iran. In 1998, Pakistan's anti-Shia Sipah-e-Sahaba, riding together with the Taliban, killed eight Iranian 'diplomats' inside the Iranian consulate. That brought Iran and India closer; and once again India was threatening Pakistan on the western border.

Morbidity of Jihad

Tariq Rahman, dean of the School of Liberal Arts and Social Sciences at the Beaconhouse National University in Lahore, has written the most comprehensive book on jihad, the religious war of Islam, exercising the minds of Muslims and non-Muslims alike. *Interpretations of Jihad in South Asia: An Intellectual History*[10] begins with erstwhile, but now-ignored, thinkers such as Sir Syed Ahmed Khan and Maulvi Chiragh Ali, who thought that jihad was defensive war and not conquest to collect more *jizya* (tax levied on non-Muslims).

This useful book looks at the lack of scholarly consensus on what jihad means, especially in the hands of radical organizations such as al-Qaeda and the ISIS. It takes 323 pages of the most absorbing scholarship to understand the radical jihad springing mostly from the authority of Ibn Taymiyya (1262–1328) and culminating in the disputed Hadith about Ghazwa-e-Hind, legalizing and prompting an uprising against India in Kashmir.

The book rivets attention on the details of the phenomenon of extremism among Muslims, which has ended up in jihad, killing more Muslims than 'non-believers'. Pakistan has been the testing ground of theories of jihad that, some say, have been ordained in the Quran, which also lays down qital as an injunction. Pakistan has been the victim of a covert war that was supposed to be directed at the infidels. And it is instructive, after a lot of aimless bloodshed, unless Pakistan doesn't care about it.

Jihad has been enjoined in the Quran and, therefore, lies at the base of the sharia. However, it is not clear in Pakistan whether the state should wage jihad, or if it is incumbent on each individual to do so. This is very important because it relates to the doctrine of low-intensity and deniable warfare that the state of Pakistan has been practising in the recent past. It violates international law that enjoins the state to declare war instead of fighting it covertly, and does not recognize individuals in this respect.

In terms of governance, the jihadi state has to surrender internal sovereignty because private jihadi organizations have to be located in civil society and have to be exempted from municipal law with respect to their use of weapons and training. States can tolerate diminution of external sovereignty—mostly owing to economic weakness—but they cannot survive surrender of internal sovereignty. There can be no governance when the state is not sovereign even internally. The problem of 'extraterritoriality' has been the most pressing problem in Pakistan's governance under the doctrine of jihad.

More than 50 per cent of Pakistan's territory was outside the municipal jurisdiction of the state. This was because Pakistan had failed to bring the whole of Balochistan under the normal writ of the state and had preserved till 2018 the FATA as a relic of the British Raj 'buffer' territory. Jihad created an extended 'extraterritoriality', or 'no-go areas', that assaulted the big cities of Pakistan. In the smaller cities, the entire administration may have been run by non-state actors, as it happened in 'Toba Tek Singh', when the champion of Pakistani jihad, LeT, was the most powerful militia in the country. (LeT also ran a court that dished out punishments in Lahore and advertised it in newspapers.)

In the past, any discussion of law and order in Pakistan ran headlong into the state's policy of (proxy) jihad. Because jihad was fought with mercenary troops, there was a sharing of the sovereignty of the state with jihadi leaders, reminiscent of the Italian city states in the Middle Ages. There is resistance among politicians to the post-9/11 perceived policy of giving up jihad because the world, through the FATF, increasingly equates jihad with terrorism. There is apparently no realization that jihad militates against governance, above all.

Al-Qaeda and the ISIS have killed more Muslims than infidels. Afghanistan has been subjected to massacres with hardly any non-Muslim becoming the victim. In the Middle East, the ISIS has killed Muslims and waged war against the Iranian 'Muslim' elements active in Iraq, Syria and Lebanon. For the ISIS, jihad includes sexual enslavement and rape, which must rate as the moment of climax—or nadir—of Islamic revival in modern times.

Rahman says in the conclusion to his book:

> This study has concerned itself only with ideas about jihad. Perhaps the crucial question, not addressed here, is whether people are really influenced by these ideas? In short, is it because there are radical interpretations in circulation on the Internet, among role models of the peer group, among friends and relatives, that people get radicalised? Or is it that they join for other reasons such as poverty, lack of education, mental illness, sexual frustration, or money?[11]

Rahman takes note of Suhail Abbas, a Pakistani psychologist who examined 517 men in jail 'for having attempted to go to Afghanistan to fight US troops'. His conclusion was that all 'jihadis' suffered from 'psychological morbidity'.

An Orgy of Self-Flagellation

India's revoking of Articles 370 and 35A to absorb India-administered Kashmir into the union did not appear to be well-received by many across the world. The most effective objection to it came from India's own secularists and liberals, who took note of the rise of Hindutva in India under the Bharatiya Janata Party (BJP) government as being destructive to the very foundation of India. The world also took note of it, but the main cause of worry for most writers was the possibility of a nuclear war between India and Pakistan.

Pakistan reacted passionately, but much of this passion was 'political' as the Opposition bared its fangs and attacked the Pakistan Tehreek-e-Insaf (PTI) government of Prime Minister Imran Khan rather than India. Out in the street, textbook nationalism caused people to speak in hyperbole to the TV cameras, swearing revenge on India and pledging a war that would 'teach India a lesson'. Army chief General Qamar Javed Bajwa said his army would stand by the government in power in Pakistan and by the people of Kashmir. He said that they had never consented to Articles 370 and 35A, unmindful of the political cleavage in India that could benefit Pakistan, and now the army was ready for any eventuality.

Imran Khan convened a joint session of parliament and made a bold statement telling India that if war was to ensue, it would end up being a nuclear war. He also hinted that Pakistan was ready for it, to fight for the rights of the Kashmiris.[12] But the Opposition—mainly the Pakistani Muslim League (Nawaz) PML (N) of Nawaz Sharif and the Pakistan Peoples Party (PPP) of Bilawal Bhutto—was not prepared to give him relief. They attacked him for coming late to the session, as if he didn't care that the Kashmiris were suffering, and castigated him for the absence of his foreign minister Shah Mahmood Qureshi who had gone for hajj while the state was in crisis. (Qureshi aborted his holy journey and returned from Saudi Arabia, but he missed the session.)

Prime Minister Khan doesn't grace the parliament too often because of the bad blood between him and the Opposition leaders, for which he himself is to blame because of the way he hauls them over the coals every time he speaks. When the proceedings started, everything the government benches did was rejected, even the joint statement in which the Opposition found faults, attributing them to the absence of the foreign minister from the session. Khan was uncomfortable in his seat and would have left, as is his wont, had the occasion not been serious in the eyes of his public following.

On the TV channels, it was sheer national self-flagellation. Everyone asked to speak on the street simply wanted a war in which the Hindus were to be taught a final lesson. The common man simply repeated the nationalist mantra of hatred the same way the supporters of the BJP do on the streets of India.[13] Opposition leaders appearing on TV were anti-government to the extreme, recalling the vitriol Khan had heaped on them during his visit to the US, while addressing a large Pakistani gathering in Washington. The PML (N) politicians, whose leader Nawaz Sharif had once welcomed former Indian prime minister Atal Bihari Vajpayee to Lahore and later Prime Minister Narendra Modi too—and was called Modi *ka yaar* (friend of Modi) and therefore a *ghaddar* (traitor)—now cursed Khan for having welcomed Modi before he had even been elected.

Imran Khan had earlier said, 'Perhaps if the BJP—a right-wing party—wins, some kind of settlement in Kashmir could be reached.'[14] Now, the PML (N) was not ready to forgive him. These words were held against him by politicians more interested in ousting the government in Pakistan than ousting India from Kashmir. The world outside didn't like what had happened. A *New York Times* editorial expressed: 'The Indian government's decision to revoke the semiautonomous status of Kashmir, accompanied by a huge security clampdown, is dangerous and wrong.' Outrageously, the 'Arab friends' were not moved at all.[15]

Everyone cursed the government for not actively pursuing the UN Security Council, the International Court of Justice (ICJ) and the Organisation of Islamic Cooperation (OIC), as if all these organizations were actually groups of men sitting in a room with doors locked, which the government of Pakistan was supposed go and break down, and tell the shirkers to shake a leg and do the needful to teach India a lesson for what it was doing to the Muslims of Kashmir.

Alas, Pakistan's non-state actors were nowhere to be seen, removed from the battlefront by an international opinion more worried about their global outreach than the Muslims of Kashmir. The outrage over the statement of the ambassador of the United Arab Emirates (UAE), that it was an internal matter of India, was muffled because most of the remittances come from the Pakistanis working there. As realism slowly dawns, Prime Minister Khan should stick to his earlier perception that he can make a deal with the BJP and make the telephone call that was rebuffed earlier. Perhaps, this time, Prime Minister Modi will pick up.

1

Osama bin Laden in Abbottabad

The Abbottabad Commission Report on the killing of Osama bin Laden in Abbottabad, Khyber Pakhtunkhwa, during a US raid on 2 May 2011, was made public by the Al Jazeera news network.[1] The report, prepared by a panel of citizens led by a retired judge of the Supreme Court, Justice Javed Iqbal, holds the state institutions responsible for the clandestine stay of the world's most dangerous terrorist and the head of al-Qaeda in Pakistan. It doesn't name any one institution but uses blanket expressions indicting everyone responsible for national security.

When the subject of inquiry is the army or its intelligence agencies, inquiry commissions routinely avoid taking names and pretend to be mystified by the subject. In the case of the murder of journalist Syed Saleem Shahzad in May 2011, a commission headed by Justice Saqib Nisar of the Supreme Court took six months, instead of the mandated six weeks, to say it didn't know who killed him.

Al-Qaeda had attacked the Mehran naval base in Karachi in May, killing ten people. Shahzad had reported in *Asia Times* that it was triggered by the Pakistan Navy not releasing a group of naval officers it had arrested on the suspicion of them being al-Qaeda members. Shortly after the article was published, he was picked up in Islamabad and beaten to death.

The Abbottabad Commission Report says no proof was found of anyone's complicity in bin Laden's nine-year-stay in Pakistan, even as the intelligence agencies responsible for knowing his whereabouts remained clueless. Yet, the commission does not completely rule out 'complicity', while asserting that it found no proof. Let us look at the following formulation to see if complicity has been ruled out: 'This failure included negligence and incompetence, and at some *undetermined level a grave complicity may or may not* have been involved.' Clearly, even this innuendo must have required some courage.

What the commission wants to say in the report is simply this: We did not find any evidence of anyone being complicit in bin Laden's successful efforts at finding safe hiding places, but complicity may or may not have taken place. It didn't use the word 'may' alone, adding 'may not' also, probably to achieve a member's consensus on whether the commission should clearly indicate the possibility of complicity.

In the conclusion, the report carries the following sentence to insist on the possibility of complicity without clearly saying so: '[It is] a story of complacency, ignorance, negligence, incompetence, irresponsibility *and possibly worse* at various levels inside and outside the government.' The phrase 'possibly worse' points to something that the five adjectives preceding it did not convey.

The reluctance of the report to use the word 'complicity' unambiguously may point to a consensus within the commission to stay circumscribed in its pursuit of truth, so as to not tilt the country into a fresh bout of instability—and the state into a new crisis of accountability. There may have been a consensus on not to pursue certain lines of inquiry that would have required going the whole hog on possible new leads. One such lead lay in the suspicious proximity of the 'Mansehra terrorist training camp' to the final residence of Osama bin Laden.

Mansehra: The Ghost at the Banquet

It is intriguing that the Mansehra camp was not referred to in connection with bin Laden. The report carries the following itinerary of his movements: Osama was in Pakistan for nine years, out of which he spent five or six in Abbottabad, starting from 2006. Reports about a terrorist camp being located in Mansehra started floating around in 2001, when a group of terrorists attacked the Indian parliament and almost triggered a sub-nuclear war between India and Pakistan. Osama bin Laden was in Bajaur (in Khyber Pakhtunkhwa) first and probably escaped an air force attack because of 'prior information'. He was then in Peshawar and Karachi, before going to Swat. From Swat, he is supposed to have gone to Haripur before finally settling in Abbottabad.

The commission should have looked into the flurry of reports about Mansehra, simply because it was a mere 20 kilometres from where bin Laden had decided to live. The *Daily Times* correspondent in Washington, Khalid Hasan, filed a report (on 22 August 2005) identifying one Sher Ali of north Waziristan, who was sent to Mansehra by warlord Jalaluddin Haqqani for 'a twenty-day weapons training course at a secret mountain camp'. Sher Ali was later captured in Afghanistan. Osama bin Laden had run training camps for Pakistani non-state actors during the war against the Soviet Union; he could well have been funding the Mansehra camp for the same non-state actors in 2006.

An early testimony about Mansehra has come from Adnan Rasheed, the former air force officer-turned-terrorist who was sprung from a jail in Bannu last year after a Taliban raid that was hardly resisted by the prison guards. The Taliban declared after the jailbreak that they had spent 'over Rs 2 crore on the operation'. The money almost certainly went to those who transferred a dangerous terrorist from the military stronghold of Rawalpindi to Bannu, a semi-tribal area where the Taliban virtually rule in a doubtful diarchy with the local administration. After this clear case of 'complicity', Rasheed talked to an English-language Taliban journal (in March 2013) and revealed how he had landed in Mansehra after joining the jihad:

> Brother X urged me to join the Taliban air force that needed skilled men. He kept on giving me *dawa* (invitation to Islam) and kept on calling me to the path of Allah and His Prophet. Then I and Brother X left the [PAF] squadron. Brother X had some terms with Maulana Masood Azhar, so he took me to the Jaish-e-Mohammed office and then to the Mansehra training camp. He introduced me to them and then went back to his duty in Peshawar. I stayed in their camp for twenty-three days, waiting to go along with some other brothers to Afghanistan; meanwhile, I was interviewed by many commanders. Finally, they said that they had made my *tashkeel* (delegation) back to my [PAF] air force squadron. They told me that I should work there and give the dawa of jihad.[2]

Masood Azhar and Fazlur Rehman Khaleel

Maulana Masood Azhar is a wanted terrorist. Pakistan's official position on him is that it is not known where he is; he is probably not in the country. He belongs to the 'deniable list' of internationally wanted people that once included Osama bin Laden and now includes Mullah Umar. Bruce Riedel of the Washington-based think tank Brookings Institution wrote:

> Mullah Omar, who most believe lives under ISI protection in Quetta . . . He has not been seen in public in years. On rare occasions, a message is issued in his name, but he never appears in front of his followers. For all the world knows, the self-styled Commander of the Faithful may be dead, mad or incapacitated.[3]

Karachi is supposed to be under siege from a number of Taliban terrorist groups, all of them affiliated to the al-Qaeda. If the Mansehra camp belongs to JeM, it establishes a link: first between the JeM and al-Qaeda, and then between the operators of jihad within the deep state and the al-Qaeda under 'Sheikh Osama'. In 2012, a target killer caught in Karachi revealed that he was working for the Taliban on a monthly salary of Rs 15,000, and that he had been trained at the Mansehra camp ten months earlier. Sitting atop a loose terrorist hierarchy in Pakistan, the al-Qaeda is ceremonially accepted as the patron mainly because of its ability to fund camps. In the good old days of US-backed Afghan jihad, against the Soviet Union, Pakistan's ISI commandos (such as Col Imam) were training fighters in camps financed by the al-Qaeda.

While the Abbottabad Commission Report has ignored Mansehra, foreign journalists have not. Right after the killing of Osama bin Laden, the Associated Press (AP) filed the following story on 23 May 2011 from Ughi in Mansehra district:

> Three men who identified themselves as mujahideen told the AP that the training complex is one of at least three in the region that, between them, house hundreds of recruits. The mission, the three say, is aimed at taking recruits to Kashmir to fight Pakistan's arch-enemy, India. But Kashmiri veterans have been known to join forces with Al Qaeda and other terror groups, including those fighting the US and its allies in Afghanistan and elsewhere.[4]

The last sentence of the AP report is typical: 'When contacted by the AP last week, the army denied there are any training camps or any facilities hidden away in the Mansehra area. "The allegations are baseless," said spokesman Major General Athar Abbas.'

Why did bin Laden opt for Abbottabad, a garrison city home to the prestigious Pakistan Military Academy that trains newly recruited officers and was therefore unsafe for him? The reason was that he had to be closer to the training camp run by a

Punjab-based terrorist group, one that he was fond of; and he was sure that another terrorist group similarly close to him dominated Abbottabad and its environs. The two groups, one run by Maulana Masood Azhar and the other by Maulana Fazlur Rehman Khaleel, were once united under the name Harkat-ul-Mujahideen (HuM). Warriors belonging to these groups had accompanied bin Laden to Sudan, when he fled the onset of civil war among the Pakistan-backed Afghan mujahideen after the Soviet withdrawal from Afghanistan.

On 23 June 2011, Carlotta Gall, Pir Zubair Shah and Eric Schmitt reported in the *New York Times*:

> Harkat has especially deep roots in the area around Abbottabad, and the network provided by the group would have enhanced bin Laden's ability to live and function in Pakistan, analysts familiar with the group said. Its leaders have strong ties with both Al-Qaeda and Pakistani intelligence, and they can roam widely because they are Pakistanis, something the foreigners who make up Al-Qaeda's ranks can't do. Even today, the group's leader, Maulana Fazlur Rehman Khaleel, long one of bin Laden's closest Pakistani associates, lives unbothered by Pakistani authorities on the outskirts of Islamabad.[5]

It was only natural that Maulana Khaleel should handle bin Laden's correspondence. It is difficult to imagine Khaleel acting as the arch-terrorist's post office while living under close intelligence surveillance. The Americans, too, traced cell phone calls made by HuM operatives in Abbottabad to ISI officers. But what about the other favourite of bin Laden, Maulana Masood Azhar?

The Rise of Jaish

Jaish-e-Mohammed (JeM) was created by Maulana Masood Azhar after a fall out with Maulana Khaleel in 2001. The split was formalized by Mufti Shamzai of the Banuri seminary in

Karachi, who had facilitated the first meeting between Mullah Umar of the Afghan Taliban and Osama bin Laden in Karachi in the early years of Afghan jihad—the same Shamzai who, while accompanying the delegation led by ISI chief General Mahmud Ahmed, ended up persuading Mullah Umar to go on fighting the Americans instead of causing the al-Qaeda to leave Afghanistan. (It was later revealed that it was General Mahmud who hated the Americans so much—like other ISI chiefs from General Hamid Gul to General Ahmad Shuja Pasha—that he advised Mullah Umar to take on the Americans.)[6]

Shamzai was killed by a sectarian hit squad in 2004, at the height of attacks on the Shias in 2003 and 2004, in which organizations linked to him through instruction and tutelage were involved. Masood Azhar was his favourite student at the Banuri madrasa. He was also close to Osama bin Laden, in the same way as the Abdullah Ghazi family that ran the Lal Masjid in Islamabad as an R&R muster point for al-Qaeda members and their non-state actor affiliates.

Masood Azhar was born in 1968, completed his religious training at the Banuri madrasa and then taught there for two years till 1989. He was inspired to do jihad while at Banuri. Azhar's brother Ibrahim Masood went to Afghanistan at the age of nineteen; later, he took his father too. His sister, Rabiya Bibi, worked for the Taliban government in Afghanistan. His elder brother Ibrahim Azhar too made many trips to Afghanistan for jihad and was included in the team put together to hijack an Indian Airlines airplane in 1999, making it land in Afghanistan where the Taliban—some versions say ISI officers—released Indian passengers in return for the freedom of Masood Azhar from a jail in India.

Azhar is said to have met Osama bin Laden in Medina in 1994, when both of them were in disguise. His mission was to bring his jihadi organizations under the aegis of the al-Qaeda, which he accomplished in 1993 by placing himself close to warlord Farah Aidid in Somalia, while Osama bin Laden was based in neighbouring Sudan. The same year, Aidid ended up killing twenty-four Pakistani troops on UN peacekeeping duty in Mogadishu. Azhar was a great fundraiser and a man of action, and was liked by both Shamzai and Osama bin Laden. Shamzai placed him in Mansehra to guard his 'sectarian belt' that stretched from Mansehra to Besham and Jaglot Kohistan, which also connects with Swat, in addition to doing 'asymmetric' terrorism in India. It was his boys who attacked the Indian parliament in 2001, almost triggering a war.

Osama bin Laden attracted Pakistan's attention because of his ability to get money for terrorist training without asking if the planned terrorism was against the US or India. His hatred for the US was shared by many serving senior Pakistani military officers. Secular officers hated the US for its post-1965 tilt in favour of India and the subsequent non-recognition of Pakistan as a long-term nuclearized ally; Islamist officers interfaced with the al-Qaeda and its affiliated non-state actors at a much deeper level. Nothing demonstrates this pathology more than the contents of the Abbottabad Commission Report that recorded the deposition of then director general of the ISI, General Ahmad Shuja Pasha.

The Mind of the Top Brass

With regard to the role of former army chief General Pervez Musharraf, General Pasha told the Abbottabad Commission:

> Musharraf had caved in so promptly and so completely to the US demands that Shamsi airbase was given to them for drone strikes against people in Pakistan. Someone should have told the Americans that enough is enough, but in vain, and both the 'political and military elite were responsible for this lapse'.[7]

As if in response, the commission too succumbed to the fallacy of 'national sovereignty' and joined the former ISI chief in his rhetoric without sparing a thought for the loss of state writ in almost 60 per cent of Pakistan's territory to Al-Qaeda and its Taliban allies. The commission probably needed some help to interpret General Pasha's statement.

This year, a more revealing book by a much-lionized and decorated retired officer, General Shahid Aziz, paraded this pathology more clearly. In his acclaimed Urdu biography titled *Yeh Khamoshi Kahan Tak* (How Long Will This Silence Last?), with a telltale subtitle *Ek Sipahi ki Dastan-e-Ishq-o-Junoon* (The Story of a Soldier's Passion and Madness), he writes:

> The bombs that kill innocent Pakistanis in bazaars and mosques are planted by friends of America, and this terrorism is done to persuade Pakistan to embrace America more closely, allow the government to pursue pro-America policies and to alienate Pakistan from the mujahideen. But this trend of support to the killers of Muslims is open rebellion against Allah.[8]

What should interest any psychiatrist is the following confession he makes about himself:

> Why am I full of contradiction? Why can't I be balanced? Then I console myself with the thought that a pendulum has a balance too; what use is balance that is static and frozen? Real balance is in movement. One should be flying back and forth on a swing.

The change of mind about such officers among the new political leadership was revealed when, on 18 June 2013, the then newly appointed interior minister Chaudhry Nisar Ali Khan uttered the following sentence: 'We need to purge the army and its leadership of people like ex-ISI chief General Shuja Pasha. Although Chief of Army Staff General Ashfaq Parvez Kayani has kept himself away from politics, people like Pasha still exist in the army.'[9]

There are a lot of other senior officers in the military who have gone one step ahead from where General Pasha stands. Many have joined banned terrorist organizations like Hizbut Tahrir—including some officers at the Shamsi base that General Pasha mourns—and have thought of taking over military command by staging a coup. The most blatant first indication came in a letter from a commando officer, Major General Ameer Faisal Alavi, that informed London's *Sunday Times* that the army might kill him because he had reported two generals to the army chief General Kayani as actually working for the al-Qaeda. He was promptly killed by a deserter to al-Qaeda, Major Haroon Ashiq, in Islamabad in November 2008, on orders from former chief of al-Qaeda's Lashkar-e-Zil, Ilyas Kashmiri. (Major Ashiq was acquitted by an anti-terrorism court in 2010; Ilyas Kashmiri was killed by a drone in north Waziristan in 2011.)

Just as bin Laden seems to have been clandestinely favoured and kept in hiding by certain US-hating Islamist elements, so were those favoured by the US chastised, once again, through al-Qaeda and its terrorist adjuncts. The case of Benazir Bhutto's assassination in 2007 highlights an interface between such elements and the chief of the Taliban, Baitullah Mehsud. But such cases never come to justice. General Musharraf may actually get punished for ordering a commando attack on Lal Masjid but be let off the hook in the case of Bhutto's assassination. After her death, the al-Qaeda had announced: 'We have eliminated an American asset.'

2

Who Sneaked on Osama bin Laden?

Shuja Nawaz, currently a distinguished fellow, South Asia Centre, at the well-known bipartisan think tank, the Atlantic Council, Washington DC, and a known security expert, revealed additional secrets about the killing of Osama bin Laden in his book *The Battle for Pakistan: The Bitter US Friendship and a Tough Neighbourhood.* Pakistan has always wondered who sneaked on its friend Osama living peacefully in Abbottabad, but there were 'foreign' sources who kept hinting that someone from inside the military establishment had reported his location to the Americans 'for money'. Let's first consider a sample:

> The first shocker came when the Pulitzer prize-winning American journalist Seymour Hersh made it public that a former Pakistani intelligence official had actually informed the Americans about the Abbottabad hideout of Osama bin Laden, and that a former ISI official had provided the information

> about his hideout for $25 million in addition to US citizenship 'with a new identity'. Who was the bloke?[1]

It was later alleged that Brigadier Usman Khalid,[2] a retired ISI officer, got Dr Shakil Afridi, a Pakistani physician, to conduct a fake polio campaign in the Bilal Town area of Abbottabad to help the Central Intelligence Agency (CIA) hunt down Osama. Then, on 17 February 2012, David Ignatius wrote in the *Washington Post*[3] that former ISI chief General Ziauddin Butt, quoted in the Pakistani press, had said that Osama's stay at Abbottabad was arranged by Brigadier (retd) Ijaz Shah—today interior minister in Imran Khan's government—on Musharraf's orders. Butt repeated his claim in the February 2012 issue of the *Newsweek* magazine, in an online interview conducted by Bruce Riedel. Riedel quoted him as saying: 'General Musharraf knew that Osama bin Laden was in Abbottabad'.[4] He repeated that Ijaz Shah was responsible for setting up bin Laden in Abbottabad, ensuring his safety and keeping him hidden from public view. Musharraf, of course, denied having any knowledge about bin Laden living in Pakistan during his tenure.

The *New York Times* claimed in a March 2014 report that the US had direct evidence about 'former ISI chief Lt Gen. Ahmed Shuja Pasha knowing [about] bin Laden's presence in Abbottabad at the time'. The newspaper also quoted General Butt saying that Musharraf had arranged for bin Laden to hide in Abbottabad. This was again dubbed a pack of lies aimed at making the international community believe that the world's most wanted terrorist 'was living unnoticed for five years in a vast compound in Abbottabad without any support system'.

ISI Chiefs Who 'Came Clean'

More recently, an ex-ISI chief dropped a bombshell that greatly offended Pakistan. Former ISI chief Lt Gen. (retd) Asad Durrani, talking to A.S. Dulat, India's former special director of the Intelligence Bureau (IB) and former chief of the Research and Analysis Wing (R&AW) from 1999 to 2000, in the book *Spy Chronicles* (2018),[5] came out with more details about how the Americans found out about Osama bin Laden living in Abbottabad:

> I have no doubt that a retired Pakistani officer who was in intelligence walked in and told the Americans. I won't take his name because I can't prove it and also I don't want to give him any publicity. How much of the 50 million dollars he got, who knows. But he is missing from Pakistan. I should know.

After this statement, Major General Asif Ghafoor, director general of Inter-Services Public Relation (ISPR) of the media wing of the Pakistan Army, issued a statement saying: 'Lt Gen Asad Durrani, retired, is being called to the GHQ on 28 May 2018. He will be asked to explain his position on views attributed to him in the book *Spy Chronicles*.'[6]

Was It Lt Col Eqbal Saeed Khan?

Finally, was it Brigadier (retd) Usman Khalid or not? Shuja Nawaz gives us a more detailed and credible version of what happened, unless there was more than one Pakistani officer who sneaked to the Americans for big money.

Lt Col Eqbal Saeed Khan of the ISI was the man according to Nawaz's book *The Battle for Pakistan.* Saeed was commissioned into the Pakistan Army as part of the 4th War Course. He did his Intelligence Staff Course in 1993, and his colleagues recall him as being 'a bright guy and lively company'. He was well known by his nickname of Bailee, a Punjabi equivalent of 'buddy' in English. He was reportedly told to retire prematurely by the army chief for dealing in fake currency. Another report says he was passed over for promotion to brigadier and then prematurely retired. According to the book:

> Col Saeed, who ran a security firm in Islamabad, may have been responsible for providing logistic [and] surveillance assistance to the Americans in tracking and locating movements related to what turned out to [be] the final lair of bin Laden in Abbottabad. Col Saeed's office in Abbottabad is reported to have been used as a listening and staging post. He is reported to have been recruited by Lt Col Hafeez, his predecessor at the helm of the 408 Intelligence battalion, who had been hired by the US, and according to one report, was even in the US, and that CIA Director George Tenet once brought him to a meeting with General Kayani.
>
> According to another senior retired ISI officer, Col Saeed may have been rewarded by the Americans for keeping mum about the final stages of the search for bin Laden's hideout in Abbottabad. Another retired brigadier was also prominently mentioned in assisting during the search for bin Laden, but no formal inquiries in Pakistan have been shared with the public. Indeed, the Abbottabad Commission that was set up by Pakistan to investigate the raid that killed bin Laden appeared to clear Col Saeed. A very senior military officer, who spoke with me about a brigadier implicated in that case, also indicated that they had not found much on him. The brigadier was not mentioned in the report.[7]

So, was it not Brigadier Usman Khalid after all?

Living It Up in the US

Nawaz has more dirt on Col Saeed:

> Yet, Col Saeed decamped from Pakistan immediately after the raid on Abbottabad, leaving behind an empty home in the DHA [Defence Housing Authority] at Morgah, days before his child's high-school exams, and even as his second wife was reported to be recuperating from a medical procedure. The

> house was then disposed of by the manager of his security firm, according to a former colleague of the colonel. He is [now] living in San Diego, California, owns a $2.4-million home under his own name and also operates under the name Bailey [sic!] Khan, a Western variation of his nickname, Bailee, in Pakistan. In May 2018, photographs emerged of the colonel and his wife enjoying their new life. A white BMW convertible with a California licence plate is visible in some of the photos of the dapper colonel.

The House That Osama Built

Nawaz also offers details regarding how Osama bin Laden landed in Abbottabad and how he came to live in the house built by Arshad, a Pakistani tribal who became his lynchpin:

> The ISI was also tracking a local person named Arshad and had established that he travelled once a month to Peshawar and bought medicines. It was during this period of inquiry that the ISI requested satellite surveillance by the CIA of the house on 'Pathan Street' in Bilal Town. [The] Clues were the transcripts of wiretaps of conversations in Arabic between someone in Nowshera and later Peshawar, Waziristan, and finally [the] bin Laden Compound in Abbottabad, and someone in Saudi Arabia that the ISI shared with the CIA in 2009 and 2010. The information and location data in those wiretaps allowed the CIA to hone in on the compound and find bin Laden.

What is revealed further by Shuja Nawaz is spellbinding. Osama bin Laden lived in Abbottabad for six years—the ISI ostensibly knew nothing about it—with his wives and sixteen children aged six to eight years. If there was just one wife, she was sharing the house with two other women. Arshad, the Pashtun from Charsadda who died in the US attack, had bought a plot of 7 *kanal*s and 5 *marla*s in 2004 for about Rs 5 million, which is 'at least 25 per cent more than the value of property in that locality'.

In Nawaz's own words:

> [Osama] Bin Laden drew a sketch of the outline of the house-within-a-house that would shelter him and his family, as well as the Pakistani brothers who were his keepers and couriers. The site was considered safe for him and his family since it was far from the battlefront. Also, it turns out that the ISI did not have a permanent presence there till after the Libyan terrorist Al Libi was tracked to that town in the Nawan Shehr neighbourhood, not far from Bilal Town. The ISI team later grew in size. In February 2011, terrorist Umer Patek, as Jaffer Alawi, a.k.a. Hisyamein Alazein (of Kuwaiti origin), implicated in the Bali bombing, was captured near Abbottabad. But even this did not raise [any] alarm at the ISI headquarters about a more important presence in the area.

3

Kargil: High on Low IQ

Pakistan, in its seventy-one years of existence, has fought an abnormal number of wars. Each of these has extracted a high cost, often derailing gains to the country's economy. The situation was no different more than two decades ago. Islamabad was in dire straits economically—and as politically unstable as ever—when the country went to fight its 'post-nuclear' war in the Kargil district of Kashmir. Taking place between May and July 1999, the conflict was a disaster for Pakistan. But rather than facing the punishment for his failings, its planner–executioner, the then army chief General Pervez Musharraf, staged a coup against the democratically elected government of Nawaz Sharif in October 1999, grabbing the reins of power for nearly a decade. An already crippled economy, struggling under the weight of the sanctions imposed by the US after the previous year's nuclear tests, had to cough up $2 billion for the botched war. The damage to Pakistan's international standing was no less significant: In the eyes of the world, Pakistan was perceived as a dangerously unstable state led by military officials with little to no accountability.

When the war started, India was caught unawares. Based on media reports, 4000 infiltrators—'shepherds' according to some retired Pakistani generals who supported the war—established 196 checkposts 14 kilometres inside the Indian side of the Line of Control (LoC), which divides Pakistan-administered Kashmir from India-administered Kashmir. As reports of these gains spread, the media and the people in Pakistan cheered. But when the Indian Army responded to this penetration, the Kargil 'operation' quickly wilted, revealing glaring flaws in its planning and execution. The troops, trapped in their high-altitude dugouts, were forced to survive on grass before having to surrender. The Pakistan Army soon realized the 'critical problems of logistical stretch' this operation had presented. In its loss, Pakistan had snatched another defeat from the jaws of flawed strategy.

Nearly twenty years after the war, journalist Nasim Zehra wrote an extraordinary tell-all book, *From Kargil to the Coup: Events that Shook Pakistan* (2018),[1] making no bones about her 'insider' eyewitness sources who included the who's who of retired military officials: Former army chief General Pervez Musharraf, Lt Gen. Nadeem Ahmad, Lt Gen. Gulzar Kiani, Lt Gen. Javed Hassan, Lt Gen. Amjad Shuaib, Brig. Syed Azhar Raza and Brig. Khalid Nazir. She also mentions some 'critics' of the Kargil operation—officially dubbed Operation Kohpaima (mountaineering trip)—who were the earliest to spill the beans, including former chief of general staff General Ali Kuli Khan and Musharraf's 'blue-eyed boy', Lt Gen. Shahid Aziz.

Bypassing the Prime Minister

Let's ask the last but all-important question first: Did General Musharraf 'clear' the Kargil War with then prime minister Sharif? Zehra's book hands down a grim and clear verdict:

> The country's chief executive, the prime minister, had neither cleared the operation, nor was he taken in the loop by the Army chief. All SOPs [standard operating procedures] had been ignored.

Four officers, whom she calls the 'Kargil clique', actually put into motion the strategically toxic plan that had been brewing for years—ever since 1984 when India grabbed the Siachen glacier and the General Headquarters (GHQ), under General Zia-ul-Haq, could do nothing to stop it. However, after the ouster of the Soviet Union from Afghanistan, a new headiness prevailed and some senior officers began raising the possibility of an operation against India.

At its core, the idea was to 'block India's lifeline to its troops in Leh', in India-administered Kashmir, by cutting off the national highway route that was used to travel to and from Srinagar. According to Zehra, General Musharraf's appointment as army chief in October 1998 further led to the idea taking shape based on the supposition that 'the Indians would never fight back'. Even before being appointed as the chief, General Musharraf had advocated a military operation to resolve the Kashmir dispute, telling an incredulous Prime Minister Benazir Bhutto in 1996, when he was the director general of military operations: 'The time window for the resolution of the Kashmir dispute is short because, with the passage of time, the India–Pakistan equation, military as well as economic, is going against us.'[2] She didn't bite.

The then foreign minister Sartaj Aziz, in his book *Between Dreams and Realities: Some Milestones in Pakistan's History* (2009),[3] tells a slightly different story. According to Aziz, General Musharraf briefed the prime minister on Kargil in May 1999. This may very well not have been the first briefing on the matter, but it was the first Aziz was a part of. Aside from Aziz, Abdul Majid Malik (former minister for Kashmir Affairs), Raja Zafarul Haq (former minister for religious affairs), Shamshad Ahmad (former foreign secretary) and Tariq Fatemi (former additional secretary in the PM Secretariat) also attended the meeting. Aziz was among the plan's dissenters, and what he said must be flagged as the intellectual thesis of his book: that the Pakistan Army is 'tactical' rather than 'strategic' in its thinking.

He writes:

> I saw that the tactics were brilliant but the strategy did not seem viable. And the objectives of the operation were even less clear. Other Foreign Office diplomats were perhaps in the loop [unlike Sartaj as foreign minister]. In the RAW [India's foreign intelligence agency] telephone intercept of General Musharraf, General Aziz in Islamabad was heard telling the chief in Beijing [in Appendix III of the book] that while Mian Sahib was okay, foreign secretary Shamshad as usual was supporting.[4]

(The foreign service's support of the army, without any input from the prime minister, might also shed some light on why Sharif, in his most recent tenure as prime minister, chose to keep the foreign ministry as a personal portfolio.)

The Kargil Clique

It must be recalled that the Kargil War happened less than a year after Pakistan's nuclear tests at Chagai formally declared to the world that the country was a nuclear power. Touted as a deterrent to armed conflict, the tests were a boon for Sharif who reaped political mileage from it on the 'theory' that India 'will never attack now'. The Kargil clique, seizing on this misguided belief, decided to enact a plan that had been rejected earlier by former army chief General Jehangir Karamat, who retired in 1998. Lt Gen. Aziz Khan, appointed as chief of general staff at the GHQ, spearheaded it under the guidance of the clique's boss, General Musharraf. Next was Lt Gen. Mahmud Ahmad, who had earlier served as the commandant of National Defence College (now University), the 'think tank of the Pakistan Army', and as director general of military intelligence.

Perhaps the most important member of the clique was its fourth member, Major General Javed Hassan, who presented himself as a 'geopolitical strategist' and was accepted as such because he 'interpreted most developments within Pakistan as an extension of the agenda of major powers'. He headed the Force Command Northern Areas (FCNA) and was convinced that Pakistan, and the world, was ready for a successful assault on the 'Indian adventure' on Siachen. He would say that it was the 'defeated-by-Pakistan' Russia that had asked India to 'do something against Pakistan', because 'Pakistan is giving us trouble in Afghanistan'. And the US, instead of being happy with Pakistan for having helped defeat the Soviet Union, had 'got the anti-Zia Movement for the Restoration of Democracy to begin arm-twisting general Zia over Afghanistan'.

Zehra's book features much insight into Javed Hassan's thinking. He insisted that India 'had run out of options on Kashmir', but 'the Pakistani political government's stance on Kashmir was weakening the cause.' As he saw it, the world was noticing a change in Pakistan's position. Quoting Kashmiri leader Mirwaiz Umar Farooq, he reported that the Pentagon and US State Department thought that 'Pakistan neither has the will nor the wherewithal, so you move away from Pakistan and we will get you the best deal.' The lesson here was: Now is the time to attack or forget about Kashmir.

Hassan was formerly involved in monitoring the Kashmiri insurgency and that may well have coloured his world view. Between 1992 and 1993, Pakistan concluded that the 'insurgency's spirit was depleting', and sought to make up for it by deploying its *mehman mujahideen* (guest fighters) in India-administered Kashmir. He was further convinced about the need for the Kargil operation because the Army's assessment was that the Kashmiris were 'tending to stay away from the insurgency'.

Meet the Mentors

As commander of the FCNA in October 1997, Hassan would reportedly reconnaissance the area around the LoC and return with fresh orders for his officers: 'Get offensive, we have to cross the borders.' It seems that he was inclined to act without instructions from his superiors and abstained from passing down written orders. Zehra writes:

> Hassan openly exhibited his enthusiasm for undertaking military operations to capture Indian-held posts on and around the LoC. Once, when present at the 19 Gayari sector, he got news that one of his brigade commanders had captured a post earlier held by the Indians. He ordered a gathering of his troops and chanted 'Allah-o-Akbar' (God is great), and urged the other commanders to also mount post-capturing operations.

Lt Gen. Mahmud Ahmed, who Hassan reported to at 10 Corps, was not averse to accepting the latter's geostrategic daydreaming. Commissioned in 1962, he was a regimental colleague of then army captain Musharraf and was part of the 1971 war between Pakistan and India. The bulk of his military career was spent in military intelligence. Deeply religious and hailing from a middle-class background in Faisalabad, he is remembered as a bully by many at the foreign office, where he often lost his cool during encounters with not-so-strategic diplomats. After retirement, he publicly came out against the US invasion of Afghanistan, retreated into bearded piety and was never questioned over the fated Operation Kohpaima.

Lt Gen. Aziz Khan, second-in-command of the Kargil clique, had already—unsuccessfully—advised ex-chief Karamat that 'Pakistan should occupy the heights that the Indians would vacate during winter'. He wanted the troops to cross the LoC knowing full well that such an action would amount to triggering a conventional war under the nuclear umbrella Pakistan had acquired a year earlier. Shockingly, the 'consensus' he was putting forward was that, after the nuclear tests, 'a successful Operation Kohpaima would force the world powers to intervene to resolve the outstanding Kashmir issue.' Zehra calls it a strategy of nuclear blackmail.

Were there any doubts about the planned operation in the army? Not according to Zehra, who notes that it was planned and executed in great secrecy. But once it was on, the plan found support in the media and a populace fed on the textbook 'realities' of Pak–Indo ties that had triggered earlier wars (and defeats). Prime Minister Sharif was on the 'wrong track' while Kargil was brewing. Buoyed by his encounter with his Indian counterpart Atal Behari Vajpayee in February 1999, he sought to change the Pak–Indo equation forever. He had gone so far as to tell the generals in the GHQ that 'Pakistan would gradually move towards discontinuing armed support for the Kashmiris.'

But the warriors planning to attack Kargil were convinced that they could win Kashmir by bringing India to its knees and the world opinion on the side of Pakistan.

Too Many Necks

'The strategic philosopher and executioner of Kargil, then major general, later lieutenant general, Javed Hassan was quick to assure the [army] chief that Pakistan's positions were strongly established, while the Indians were completely unprepared to respond. He then raised his hands to his throat and said, "If anything goes wrong, my neck is available." His commander, General Mahmud, was quick to take responsibility. "Why yours? My neck will be on the line since I have cleared it." As if taking the cue, in stepped the next man up in the hierarchy, the chief [of the army] himself: "No, it would not be your neck, it would be my neck."'

This bonhomie did not last. After General Musharraf dismissed Lt Gen. Mahmud in 2001, reportedly under American pressure, he lashed out at his chief's decision to ally with the US against the Taliban. In 2006, he published *History of the Indo–Pak War 1965*,[5] assessing the conflict as a defeat rather than victory. Published by the Services Book Club, few copies of the book remain in circulation, as an embarrassed General Musharraf persuaded the GHQ to buy over 20,000 copies. The Kargil defeat hadn't stopped rankling yet and he was worried about any comparisons that might be drawn.

General Musharraf also tried to give a veneer of victory in Kargil by 'not taking the neck of Lt Gen. Javed Hassan', instead rewarding him with the Staff College in Lahore, where he was to 'correct' the minds of the country's senior civil servants by infusing them with his strategic wisdom. Zehra, however, inserts a significant quote from him, offering regrets, after his dream ended in defeat and the rank and file started questioning the situation in Kargil:

> Even as adversity struck, with military pressure mounting on Pakistani troops, Commander FCNA lost his nerve . . . In a meeting, Javed Hassan implored the others: 'For God's sake, forgive me. I have made a big mistake. Now is the time for prayers.'

The book has its unchallenged sources casting Hassan in a different light:

> Major General Javed Hassan's unprofessional, prejudiced refrain was: 'The timid Indian will never fight the battle.' Hassan used to go to the battle headquarters but mostly not across the LoC, yet all the posts were established with his clearance.

Despite these attempts at face-saving, the end result is undeniable. The Indian Army recaptured all the contested posts in Kargil on 26 July 1999. It said it had won 1920 square kilometres of territory to Pakistan's 540. India had lost 2862 soldiers; Pakistan

5800. India lost 97 tanks; Pakistan lost 450. Pakistan confirmed that 453 soldiers were killed. The US Department of State made a partial estimate of close to 700 fatalities. Nawaz Sharif's 'emotional' estimate was over that 4000 Pakistani soldiers had died.

Brainwashing Books

Zehra notes in her book the gaping chasm that exists between the Pakistan Army and its elected civilian prime minister:

> A senior ISI general . . . found the country's elected chief executive, constitutionally the ISI's direct boss, unrealistic and somewhat amusing. For these men, there was no buy-in to Nawaz Sharif's diplomacy-oriented foreign policy. By virtue of their almost unaccountable control of Pakistan's security institutions, they effectively controlled Pakistan's security-dominated India and Afghanistan policies. Military men, trained to see the world in binary terms, are accustomed to unaccountably and independently managing Pakistan's security policy.

Pakistan's former foreign secretary Riaz Muhammad Khan, in his book *Afghanistan and Pakistan: Conflict, Extremism and Resistance to Modernity* (2011), agrees with Zehra:

> A siege mentality is also manifest in aggressive patriotism and narrow nationalism. The sentiment is especially evident among retired mid-level officials, both military and civilian, and religiously inclined middle-class citizens, who have imbibed suspicion towards the West, hostility towards India and pride in a culture of patriotic self-righteousness typical of middle classes in many societies. This mentality induces further stress in an environment of anger, suspicion, dissension, and delusions, in which extremist tendencies breed and thrive.[6]

What Pakistan got out of Kargil was humiliation and isolation. Unable to sack General Musharraf, Nawaz Sharif took off to the US, taking his entire family along. This, to most Pakistanis, meant that he feared a coup from an army chief who had refused to accept defeat and face the consequences, instead opting to paint him as an abettor. Riaz Muhammad Khan has succinctly laid out the factor that most likely induced him to make this trip with his family. The nation, brainwashed with 'binary' nationalism planted in the Constitution and textbooks, was not with him as he pleaded with the then US President Bill Clinton to intercede and end the war.

Too Big for Its Boots?

The most shameful expression of the selective amnesia prevalent in Pakistan came from ex-foreign secretary Abdul Sattar after he joined Imran Khan's PTI. His statement is reproduced in Zehra's book:

> He predicted that Sharif would be ousted from power like former rulers who compromised Kashmir's interest. Sattar's recall of history was faulty. Of the assassinated prime minister Liaquat Ali Khan, the seasoned diplomat claimed [that] 'in 1949 Liaquat Ali Khan was involved in a sell-out and he had to leave in 1951. Military ruler Ayub Khan's exit he singularly linked to the 1965 ceasefire. Ayub Khan, he said, 'sold out with a ceasefire in 1965, and he also had to go in 1968'.

(After the coup of October 1999, General Musharraf appointed Sattar as his foreign minister.)

Shuja Nawaz, in his classic *Crossed Swords: Pakistan, Its Army, and the Wars Within* (2008),[7] has also dwelt on some of the aspects of the Pakistan Army and the Pakistani mind. The Pakistan Army, a well-organized entity, has tried to fit into an underdeveloped political system. While responding to the unequal challenge of neighbouring India, it has ended up cannibalizing the very state it is supposed to defend. Its acts of trespass and usurpation have sapped its professional function and habituated it to reinterpreting its defeats as victories. Nawaz tentatively compares it with the Kemalist army of Turkey that often clashed with the democratic aspirations of the Turks—with roles reversed today as far as religion is concerned—and, more relevantly, with the Indonesian Army that has its tentacles deep inside the national economy and its system of privileges.

Zehra's book sheds light on a topic in Pakistan's history that has remained taboo for far too long. It is commonly said that one must learn from their mistakes or risk repeating them. Pakistan, with several military losses to its name, cannot continue to bury the past or obfuscate reality to match its internal narrative. We must take stock of our mistakes, our follies, and not only learn from them, but also pledge to never repeat them.

There is no honour lost in this. Only through introspection can a person, an organization, or even a state, grow into a better version of itself. Zehra's book is an excellent first step in that direction.

4

The Sad Saga of Hafiz Saeed

When an 'under pressure' Pakistan initiated '23 cases against Hafiz Saeed and his 12 aides over terrorism-financing', the news was immediately flashed in all the major Indian and Pakistani newspapers. *Daily Times* in Pakistan carried the story on 4 July 2019:

> The counter-terrorism department (CTD) said it had launched 23 cases against Hafiz Saeed and 12 of his aides for using five trusts to collect funds and donations for Lashkar-e-Taiba (LeT). Two banned LeT-linked charities, Jamaat-ud-Dawa (JuD) and Falah-e-Insaniat Foundation (FIF), were also targeted, the department said in a statement. 'All the assets of these organizations and individuals will be frozen and taken over by the state,' said a counter-terrorism senior official, speaking on the condition of anonymity because he was not authorized to speak publicly. The CTD was quoted as saying that 'the action

> is in accordance with UN sanctions against the individuals and entities'.[1]

No mention was made of the courts Hafiz Saeed had been running across the country. The daily the *News* (on 9 April 2016) had earlier disclosed that Saeed had been doing something unforgivable, that is, running stealth courts in violation of the constitution of Pakistan:

> The supra-constitutional Sharia courts, established by Jamaat ud Dawa (JuD), operate across the country and only the Lahore court of this parallel judicial system has issued verdicts in 5,550 cases, including murder trials.

The FATF Fiat

The pressure in 2019 to 'do something' had come from the Paris-based FATF, which placed Pakistan on its 'grey list' of countries with inadequate controls over money laundering and terrorism-financing. The US had offered $10 million for Hafiz Saeed's head in 2012; Pakistan finally offered it on a platter and, as quid pro quo, got the US to declare the Balochistan Liberation Army (BLA) a terrorist organization. The BLA had long been seen as India's tit-for-tat response to the Pakistani 'non-state actors' launching attacks in India.

Geo TV's anchor Kamran Khan, in his 12 November 2012 programme, had revealed that Pakistani officials had told the anti-terrorism court judge Chaudhry Habibur Rehman, on 10 November 2012, that 'the terrorists who attacked and killed over 166 innocent people in Mumbai on 26 November 2012, belonged to the LeT and that they had trained at various cities of Pakistan. The mastermind of this attack, Zakiur Rehman Lakhvi, was under trial at Adiala Jail in Rawalpindi.' However, on the order of the Lahore High Court, Lakhvi was finally released on bail on 10 April 2015.

And just as one thought that the Mumbai massacre planner, Pakistani-American David Headley/Daood Gilani, had disappeared from the world terror radar to spend thirty-five years in an American prison, more information about him surfaced in a documentary by *PBS-Frontline*.[2] The new lowdown came from a typed 'memoir' apparently put together by him. He wrote that he joined the LeT before the 9/11 attacks in the US, and ended up reconnoitring for the November 2008 Mumbai attack, which killed 166. It turns out that without him laying out the 'mission map', the attack wouldn't have taken place. Headley went to Pakistan in July 2002 and visited the Qadisiya mosque, then the headquarters of LeT—which was later renamed the JuD—in Lahore, meeting its head, Hafiz Muhammad Saeed, to reveal his interest in covert jihad.

Khawaja Asif in Trouble

This was not the first time Pakistan had moved to arrest Hafiz Saeed. In February 2017, the founder-leader of the charity organization JuD had been confined to his house, but support for him had swelled around the country. His followers and members of the JuD staged protests against his confinement. No one dared point to evidence, which was internationally in circulation, about his involvement in acts of terrorism in India and India-administered Kashmir. A statement made by the then defence minister Khawaja Muhammad Asif, however, opened the floodgates of castigation on the Nawaz Sharif government.

Reports said that Khawaja Asif was in Germany when he committed the 'blasphemy' of saying: 'Hafiz Saeed can become a threat to society.' The world and the UN accused Saeed of committing atrocities in India and Afghanistan. The latter had him on its 'reward list' of terrorists, but in Pakistan he was the wealthiest philanthropist alive. However, two terrorists, Daood Gilani and Ajmal Kasab confessed to details of his involvement in international terrorism. But Pakistan's devotion of him ran deep.

His reported running of private courts in Pakistan seemed to have been forgiven.

After Khawaja Asif's statement in Germany, Pakistan experienced a pro-Saeed earthquake. The dreaded Defence of Pakistan Council (DPC), which scared anyone critical of the policies of jihad, fired a broadside at the government Asif served. A roll call of those who would have liked Sharif's term in office to end prematurely joined in. Their beef was that instead of 'speculating' whether Saeed could become a threat or not, Khawaja Asif should have highlighted the atrocities committed against Muslims in Kashmir. Former Azad Kashmir prime minister Sardar Muhammad Atique said that Khawaja Asif was appeasing India; and PTI leader Mahmood Ur Rasheed thought the Sharif government had become 'defensive' on India and the US, making Khawaja Asif sound more like the defence minister of India than of Pakistan.

The Mainstreaming Menace

In September 2017, it had become certain that unless the powers-that-be intervened, the dubious empire of under-house-arrest and internationally dubbed terrorist Hafiz Muhammad Saeed had come to an end, and that the process of 'mainstreaming' recommended by retired generals debating on talk shows had been shipwrecked. The foreign office, under the ruling PML (N)'s foreign minister Khawaja Muhammad Asif, had finally decided that Hafiz Saeed's Milli Muslim League (MML) should not have taken part in the by-polls of the NA-120 constituency, bagging 5822 votes and beating the mainstream PPP.

In the same month, the foreign office followed up on the letter of the interior ministry under PML (N) minister Ahsan Iqbal, in answer to a query sent by the Election Commission of Pakistan (ECP) about whether the MML should be allowed to take part in the by-polls. The interior ministry stated:

> There is evidence to substantiate that [the] Lashkar-e-Taiba (LeT), the Jamaat-ud-Dawa [JuD] and Falah-e-Insaniat Foundation (FIF) are affiliates and ideologically of the same hue, and [therefore] the registration of the MML is not supported.[3]

In 2008, the UN Security Council had added JuD to the banned list under Resolution 1267, as a 'supporting agent of the banned Lashkar-e-Taiba'.

Hafiz Saeed and his various 'charity' organizations, including hundreds of schools and colleges, were a prime example of the 'mainstreaming' of an outlawed organization by Pakistan. Its negative fallout was also endured, like the running of private courts under 'Islamic law' by the banned outfit. The state helped further by enlisting Saeed's enormous wealth for the 'renewal' of regions depredated by state neglect and local rebels in Sindh and Balochistan.

What had been highlighted by a lame-duck PML (N) government was the negative consequence of what was called 'mainstreaming' by some elements of the state. Instead of de-radicalizing the declared terrorists, the process sought to further radicalize society and undermine the power of the state as per the Constitution. Also, the 'indirect' and 'implied' Chinese warning at a BRICS summit earlier that year had to be heeded.

Lashkar As Jamaat

In March 2005, the *amir* (commander) of the banned LeT and the renamed JuD, Hafiz Saeed, routinely issued criticism of the government's policies. After having abandoned the grand Muridke seminary, which he ran under the cover of Markaz Dawat wal-Irshad, he was now firmly established near Chauburji in Lahore, not lacking in financial and manpower muscle. Urdu newspapers felt obliged to print his almost-daily diatribes against 'the misdirection of the country'. He was part of the trio (the other two being Masood Azhar of JeM and Fazlur Rehman Khaleel of Harkatul Mujahideen) that seemed exempt from the punishment that usually followed the label of terrorism.

In 2005, Hafiz Saeed was supposed to be fighting for his political survival. There were reports that a group of disgruntled JuD bigwigs, led by Maulana Zafar Iqbal, had revolted against him and a new splinter, by the name of Khairun Naas (meaning people's welfare), had been formed. It included some top JuD leaders like Abdus Salam Bhutvi, Amir Hamza, Nasr Javed, Saifullah Mansoor and Ustad Abdul Qadir. Oddly, the new group also enjoyed the support of Zakiur Rehman Lakhvi, the amir of the banned LeT, who walked from a special court that did not find him guilty of the Mumbai attack. Maulana Zafar Iqbal had visited Saudi Arabia to seek support from the Saudi clerics to consolidate his splinter party. This is how Hafiz Saeed's declining post-9/11 fortunes were described then.

From Simla to Sargodha

Hafiz Saeed, a Kashmiri *gujjar* (one belonging to a pastoral community) whose family lived in Simla before Partition, grew up in Sargodha where his family tilled the land they had got 'in claim' for the property left behind in 1947. Saeed's father, Maulana Kamaluddin, was a religious scholar, so was his uncle Maulana Hafiz Abdullah, who later helped him set up LeT. Abdullah's sons, Abdur Rehman Makki and Abdul Mannan, married the sisters of Hafiz Saeed. Makki later became the second-in-command of the LeT.

Hafiz Saeed graduated from Sargodha Government College and later pursued his MA in Arabic and Islamiat from Punjab University. At the university's Old Campus, he was a *nazim* (administrator) of the Islami Jamiat Tulaba, the students' wing of the Jamaat-e-Islami. PML (N) leader Javed Hashmi won the Punjab University Students' Union elections under his *nizamat* (leadership) and rose on the Pakistani political scene.

After graduation in 1974, Hafiz Saeed was appointed lecturer at the University of Engineering and Technology (UET), Lahore, in the Islamiat Department. (One should recall that the son of a former Punjab governor, Shahbaz Taseer, following his father Salman Taseer's assassination, was kidnapped in August 2011 by UET students. Shahbaz was taken to Faisalabad, the earliest Wahhabi base that had attracted the al-Qaeda, where the first al-Qaeda leader working for Osama bin Laden was arrested and handed over to the US: Abu Zubayda.)

A Star Is Born at UET

It is from UET that Hafiz Saeed was sent for higher studies to Saudi Arabia. He graduated from King Saud University, Riyadh. While in Saudi Arabia, he was close to famous Saudi scholar Sheikh Abdul Aziz bin Baz, who was the first to pronounce the fatwa of jihad in Afghanistan in 1979. After his sojourn in Saudi Arabia, Saeed returned to Pakistan and was selected as a research scholar at the Council of Islamic Ideology, a selection made by a panel of high court judges. As part of the council, he retained his bond with UET.

According to *Nida-e-Millat* magazine (issue dated 22 March 2001), Hafiz Saeed took part in the election campaign of the Jamaat-e-Islami in 1970 but was put off by its politics after losing. He turned against democracy and was traumatized by the fall of East Pakistan in 1971. It was after the fatwa of jihad was issued in 1979 by bin Baz that he turned to jihad in Afghanistan and went to the training camp of Abdur Rasul Sayyaf, which is where he met the teacher of Osama bin Laden and other Arab fighters, Dr Abdullah Azzam. He admitted that during his training he met Osama bin Laden a number of times. In 1986, the teachers of the Islamiat faculty at UET had founded the Markaz Dawat wal-Irshad, an Ahle Hadith organization devoted to the Saudi brand of Islam raising armies for the jihad in Afghanistan.

In 1990, when Hafiz Saeed set up the LeT, it was in consultation with the professors in Lahore and the organizers of the Kunar camp in Afghanistan, where the Wahhabis had set up their own government. By 2001, the LeT was the most well-known jihadi outfit in the region, boasting 1100 martyrs and 15,000 Indian troops killed in Kashmir. Hafiz Saeed claimed that his fighters had also figured in jihad in Bosnia and Chechnya.

Nuclear Scientists and Saeed

Paul L. Williams, an American journalist with a PhD who teaches and advises Federal Bureau of Investigation (FBI) officers, writes in his book *Osama's Revenge: the Next 9/11* that Pakistani nuclear scientists and Pakistan's premier Wahhabi militia, the LeT, helped Osama bin Laden equip the al-Qaeda with miniaturized nuclear weapons and 'dirty' nuclear explosives.[4] Quoting from BBC News (20 December 2002), he stated that Dr Abdul Qadeer Khan had got his Kahuta Laboratories funded clandestinely by Saudi Arabia, which was interested in developing an 'Islamic bomb'. The then prime minister Benazir Bhutto too got Dr Khan to visit North Korea and purchase twelve to fourteen Nodong ballistic missiles.

Dr Khan also appeared in LeT rallies run by Hafiz Saeed. In 2003, after the LeT was banned and came back as the JuD, it devoted itself to serving the al-Qaeda as a coordinating agency with pro-al-Qaeda networks in Pakistan. As noted above, on 2 February 2002, at the high tide of the al-Qaeda's revenge killings inside Pakistan, Osama bin Laden's lieutenant, Abu Zubaida, was caught in Faisalabad from one of Hafiz Saeed's safe houses. (The rumour then was that a son of Osama bin Laden was also in the safe house but had managed to escape a few days earlier.)

Dr Khan attended LeT gatherings with other nuclear scientists, including Sultan Bashiruddin Mahmood, former director of the Pakistan Atomic Energy Commission (*Washington Times*, 30 December 2003). In this context, Hafiz Saeed came within the orbit of the 'deterrence' assets Pakistan had to safeguard. The other factor was the possible connection with Saudi Arabia, which enjoyed a lot of traction in Islamabad.

The Global Squeeze

In January 2017, Islamabad got scared enough by a global anti-terrorist consensus to restrain Hafiz Saeed under Section 11-EEE (1) of the Anti-Terrorism Act, 1977. He had more money than any other religious leader and had financed the DPC, which hit the road every time the government 'betrayed' the country by relaxing on the 'Kashmir dispute'. He was put under house arrest at Masjid Qadisiya, on Lake Road in Lahore, his headquarters named insultingly after Qadisiya. He later shifted to a more comfortable residence in Johar Town. Earlier in April, nothing came of the 'discovery' that he had been running stealth courts across the country in violation of the Constitution of Pakistan.

The UN dubbed him a terrorist, putting $10 million as bounty on his head, but the courts in Pakistan were not tough enough to restrain him or punish him for changing the names of his jihadi outfits. Saeed, meanwhile, carried on with anti-India hate speech, which actually smeared Pakistan in the eyes of a scared world. The perpetrators of the 2008 Mumbai attack, who shot dead 166 people, had confessed to details that should have been enough to hang him, but Pakistan enjoyed his anti-India rhetoric and let him spread his tentacles.

Expanding the Domestic Domain

He was rumoured to have 2,00,000 men deployed in Tharparkar in those days, and later in Balochistan, 'conquering' people that Pakistan didn't like: the Hindus who 'converted' because of his 'kindness' and the Baloch who 'appreciated' his help. He headed the largest charity in Karachi where he had also his university, in addition to thousands of schools and kindergartens all over Pakistan.

In July 2016, after *Dawn* published a front-page story about how in a meeting between then prime minister Nawaz Sharif and then ISI chief General Rizwan Akhtar, it was discussed that the impunity enjoyed by non-state actors (like Masood Azhar of the JeM and Hafiz Saeed of the JuD) was isolating Pakistan in the world at a time when it needed to expose India's atrocities in Kashmir, Hafiz Saeed responded with a tactful rejoinder.

He said (in *Dunya* on 8 October 2016) that the government and the army were on the same page when it came to India, but Prime Minister Sharif's advisers were making him 'embrace the general in his arms while tripping him on his foot'. As reported in *Jang* (on 10 June 2006), the JuD held a funeral prayer in absentia for Abu Musab al-Zarqawi (the founder of today's ISIS) in Lahore and condemned the foreign office for saying that the death of the Shia killer in Iraq was an achievement in the war against terrorism. The congregation that blessed Zarqawi kept weeping loudly for the great shaheed (martyr). In the National Assembly, the clerical alliance MMA demanded a funeral prayer called Fateha for Zarqawi, but this was denied by the speaker. Reported in the daily *Nawa-e-Waqt*, a Jamaat-e-Islami leader, Syed Munawwar Hasan, said Pakistan was reluctant to call Zarqawi shaheed 'as that would offend Washington'.[5]

The Pathankot Puzzle

In January 2016, a terrorist attack took place at the Pathankot Air Force Station, a part of the Western Air Command of the Indian Air Force. Four attackers and two security forces personnel were killed in the initial battle, with an additional security force member dying from injuries hours later. The Indian reaction to the attack was intense. Babar Sattar wrote in the *News* (8 October 2016):

> Pathankot highlighted that actions of non-state actors can trigger a full-scale war between nuclear-armed India and Pakistan. Uri is establishing that it is non-state actors that are now in control of the fate and fortune of the Subcontinent and not the two states. It is time to snap out of our present state

> of insanity. Let us not allow India's fighting words to prevent us from undertaking a Machiavellian appraisal of our national security doctrine and how we have transformed homebred non-state actors into the biggest threat to our security.

By 2012, Hafiz Saeed was at par with Mullah Omar and the al-Qaeda chiefs of Iran and Iraq, all of whom carried a reward of $10 million on their heads. His brother-in-law and co-founder of the LeT, Abdul Rehman Makki, also carried a bounty of $3 million. Ayman al-Zawahiri, the head of the al-Qaeda after the killing of Osama bin Laden, remained the most-wanted terrorist in the world, with $25 million on his head.

Hafiz Saeed was arguably the most powerful man in Pakistan, heading the country's biggest charity organization (JuD). He was the mover and shaker of the DPC. And he was the spearhead of Pakistan's non-state actors who prevented the country from allowing the resumption of the North Atlantic Treaty Organization (NATO) supply route through its territory.

The Extreme Exegete

Tariq Rahman, in his book *Interpretations of Jihad in South Asia: An Intellectual History* (2019), sums up Saeed's intellectual background:

> Hafiz Saeed was influenced by Abdullah Azzam, Shaikh Abd al-Aziz bin Baz (1910–1999), the grand Mufti of Saudi Arabia, and his organization was supported at some level by Osama bin Laden. Thus, he imbibed radical Islamist ideas from these Arab militant sources in addition to developing them himself.
>
> His ideas have been disseminated in the form of sermons and pamphlets, discussed in great detail by Western scholars. The gist of studies about the narratives offered by Saeed himself, as well as other members of his organization, is that jihad is a duty of every Muslim in the absence of the

Islamic State. Moreover, Saeed negates the ideas that: (a) jihad needs to be ordered by the state; (b) that it is not incumbent upon Pakistani Muslims since they have not been attacked; (c) that international treaties would have to be renounced first before any attack; (d) that Pakistan is too militarily and economically weak to win a war so it should not be initiated. He maintains, like Abdullah Azzam and Osama bin Laden, that if there is no Muslim ruler ready to order jihad openly, the Muslim community can choose one for that purpose and, as he himself is the head (amir) of his organization, it is implied that he is the one who has been de facto chosen. He claims, again like the two Arab militant leaders mentioned above, that Muslims have, indeed, been attacked.

In this context, he presents the case of Kashmir which, he says, has been occupied by India illegally and is subject to human rights abuses. This being so, he argues, India has already broken international agreements about peace, so he is merely responding defensively on behalf of Pakistan. As for the last point, he refers to the small size of the Muslim army in the Battle of Badr vis-à-vis the Quraysh, arguing that it is courage and faith which are needed and not military superiority. Indeed, when his fighters, as well as regular Pakistani soldiers, had to withdraw from the Kargil peaks which they had occupied in 1999, he quoted seven verses of Surah Maidah (5:51-57), to argue that Prime Minister Nawaz Sharif (b. 1949) had gone against Quranic injunctions that prohibit Muslims from befriending Jews and Christians.[6]

Ghamidi: Rejected by Asymmetric Jihad

Hafiz Saeed was lionized by the state and the believers of Pakistan, but there were others who, despite disfavour shown to them, rejected interpretive radicalization of Islam to somehow let the state nurse warriors. One of these was Jawed Ahmad Ghamidi (b. 1948) who can't live in Pakistan because he doesn't allow 'aggressive' jihad. In his widely distributed publications *Al-Mawrid* and *Renaissance*, Ghamidi rationally rejects the 'aggressive war' message of Mawdudi and Syed Qutb, and holds that aggression was addressed primarily to Ismaelites, Israelites and the Nazarites (Muslims, Jews and Christians) of Arabia in the Prophet's times and was no longer binding in modern times.

Ghamidi, however, permits 'defensive war' as jihad only in the case of *fitnah*, which he defines as 'cruel persecution of Muslims and effort to alienate them from their religion'. One can add 'cruelty, exploitation and antagonism' suffered by the Muslim community. He leaned on verse 22:39 of the Quran to say that 'those being oppressed are allowed to fight', or 'those who [are] expelled from their homes'. There was nothing new in these messages of moderation. Many moderate exegetes, like Sir Syed Ahmed Khan and Maulvi Chiragh Ali, had adopted this interpretation but were rejected over time, till a point where Sir Syed was quietly taken off the pantheon of the Pakistan Movement. Ghamidi outraged the 'new' Pakistani by implying that the message of the Quran was not for all times, that certain messages were meant for the times that are now past and not relevant to modern times.

Declan Walsh of the *Guardian* reported in 2011 that 'Javed Ahmad Ghamidi, reformist scholar and popular television preacher, has launched a blistering attack on Pakistan's blasphemy laws, warning that failure to repeal them will only strengthen religious extremists and their violent followers.'

He quoted Ghamidi:

> The blasphemy laws have no justification in Islam. These ulema [council of clerics] are just telling lies to the people. But they have become stronger, because they have street power behind them, and the liberal forces are weak and divided. If it continues like this, it could result in the destruction of Pakistan.[7]

Ghamidi left for Malaysia in 2010 and can't return to Pakistan unless he wants to die at the hands of any one of the trainees in the sprawling world of the madrasas. And the state will keep quiet if he meets his end simply because he is irrelevant today. His ally, Farooq Khan, brilliant on TV and favoured by not-so-canny Pakistanis when he appeared in TV discussions, was 'wrongly' favoured by the state too and made vice chancellor of the University of Swat that was founded in 2010. He was killed in 2010, which may have triggered the wisdom of exile in Ghamidi.

A World That Didn't Believe

The world didn't buy Pakistan's denial on Pathankot, and since it believed that Hafiz Saeed had masterminded the Mumbai attack of 2008, led by the US, it wanted Pakistan to prevent Hafiz Saeed from moving freely in the country, freeze the assets of the groups associated with him and stop allowing the LeT from acquiring weapons—in accordance with UN Security Council Resolution 1267/1989. In Pakistan, the JuD was not considered to be a changed LeT and Hafiz Saeed was a highly respected person because of his jihadi slogans against the 'enemies of Pakistan', which at that point were the US and India.

International reports about the 'connectivities' of the JuD with the al-Qaeda, and Hafiz Saeed's past associations with the founders of the al-Qaeda were hardly discussed in the Pakistani media. Revelations about the various sojourns of Osama bin Laden before his death—in Kohat, Swat, Karachi and Abbottabad—and his phone calls to Hafiz Saeed were dismissed without comment. As titular head of the DPC, Saeed headed one of the six centres of power in a slowly imploding state. He was the national symbol of Pakistan's defiance of its erstwhile ally, the US.[8]

Pride and honour breed defiance no matter what the odds. Defiance in foreign policy, when no one in the world backs you, is called isolationism. This is basically another name for defeat in the given international order. When Pakistan's non-state actors defeated the Soviet Union, the world was on Pakistan's side in the proxy war; in Kashmir, the world was not with Pakistan, and

Pakistan was not successful in humbling India. The blowback from the planned 'victory' against the US was far more lethal than the blowback from the victory against the Soviet Union. The problem was not only that foreign policy was not being handled by the parliament in Pakistan, but that foreign policy was being spearheaded by elements who had their own agenda.

5

The Murder of Syed Saleem Shahzad

On 29 December 2019, the daily *Pakistan Today* wrote:

> The book launch functions of Washington-based Shuja Nawaz's latest book, *The Battle for Pakistan*, were cancelled after the author was told to do so. The reason for this censorship was not easily understood, for Shuja Nawaz has hitherto enjoyed an impeccable reputation as one who has strongly supported the Pakistani position in the USA, where he is based, being a Distinguished Fellow of the South Asia Centre at the prestigious Atlantic Council. His previous books have been praised, including his two works on the Pakistan Army, *Crossed Swords* and *Wars Within*. There is some speculation that the book contains material uncomplimentary to the present government, but there is none of the certainty of an official statement.[1]

The most probable cause of the 'ban' was Nawaz's account of what happened in Pakistan on 22 May 2011, when a fifteen-man-strong Tehreek-e-Taliban Pakistan (TTP) force stormed into three hangars at PNS Mehran in Karachi. After cutting the barbed wire on the perimeter fence, at a place where there were no security cameras, they first attacked the aircraft parked on the tarmac and the equipment in nearby hangars using rocket-propelled grenades, damaging and destroying several warplanes and premiere anti-submarine and marine surveillance aircraft, the US-made P-3C Orion and several multimillion-dollar aircrafts.

Syed Saleem Shahzad, bureau head at Asia Times Online in Pakistan, wrote an article challenging the official story. Headlined 'Al-Qaeda Had Warned of Pakistan Strike', the article alleged that the attack was not carried out by the TTP or its affiliates, but by al-Qaeda. The reason was presumed to be the failure of talks between the authorities and al-Qaeda on the release of the latter's sympathizers, whom the military had uncovered and taken into custody. He alleged that the military had been penetrated by such elements and cited an anonymous source (from the military):

> 'Islamic sentiments are common in the armed forces,' a senior navy official told *Asia Times Online* on the condition of anonymity as he is not authorized to speak to the media. 'We never felt threatened by that. All armed forces around the world, whether American, British or Indian, take some inspiration from religion to motivate their cadre against the enemy,' the official said. 'Nonetheless, we observed an uneasy grouping on different naval lases in Karachi. While nobody can obstruct armed forces for rendering religious rituals or studying Islam, the grouping [we observed] was against the discipline of the armed forces. That was the beginning of an intelligence operation in the navy to check for unscrupulous activities.'
>
> The official explained [that] the grouping was against the leadership of the armed forces and opposed to its nexus with the US against Islamic militancy. When some messages were

intercepted, hinting at attacks on American officials, intelligence had good reason to take action after careful evaluation of at least 10 people—mostly from the lower ranks—[they] were arrested in a series of operations. 'That was the beginning of huge trouble,' the official said.[2]

Shahzad Spills the Beans

Shahzad's article revealed:

> Within a week, insiders at PNS Mehran provided maps, pictures of different exit and entry routes taken in daylight and at night, the location of hangers and details of likely reaction from external security forces. As a result, the militants were able to enter the heavily guarded facility where one group targeted the aircraft, a second group took on the first strike force and a third finally escaped with the others providing covering fire. Those who stayed behind were killed.[3]

Shuja Nawaz writes in his book:

> His story and the release of Shahzad's book, that detailed infiltration by the militants into the military and alleged links between the ISI and militant organizations, created a public furore and may have raised hackles inside the security services. Shahzad had earlier been approached by the ISI to retract a story on 25 March, stating that bin Laden was on the move inside Pakistan and hinting at knowledge of Pakistani intelligence about his movement.
>
> The next morning, he got a phone call from an officer at the ISI, summoning him to the agency's headquarters, in Aabpara, a neighbourhood in eastern Islamabad. When Shahzad showed up, he was met by three ISI officers. The lead man, he said, was a naval officer, Rear Admiral Adnan Nazir, who served as the head of the ISI's media division.

'They were very polite,' Shahzad said. 'They don't shout, they don't threaten you. This is the way they operate. But they were very angry with me,' [he added]. The ISI officers asked him to write a second story, retracting the first. He refused. And then Admiral Nazir made a remark so bizarre that Shahzad said he had thought about it every day since. 'We want the world to believe that Osama is dead,' Nazir [had] said.

Bin Laden was still alive, his whereabouts presumably unknown, when that conversation occurred. I pressed Shahzad. What did he mean by that? He shrugged and glanced over his shoulder again. Shahzad said, 'They were obviously trying to protect bin Laden.'

'Do you think the ISI was hiding bin Laden?' I asked.

Shahzad shrugged again and said yes. But he hadn't been able to prove it. (The ISI called this claim an 'unsubstantiated accusation of a very serious nature'.)[4]

Shahzad Taken Off the Scene

Nine days later, Shahzad disappeared. Two days after that, his tortured body was found in a canal near Jhelum. The *New York Times* reported:

> Obama administration officials believe that Pakistan's powerful spy agency ordered the killing of a Pakistani journalist who had written scathing reports about the infiltration of militant[s] in the country's military.

The report added:

> In a statement the day after Mr. Shahzad's waterlogged body was retrieved from a canal 60 miles from Islamabad, the ISI publicly denied accusations in the Pakistani news media that it had been responsible, calling them 'totally unfounded'.[5]

The ISI said the journalist's death was 'unfortunate and tragic' but should not be 'used to target and malign the country's security agency'. Much later, when I asked a senior Pakistani intelligence official about his murder, he said he had no idea who had done it. 'Why did you not investigate it in that case, since the ISI was being blamed for it?' I asked. His answer was a shrug.

The government came under intense pressure from journalists to investigate Shahzad's murder. Shuja Nawaz writes that on 16 June 2011, 'the government accepted the demands of journalists and announced the formation of an inquiry commission.' Headed by Justice Saqib Nisar, the commission's other members were Justice Agha Rafiq, the additional IG (Punjab), the president of the Pakistan Federal Union of Journalists (PFUJ) and the deputy DIG (Federal Police). From the outset, the commission was mired in controversy since only the Supreme Court chief justice could form and announce such a commission. Regardless, the commission completed its work and issued a 146-page report in January 2012, offering many suggestions on how to remove, as quoted in Nawaz's book, 'the systemic causes of tensions between [intelligence] agencies and the media', but it failed to identify either the motive or the likely suspect responsible for Shahzad's murder.[6] Many journalists testified to receiving threats and being harassed by intelligence agencies. However, both the Military Intelligence, which normally operates only on military matters and is housed in the army headquarters, and the Intelligence Bureau simply notified the commission that they had nothing to do with Shahzad's murder. They were not questioned further.

Nawaz writes in his book:

> The ISI's written testimony and replies to the Commission's questions pointed to Al-Qaeda as the likely suspect, and [also] hinted at an American link given what they thought was undue interest in the case from 'President Obama to every man worth a name in the US [who] felt disturbed. Was he [Shahzad] a pawn who could be used at [an] appropriate time to further use the

US Objectives and create a wedge between [the] establishment (the euphemism in Pakistani parlance for the military and its intelligence agencies) and other segments of society?

Brigadier Zahid Mehmood Khan of the ISI's sector headquarters, central Islamabad, who delivered some of the ISI rebuttal against [the] charges that his agency was implicated in the murder, also pointed to Shahzad's contacts with other intelligence agencies from India and the UK. Not surprisingly, the Commission was unable to implicate the ISI. This murder, like many other disappearances and highly publicised assassinations in Pakistan's history, remained unsolved.

It also left an unresolved issue in the fractured relationship between the US and Pakistan, and reflected poorly on the lack of ability of the civilian administration in Islamabad at safeguarding the citizens of Pakistan. It also underlined the gap between the government and the autonomous military establishment to which the government had outsourced security issues. Indeed, the PPP government itself felt constantly threatened by the coercive potential power of the military, as other events in 2011 indicated.[7]

The Book That Saleem Shahzad Wrote

Anyone who has read *Inside Al-Qaeda and the Taliban: Beyond Bin Laden and 9/11* by Syed Saleem Shahzad[8] will come to the following conclusions:

1) It is the al-Qaeda, and not the Taliban, that plans militant attacks in Pakistan, and that the Taliban execute no operations without the permission of the al-Qaeda.
2) Jihadi organizations are subservient to the al-Qaeda, and some are extensions of the Pakistan Army.
3) The TTP was shaped by the al-Qaeda through Uzbek warlord Tahir Yuldashev after the 2007 Lal Masjid affair.

4) 'Retired' army officers, earlier handling proxy jihad, defected to the al-Qaeda but continued to use contacts within the military on its behalf.
5) Benazir Bhutto was killed by the al-Qaeda and not Baitullah Mehsud; he was merely an instrument.
6) The 2008 Mumbai attack was conducted by the al-Qaeda through former Pakistan Army officers, with help from the LeT and without the knowledge of the ISI despite the fact that the LeT was on ISI's leash.
7) Army officers, or freedom fighters trained by the army for Kashmir jihad, spearheaded al-Qaeda's war against the Pakistan Army.
8) Islamic radicalization of Pakistani society and media, together with the fear of being assassinated by al-Qaeda agents—who include ex-army officers—has tilted the balance of power away from the state of Pakistan to al-Qaeda.
9) Punjabi Taliban are under the Haqqani network, which is supposed to be aligned with the Pakistan Army.
10) The army has ex-officers in al-Qaeda, as well as serving officers collaborating with them.[9]

A Case of Knowing Too Much

Saleem Shahzad, who enjoyed the confidence of many al-Qaeda militants and never betrayed their whereabouts, wrote in his book:

> There were at least 600,000 youths there who since 1979. . At least 100,000 Pakistanis were active members of different Jihadi cadres. Over 1 million students were enrolled in various Islamic seminaries, and there were several hundred thousand supporters of Pakistan's Islamic religious parties.
>
> The main handler of the Afghan Jihad against the Soviets had been Pakistan's army, which itself was not immune to the influence of radicalism. Several army officers had pledged their allegiance (bait) to different Jihadi spiritual leaders, including

> Maulana Akram Awan of Chakwal. These groups were known in the Pakistan Army as *pirbhai* groups. Although General Pervez Musharraf had purged some of these elements from the Pakistan Army after 9/11, including his very close friend, the then deputy chief of army staff Lt Gen. Muzaffar Usmani, he was unable to completely eradicate the radical tendency, which had become deep-rooted in Pakistan's security services during the period from 1979 to 2001.[10]

Al-Qaeda bent its principles constantly to get more allies on board. One was Lashkar-e-Jhangvi (LeJ):

> Slowly and gradually this strategy began to work and brought thousands of new recruits into the Al-Qaeda fold. Among them were two well-known brothers, Dr Akmal Waheed and Dr Arshad Waheed, from Karachi, who were now linked to Al-Qaeda through Jandullah. Dr Arshad Waheed was later killed in Wana in south Waziristan in a CIA drone strike, and soon afterwards Al-Qaeda's media wing, Al-Sahab, released a documentary on his life and exploits to inspire the younger generation. Subsequently, several army officers joined the Al-Qaeda cadre.

Radicalization was facilitated by the Jamaat-e-Islami:

> Its student wing had been formed in the 1948 as the offshoot of Jamaat-e-Islami, and by the 1970s it dominated all the country's major educational institutions, including the University of Karachi, University of Punjab and University of Peshawar. Most of the middle-class members of Pakistan's leadership had belonged to the IJT as students, including Pakistan's ambassador to the United States, Husain Haqqani, Pakistan Muslim League leaders Javed Hashmi and Ehsan Iqbal, Pakistani law minister Dr Babar Awan, and almost 80 per cent of Urdu-language newspaper and electronic media opinion writers and television talk show anchors in Pakistan.

> [The] Uzbeks that Al-Qaeda brought to Waziristan were critical in forming the violent mood of the militants: Tahir Yuldashev played a key role in the recruiting of such tribal militants as Abdullah Mehsud. Yuldashev headed an Uzbek force of 2,500 men. The Uzbeks were to give the Pakistani militants lessons in brutality to establish a reign of terror: their tactics included routinely slitting the throats of their foes.

The Ashiq Brothers

Al-Qaeda's hero was Captain Khurram Ashiq of the Pakistan Army, whose brother, Major Haroon Ashiq, followed him to become the al-Qaeda's hand that wielded the sword. In 2001, Khurram was an assault commander of the elite anti-terrorist Zarrar Company from Pakistan's Special Service Group (SSG), but he flipped after 9/11. Because of his Salafi background, he was shaped into a warrior by the LeT. Today, he is being investigated and targeted by the FATF presided over in 2019 by China. He wrote to Saleem Shahzad about his brother too. Major Haroon Ashiq hung up his boots right after 9/11. On his release from service, he joined the LeT: 'One of my unit officers, Major Abdul Rahman, also followed suit. I joined the outfit soon after, without caring for the consequences.'[11]

For Captain Khurram, faith came before country. While on a UN mission, he clearly demonstrated it:

> Khurram built a mosque and a Madrassa in Sierra Leone, despite the opposition of his commander, Brigadier Ahmad Shuja Pasha, later chief of the ISI. Both brothers had joined the LeT, but had soon 'realised that the LeT was just an extension of Pakistan's armed forces.

Major Haroon read classical Muslim academics like Imam Ibn Taymiyya, Ibn Khaldun and Muhammad Ibn Abd al-Wahhab.

Among modern-day scholars, he studied the works of the Muslim Brotherhood ideologue Syed Qutb, as well as the founder of the Jamaat-e-Islami Pakistan, Syed Abul Ala Maududi. Haroon then severed his ties with the Kashmiri struggle and move to north Waziristan with his family. Khurram and Rahman then went to the Afghan province of Helmand in 2007, where Khurram was martyred, after which Rehman joined Haroon in the al-Qaeda, becoming the lynchpin of the Mumbai attack in 2008.

Enter Hizbut Tahrir from London

As an al-Qaeda terrorist, Haroon enjoyed contacts inside the army:

> Haroon developed a silencer for the AK-47. This became an essential component of Al-Qaeda's special guerrilla operations. He then visited China to procure night vision glasses. The biggest task was to clear them through the customs in Pakistan, Haroon called on his friend Captain Farooq, who was President Musharraf's security officer. Farooq went to the airport in the president's official car and received Haroon at the immigration counter. In the presence of Farooq, nobody dared touch Haroon's luggage, and the night vision glasses arrived in Pakistan without any hassle [Farooq was a member of the Hizbut Tahrir, a fact discovered by the military intelligence as late as nine months later his posting as Musharraf's security officer. After being spotted, he was briefly arrested and then retired from the Pakistan Army.][12]

Al-Qaeda targeted NATO supplies through Haroon in 2008:

> Haroon travelled through North Waziristan to Karachi. When night fell, he stayed in army messes in the countryside. Being an ex-army officer, he was allowed that facility. He spoke English and Urdu with an unmistakable military accent.[13]

He took revenge on Major General Ameer Faisal Alavi because the latter had killed a lot of al-Qaeda men—including Abdur Rehman Kennedy—as the leader of a Pakistan Army assault on Angor Adda in north Waziristan. Haroon ambushed Alavi in Islamabad 'jumping out of his car and killing Alavi with his army revolver'.[14] Haroon believed in the *Ghazwa-e-Hind* (Battle for India) hadith and thought that the end of the world was close, and that the advent of the Mahdi was at hand with the help of the armies of Khurasan (Afghanistan–Pakistan).[15]

Haroon landed in Adiala jail in Rawalpindi after failing to kidnap an Ahmadi, Sarwar Khan. (The police officer in Adiala jail told Saleem Shahzad that he had started admiring his prisoner.) In custody, he admitted to killing Major General Alavi and kidnapping Hindu filmmaker Satish Anand with the help of one Major Basit from Karachi. After he discovered that Anand had no money, he released him on orders from al-Qaeda's Ilyas Kashmiri, but only 'if he embraced Islam', which Anand immediately did. Later, the al-Qaeda decided that to refill its empty coffers it will abduct only non-Muslims, Ahmadis in particular.

The Mumbai Attack and ISI

The Mumbai operation was actually the revival of an old ISI plan. The idea was to deflect the Pakistan Army away from Waziristan and get it to fight India instead. This nearly succeeded:

> Pakistan's militant leaders Mullah Fazlullah and Baitullah Mehsud announced that they would fight alongside Pakistan's armed forces in an India–Pakistan war, and the director general of ISI, Lt Gen. Ahmad Shuja Pasha, confirmed this understanding in his briefing to national and foreign correspondents, when he called Fazlullah and Mehsud Pakistan's strategic assets.[16]

Shahzad saw the al-Qaeda busily pursuing the goal of weaning Pakistan away from the West with violence and ideology.

Pakistan's own teleology of moving from mild to harsh Islam helped. He saw the al-Qaeda achieving the following objective:

> Pressure on the ruling Muslim elites and the Muslim masses to break their alliance with the West and support the Islamists' cause of a global struggle for the freedom of occupied Muslim lands and establishment of a Global Caliphate.[17]

Pakistan Today concluded by wondering about the 'ban' applied to the launch of Shuja Nawaz's book in Pakistan:

> It is perhaps paradoxical that the sale and distribution of the book have not been forbidden, which indicates that it does not contain any material which would justify a prohibition in court. The way the book launches, which were originally scheduled for Karachi, Lahore and Islámabad, have been cancelled raises the unwelcome prospect of interference with distribution (as was done with that of a newspaper) in the past. It is true that freedom of speech does not mean license to make wild allegations, but it is equally true that any abuse of that freedom can only be so declared by a properly constituted court of law, and not according to the fiat of some junior official. As there is no legal method for any censorship, unless a crime has been committed, it seems that an over-enthusiastic adviser has given some really bad advice. It is to be hoped that none of the strong-arm tactics used for newspapers are tried on the retailers of this book, especially where no cause of disagreement has been expressed.[18]

Islamization of Pakistan Army

One theme that Shuja Nawaz has touched on in his book is the spread of radical Islam in the army, which brought some officers closer to the al-Qaeda and its affiliates. Many officers were caught after being recruited into two London-based terrorist organizations: Al Muhajiroun and Hizb ut-Tahrir.[19]

Radicalization also came with jihad in India-administered Kashmir. The kind of warriors infiltrating into Kashmir could not be friendly to the Shia there after Pakistan's experience with Gilgit-Baltistan, from where infiltrators entered Kargil. Nawaz writes:

> Via the ISI, [Pak Army] also became a party to the struggle inside Kashmir, helping train and equip Islamist fighters and militants who infiltrated and injected themselves into the battle between [the] Kashmiris and the huge Indian military and paramilitary force that was sent to quell the insurgency in Kashmir. This approach was predicated on the idea that India could be made to pay for its hostility towards Pakistan with a war of a thousand cuts, by forcing India to deploy large numbers of troops against a small but elusive enemy in Kashmir.

Pakistan had its own radical 'Hindutva' in the army when 'liberal' General Musharraf was nearly killed after attempts made on his life from inside the army:

> Group-think took root and prevented the kind of massive transformation of military thought and operation that was needed to cope with the new warfare, inside Pakistani territory, against its own people, [and] against fellow Muslims who said they were fighting in the name of Islam. Potentially adding to the difficulty was the infusion into the military of deeply conservative Islamic thinking and the formation of pirbhai networks of spiritual bands that included civilians and military men, and threatened the discipline and rank order of the military. This began in the Zia-ul-Haq period, but appears to be extant to some extent even today, according to those who follow these networks.

Then there was the phenomenon of the Tablighi Jamaat, 'a proselytizing group that had already penetrated the upper echelons of the military. Two DCs of the ISI and some corps commanders had been members of this group and, like their colleagues, they favoured others from their own group. Members of the group were duty-bound to take leave of absence to do missionary work each year at home or abroad. These issues bedevilled the military's operations and processes.'

Pakistan has rolled back Jinnah and his vision of 'unity-faith-discipline'. The rollback has happened in Urdu, where the first word 'unity' has been pushed back to give 'faith' the first place. The word 'faith' in Jinnah's days meant 'commitment' (*yaqin-e-muhkam*); today it means *iman* or Islam. Of course, India has to roll back an entire constitution to repeat the experience of Pakistan; but the Pakistan Army could hardly resist.

The book sums up prescriptively the brainwash affecting the civil–military relationship too:

> More needs to be done to turn back the forces of religious obscurantism and ritualism that have crept into Pakistani society and even the military. A battle of tweets or statements from media spokesmen for either side does not reflect well on either. The enhanced ability of the army to shape public opinion directly through liberal use of funding for contractual services by media firms and indirectly by exercising censorship directly or by using the Pakistan Electronic Media Regulatory Authority (PEMRA) to exert pressure on recalcitrant media has led to charges of self-censorship by media from the Musharraf period onwards.

The final warning is:

> [The] trend that needs to be monitored carefully is the movement of purged or superseded intelligence officers towards militant Islamist organizations, whom they previously had been tracking or managing. Placing these joint services bodies under civilian scrutiny via parliament and adding transparency in

handling of their affairs would make their work more credible. The military needs public support to be effective. It also needs public scrutiny to become more efficient, especially as it fights the Long War against militancy and terrorism at home and faces expanding threats on its international borders.[20]

6

Hekmatyar: The Bridegroom of Jihad

In June 2019, Afghan President Ashraf Ghani visited Pakistan during a period of thawing in the Pakistan–US relationship. He was interviewed by Geo TV's Saleem Safi who heard him say that Pakistan's past 'interference' in Afghanistan, through the Quetta Shura, had disturbed the bilateral equation which he hoped to set right. Later, Safi also interviewed an old warlord, Gulbuddin Hekmatyar, an Afghan politician and former mujahideen leader, as if to 'balance' Ghani's view with what a jihadi leader living in Kabul had to say. If Ghani carefully introduced a mild note of criticism, Hekmatyar was clear about how the former was going to harm Pakistan: by helping Iran and India to scuttle Pakistan's policy in Afghanistan, in particular, and the region in general.

That Hekmatyar 'negotiated' his return to Afghanistan after a decade of war did not mean that he was on the side of the Kabul government fighting the Taliban, al-Qaeda and the ISIS. It did not matter that he had moved back because he couldn't get along with the Afghan Taliban leaders who once lived with him in Peshawar, during the war against the Soviet Union (1979–89). He began by being a favourite of the US and ended up being its enemy, just as he began by being lionized in Pakistan only to find Pakistan to be too 'subservient' to the US. His view surreptitiously resonated with many in Pakistan.

His 'revelation' that Iran was in cahoots with India to harm Pakistan highlighted the date on which he, hounded by rival Afghan warlords, 'requested' Iran to give him shelter in 1996—only to be driven out of there in 2002. After the Taliban, under Mullah Umar, fell from power in 2001, he returned to Pakistan to 'resist' the government of then President Hamid Karzai in Kabul. In 2016, he signed a peace deal with Karzai's successor, President Ghani. How he will deal with the Afghan Taliban fighting the Ghani government after the US's planned withdrawal from Afghanistan—which will trigger the fall of the Kabul government—will be another test of his shifting world view.

A Devil's Deal

To retrieve the details of his peace deal with Kabul, let's examine the facts more closely. On 21 September 2016, President Ghani signed a peace deal with Hekmatyar and his Hezb-e-Islami militia. Before the deal, Hekmatyar apologized for bombing Kabul in 1993–94, after the Soviets had left and the mujahideen had indulged in intra-jihad war. He wanted to do this routine with former President Karzai too, but in those days the Americans didn't like the idea; they had placed a big bounty on his head. They knew that, starting 1996, he had lived in Tehran for seven years after apologizing for having kicked the pro-Iran Shia militias out of the post-withdrawal mujahideen *shura* (consultative council) of Peshawar. He had the then ISI chief, General Hamid Gul, propping him up as Afghanistan's new prime minister. Saudi handouts to the mujahideen had done the trick.

Pakistan inherited a split Afghan policy because of Hekmatyar's vendetta against Tajik warlord Ahmad Shah Massoud. It meant Pakistan had to say goodbye to the non-Pashtun tribes of northern Afghanistan, thus creating space for India to step in and balance the war in Pakistan's backyard. Pakistan's pursuit of a 'Hekmatyar policy' did not endear it to the Pashtuns of Afghanistan either. After the fall of the Soviet-backed regime in Kabul, Hekmatyar was chosen as the prime minister of the new set-up, but he was not allowed to sit on the Kabul throne by his enemy, Massoud's militia, that had 'symbolically' bombed Pakistan's embassy in Kabul to signal its opposition to a Pakistan-backed prime minister.

The Power of Saying 'No'

Hekmatyar sat on a hill outside Kabul and bombed the living daylights out of the capital city, reducing to it a moonscape, killing thousands of innocent Kabulis. He had more ammunition than all the Pakistan-supported warlords put together. As mentioned above, in 1992, as the Communist government of Najibullah in Kabul was toppled, Hekmatyar had not joined the succeeding Burhanuddin Rabbani-led government. Instead, he had tried to capture the capital city by attacking it. Efforts to persuade Hekmatyar to reconcile with the Kabul government failed despite Osama bin Laden's urging 'to compromise with Ahmad Shah Massoud' in a radio conversation from Peshawar a year ago in 1991. 'Go back with your brothers,' bin Laden had stated. Instead, in 1992, Hekmatyar persuaded Uzbek leader Abdul Rashid Dostum and his Hazara Jihadi faction Hezb-e-Wahdat to form a common front against the Kabul government.

This alliance lasted several months, and in January 1994 he restarted rocket attacks on the capital from his base in Chahar Asyab district of Kabul. The ISI was alleged to have backed Hekmatyar in toppling the Tajik-dominated government in Kabul because Massoud had attacked its embassy. Hekmatyar also cooperated with the ISI in training foreign volunteers to fight in India-administered Kashmir in the early 1990s. His failure to succeed against Massoud's forces that controlled Kabul led to a decline of support for him from Pakistan. Islamabad was reported to have abandoned Hekmatyar in 1994 and shifted support to the Taliban. After the Taliban seized Kabul in 1996, many of the Hezb-e-Islami commanders fighting under Hekmatyar either joined the Taliban or fled to Pakistan. Hekmatyar's training camps in Pakistan were taken over by the Taliban. He himself escaped to Iran in 1997.

In his book *Reaping the Whirlwind: The Taliban Movement in Afghanistan* (2001),[1] Michael Griffin revealed the narcotics nexus of Pakistan that allowed Hekmatyar to traffic heroin into Afghanistan:

> Hekmatyar's commanders established six laboratories in Koh-e-Sultan district of Balochistan in the mid-1980s to process opium from Helmand[,] before smuggling it through the ports on the Mekran coast, or across the nearby Iranian border.

The track from there led to many places inside Pakistan, and to General Zia-ul-Haq himself. People close to him were caught red-handed smuggling heroin. In one case, a banker Zia had adopted as his son was caught with help from Norway; and Zia's wife allegedly tried to get the judge hearing the case in Pakistan to let him off the hook. Hekmatyar, it was said, received half the CIA bribe through the ISI and probably shared some of it with important officers.[2] One can only imagine the scale of the man's wealth. He held the largest weapons cache in the region and had money he could hardly count. He was rumoured to be in the tribal Dir region in the Khyber Pakhtunkhwa province.

The Bridegroom Didn't Show Up

Hekmatyar failed in the long run, but not because of lack of support or big money. General Gul got Stinger missiles from the

US and gave them to Hekmatyar, who then sold them onwards till they ended up with its arch-enemy Iran. *Daily Times* (on 11 May 2006) defensively stated:

> Pakistan did not supply Stinger missiles to Iran. Only 35 missiles reached Iran, and that too by mistake, said retired General Gul. Talking to a private TV channel, Gul said the ISI had supplied 50 to 70 Stinger missiles to 'prime minister' Gulbuddin Hekmatyar.

Author Lawrence Wright once asked General Gul: 'Why did you favour Hekmatyar?' He replied: 'I went to each of the seven [warlords] and I said, "I know you are the strongest, but who is No. 2?" They all said Hekmatyar.'[3] This was clearly a fib from a powerful man whom Pakistan had allowed to decide the fate of numberless people. American journalist Peter Bergen estimated that as much as $600 million in US aid went to Hekmatyar 'who waged most of his attacks on fellow-Afghans. Islamic extremism in the region was financed by American taxpayers, largely thanks to Gul.' Everyone who didn't fight pocketed the jihad money; and men died fighting for the lesser reward in the hereafter.

In 1991, when General Gul tried to take on post-withdrawal Afghan President Najibullah's army in Jalalabad, the Afghan city bordering Pakistan, and thought Hekmatyar would deliver for all the money he had pocketed, the favoured warlord— once called 'the bridegroom of jihad'—failed to show up. In fact, over the years, he had received money and equipment for over 30,000 mujahideen, who were trained by him, 'and also by the ISI', and were ready to storm Jalalabad. Neither Hekmatyar nor General Gul was held responsible for the slaughter that Najibullah's army then inflicted on the mujahideen. And Pakistan did nothing to punish the perfidy of its 'bridegroom'.

Tariq Khosa, IG Police (2007–09), federal secretary (2010), INTERPOL executive committee delegate for Asia (2009–12),

UNODC advisor on rule of law and criminal justice (2011–13), wrote in *Dawn* (on 3 October 2016) that once when he unknowingly arrested Hekmatyar in Quetta carrying illicit weapons, he got an earful from President Zia who personally got on the line to rebuke him. Khosa said: 'Based on my four decades of law-enforcement experience, I can assert without fear of contradiction that no non-state actor can exist without support from visible or invisible state elements and certain external players.' Such was Pakistan's submission to Hekmatyar's charisma, most of it personality-based.[4]

The Culture of Pashtun Charisma

As he spoke to Saleem Safi on Geo TV, Hekmatyar was charismatic. He kept physically fit and presented an austere Islamic exterior, measured in his speech and completely unbending in his views, the last trait never failing to attract Pashtun attention devoted to defiance as a way of life. The defiance asserts pride through refusal to be led in an expression of what Ibn Khaldun called *asabiya* (binding). He was born in 1949, in the northern Kunduz province of Afghanistan, in the Kharoti sub-branch of the Ghilzai Pakhtuns. Active with the socialist People's Democratic Party of Afghanistan (PDPA) during high school and his time in a military academy in Kabul, he converted, while in Kabul University in the early 1970s, to radical Islam of the Muslim Brotherhood.

It is during his university days that he is said to have killed a 'Maoist rival' in 1972, for which he was imprisoned. The following year, after the Sardar Daud coup in Kabul, he moved to Pakistan to organize an anti-Daud force, which came into being as Hezb-e-Islami in 1977, only to bifurcate two years later into Hezb-i-Islami Gulbuddin and Hezb-i-Islami Khalis, pointing once again to the Pakhtun asabiya of not accepting leadership and splitting on the basis of personal charisma.

Pakistan has officially abjured an interventionist attitude towards Afghanistan, known as 'strategic depth', which was allowed to be spearheaded by Hekmatyar. French scholar Christophe Jaffrelot, in his book *Pakistan at the Crossroads*, explained in 2016:

> The concept of strategic depth, with all its nuances, complexities, and evolution over time (when examining Pakistan's approach toward[s] Afghanistan), gained precedence in the wake of military dictator Zia-ul-Haq's rise to power in 1977 and the Soviet Union's military intervention in Afghanistan in 1979. With clandestine support from Washington, Islamabad decided to increase its support to the mujahideen figures fighting the Soviets. Islamabad's success in bogging down the Soviet forces in Afghanistan and making the mujahideen dependent on Pakistan made it believe that it could alter the geostrategic situation by installing a friendly regime in Kabul and by fomenting an insurgency in Kashmir.
>
> The ouster of former Afghan President Muhammad Najibullah (a fierce critic of Pakistan and the rise of the mujahideen in 1991) and the rise of the mujahideen in 1991 were, in many ways, positive returns of an investment that Pakistan had made during the Daud Khan years. These events also marked the beginning of Pakistan's direct military interventionism in Afghanistan. Having failed to secure allegiance from all the mujahideen factions, and its influence over Ahmad Shah Massoud's Jamiat-e-Islami fading fast, Pakistan decided to support Hekmatyar to capture Kabul using force in the first phase of the Afghan civil war. However, it was not until September 1996, when Kabul fell to the Taliban, that Pakistan reached closest to achieving strategic depth vis-à-vis India in Afghanistan.[5]

It was Pakistan's folly to base its 'strategic depth' on the geographically apportioned ethnic divisions of Afghanistan. India inclined towards the Persian-speaking Tajik community headed by Ahmad Shah Massoud in the north; and Iran protectively supported the Hezb-e-Wahdat based in central

Afghanistan and the northern city of Mazar-e-Sharif. When the Taliban, under Mullah Umar, attacked Mazar-e-Sharif in 1998 and killed a lot of Shias, including eight diplomats in the Iranian consulate there, Iran blamed Pakistan, some of whose operatives it said had taken part in this killing. Russia, India and Iran were to fight an indirect battle with Pakistan, seeking 'strategic depth' in Afghanistan.

Pakistan may have denied that it sheltered Osama bin Laden, but it couldn't avoid the nexus with him through the Taliban and Hekmatyar. In 1992, after the fall of the Communist government in Kabul, Hekmatyar refused to join the Rabbani-led government. As 'nominated' prime minister, he instead killed a lot of innocent people by bombing Kabul.

At this point, his patron Osama bin Laden advised compromise, asking him to make up with Massoud. Typically, Hekmatyar enhanced his Pakhtun charisma by refusing to listen, even as the world thought his mindless bombing of Kabul was undertaken with help from Pakistan.[6] Finally, bin Laden too was persuaded to line up behind him as his al-Qaeda agents—two Tunisian 'reporters' from Europe—killed Massoud in northern Afghanistan in 2001, just two days before the US attacked Afghanistan and forced Mullah Umar to flee Kabul to set up the infamous Quetta Shura in Pakistan.

Double-Gaming Ashraf Ghani

Today, Hekmatyar lives in Afghanistan under the Ashraf Ghani government and tells Pakistan in a television interview that Kabul was actually involved in an Iran–India conspiracy to challenge Pakistan on its western border. Ironically, Hekmatyar's own 'asylum' in Kabul happened after an episode full of irony that he doesn't care about too much. His 'hezb' simply collapsed in 2004 when his commanders, numbering around 150, declared support for his arch-rival, President Karzai, registered with the Afghan Ministry of Justice and opened offices in Kabul and other major cities after surrendering all their weapons and swearing to have 'no ties with the Gulbuddin-led insurgents'.

In an interview in June 2009, Hekmatyar dissociated himself from his former commanders—including his son-in-law Ghairat Basheer—then politically active in Kabul. He actually ousted them from his party:

> Former Hesb-e-Islami members who are in [the] Karzai government are not members of our party any more, and their participation in the American-backed government is not an indication of Hesb-e-Islami's indirect participation in the government. In fact, they joined the government with an intention to weaken the Hesb-e-Islami and to create division within the party, but they failed to do so. In the past, some people had joined our party because they thought it was the right decision at the time. Later, however, some of them joined other parties and others formed their own parties.[7]

Bridegroom Becomes Oracle

In July 2019, Hekmatyar saw his TV statement about the India–Iran axis against Pakistan confirmed by the way it was checkmated in Beijing. The Four-Party Meeting on the Afghan Peace Process, comprising China, the US, Russia and Pakistan, came up with a 'peace settlement' in Afghanistan, which ousted India and Iran from the conflict. Reacting to the move on 14 July 2019, former Indian ambassador M.K. Bhadrakumar wrote in an article titled 'India Loses Afghan Proxy War': 'In a regional setting, it also signifies that Pakistan has inflicted a heavy defeat on India in the decade-old proxy war in Afghanistan.' In the same month, Pakistani Prime Minister Imran Khan 'accompanied by army chief General Bajwa' got ready to meet President Trump at the White House.[8]

The Beijing meeting got China and Pakistan back to the centre stage, while Iran languished under US sanctions and India was forced to stop buying Iranian oil and spend less on its Chabahar Port project. Both were thus marginalized. India stopped buying Iranian oil in May 2019, adding to its earlier hardship that started when it stopped buying oil from Venezuela after the South American state too came under US sanctions. India then came to the conclusion that Chabahar must be downgraded and decided to reduce its allocation to the deep-sea port by two-thirds: from Indian Rs 150 crore to Rs 45 crore.

In 2018, Hekmatyar received members of a Pakistani delegation at his residence in Kabul. He delivered himself the following perceptions of Iran where he had once sought asylum:

> Iran is the only neighbor of Afghanistan which has invested for 30 years for the continuation of war in our countries. Tehran has achieved economic benefits from the war in Afghanistan and has succeeded in gaining access to the Afghan market. Now the Afghan market is in Iran's hands. Iran's exports to Afghanistan's now stand at $5 billion. The official figure of the exports is $2 billion and the rest is smuggling. Now even the markets in Afghanistan's eastern Khost and Nangrahar provinces are flooded with Iranian goods and Iranian dates are sold in Laghman and Nangrahar that border Pakistan.[9]

Syed Zafar Mehdi, writing in *Tehran Times* on 10 December 2018, in an article titled 'Truth about Hekmatyar's Anti-Iran Tirade', stated the following:

> It's no secret that the Saudi regime has been investing millions in its no-holds-barred propaganda war against the Islamic Republic of Iran. The custodians of Islam's holiest shrines have not only managed to crush the voices critical of the regime's policies, but have been carrying out a systematic misinformation campaign against Iran through run-of-the-mill media outlets bankrolled by Riyadh . . . Gulbuddin Hekmatyar, the leader of Hizb-e-Islami Afghanistan, who last year [in 2017] signed

> a secret peace deal with the Afghan government, continues to be a notorious and controversial figure in Afghan politics. His return drew anger and outrage across Afghanistan as people took to [the] streets to condemn Afghan government's amnesty to a war criminal.[10]

A Go-It-Alone Hero

Once again, the go-it-alone Hekmatyar has placed himself strategically in the region. But if he persists in his image-enhancing trait of self-isolation, the 'new' Afghanistan may see another longer period of violent change in reverse. As the US focuses its negative energy on Iran, and the Arabs across the Gulf rally around it, Pakistan and India must adjust to the new strategic scenario. Aware of the 'heating up' of its western border, Pakistan is keen to cool its eastern border with India and disinvest in the non-state actors now bringing the scandal of money laundering to its door.

Chafing under the rhetoric of President Trump, but embarrassed by China forever advising improvement of relations with India, Pakistan feels itself forced to let Iran go. Add to the Chinese pressure the US 'approval' of Pakistan's Kartarpur initiative—opening the birthplace of Guru Nanak to visitors from India—and you have a global trend toward 'normalization', which is bound to isolate Iran further. Counting on the Arab states in the Gulf and China for a bailout from bankruptcy, Pakistan has to deal 'realistically' with Iran and look benignly at figures like Hekmatyar, who persist in demanding attention but who are bound to bring misfortune as a 'replacement' of the current rulers of Afghanistan.

7

A Debacle Difficult to Digest

In the last week of 2018, Pakistan's Federal Investigation Agency (FIA) recommended to the Supreme Court that its verdict in the infamous twenty-five-year-old Asghar Khan Case be set aside because it could not 'gather evidence required to launch criminal proceedings'. The case involved two generals of the Pakistan Army and several politicians, climaxing in confessions on the part of the generals who had made the payment and denial by most of the recipient politicians.

In 1996, former air marshal Asghar Khan had filed a human rights petition in the Supreme Court of Pakistan, accusing the ISI of doling out illegal money to a group of politicians. He had raised the petition after PPP leader Benazir Bhutto's interior minister, retired Major General Naseerullah Babar, disclosed in the National Assembly in 1994 that the agency had disbursed funds to manipulate the 1990 elections to defeat the PPP, something the generals didn't favour.

The petition sought investigation into the alleged distribution of millions of rupees by the ISI among anti-PPP politicians to rig the 1990 elections. Successive courts ducked the question asked in the petition because, simply put, the ISI was too powerful, manned by military personnel reporting to the army chief, though legally they were answerable to the elected prime minister.

Finally, in 1996, the Supreme Court, headed by Justice Iftikhar Muhammad Chaudhry, ruled that the 1990 general elections had been polluted by the dishing out of 'Rs 140 million to a particular group of politicians to deprive the people of true representation'. It cleverly directed the then PPP government to 'take necessary action under the Constitution and law against former army chief Mirza Aslam Beg and former director general of ISI Asad Durrani for their role in facilitating the group of politicians and political parties to ensure their success against their rivals in the 1990 elections'.

The court had accepted the challenge of taking up an embarrassing case withering on the bough of Pakistan's legal system because of the dominance of Pakistan's 'informal' centres of power that scuttle the Constitution into a polarized political environment. The earlier courts had put the case on the back burner. A predecessor of the current chief justice, Justice Syed Sajjad Ali Shah, was hearing the case in 1997 when he was shown the door by his fellow judges after a 'judicial mutiny', allegedly manoeuvred by the Nawaz Sharif government.[1]

Lists of Ignominy

Former ISI chief General Durrani confessed to having made the handouts on the direction of his boss, thus laying the blame on General Beg who said he knew nothing about the scam. Durrani's list of 'beneficiaries' of the Rs 140 million was as follows: Nawaz Sharif (3.5 million), Lt Gen. Rafaqat (5.6 million), Mir Afzal Khan (10 million), Ghulam Mustafa Jatoi (5 million), Jam Sadiq Ali (5 million), Mohammed Khan Junejo (2.5 million), Pir Pagaro

(2 million), Abdul Hafeez Pirzada (3 million), Yusuf Haroon (5 million) [he confirmed having received this for Altaf Hussain of the Muttahida Qaumi Movement (MQM)], Muzaffar Hussain Shah (0.3 million), Abida Hussain (1 million), Humayun Marri (5.4 million), Jamaat-e-Islami (5 million), Altaf Hussain Qureshi and Mustafa Sadiq (0.5 million each), Arbab Ghulam Aftab (0.3 million), Pir Noor Mohammad Shah and Arbab Faiz Mohammad (0.3 million each), Arbab Ghulam Habib and Ismail Rahu (0.2 million each), Liaquat Baloch (1.5 million), Jam Yusuf (0.75 million), Nadir Magsi (1 million), among others.

Banker Yunus Habib, who allegedly created the slush fund for General Beg and his collaborator, the late President Ghulam Ishaq Khan, had submitted his own list (in rupees): Aslam Beg (140 million), Jam Sadiq Ali (70 million), Altaf Hussain (20 million), Advocate Yousaf Memon (for disbursement to Javed Hashmi and others) (50 million); Jam Sadiq Ali (Rs 150 million in 1992); Liaquat Jatoi (Rs 1 million in 1993); the Sindh chief minister (12 million in 1993) via Imtiaz Sheikh; Afaq Ahmed of the MQM (5 million); another 1 million to the Sindh chief minister through Imtiaz Sheikh; former federal minister Ajmal Khan (1.4 million); Nawaz Sharif (3.5 million in 1993); another 2.5 million to him in 1990; Jam Mashooq (0.5 million); Dost Mohammad Faizi (1 million); Jam Haider (2 million); Jam Mashooq (3 million in 1993); Adnan, son of Sartaj Aziz (1 million); Nawaz Sharif and Ittefaq Group of Companies (200 million); Sardar Farooq Leghari (30 million in 1993, 2.0856 million in 1994 and another 1.92 million).

General Beg took over as army chief on 17 August 1988, after a plane crash killed then army chief General Zia-ul-Haq in Bahawalpur—a flight Beg had mysteriously ducked out of at the last minute, as if he knew the plane was going to explode mid-air. Zia's son, Ijaz-ul-Haq, had his suspicions and, in 2012, accused him of being a part of the conspiracy to kill his father. He appeared on Geo TV on 1 December 2012 to say that General Beg had sent Rs 5 lakh to his mother in Toba Tek Singh to get him—Ijaz—to participate in the plan to defeat the PPP through rigging. It was alleged that this was done through ISI officer Brigadier Imtiaz Ahmad, alias Billa, who had earlier assisted General Beg in getting General Zia killed.[2]

He said that he was sorry that General Hamid Gul, who was the ISI chief then, took no notice of what his officers were up to with General Beg. He added that General Beg caused the wreckage of the plane to be removed, so that the evidence of a missile being fired into the plane from another one could be concealed. He also prevented autopsies of the dead to hide the fact that everyone on the plane had died from gas poisoning. A report by an air force officer, Zaheer Zaidi, was suppressed because it focused on the 'other plane'. He said General Beg had reacted to his certain replacement with General Afzal as vice chief, and had got the chief killed.

General Gul, digesting the denouement of the case, 'disclosed' on TV that the establishment had always been wary of the PPP coming to power and, therefore, manoeuvred the system to circumvent it. He had also taken it upon himself to muster a coalition of obedient politicians under the ignominious flag of the Islami Jamhoori Ittehad (IJI) which finally got rid of the PPP government and ruled under Nawaz Sharif.

A Forgotten Verdict

In 2012, the Supreme Court, in its short order, ruled that late Ghulam Ishaq Khan, former President of Pakistan, Beg and Durrani, had acted in violation of the Constitution by facilitating the success of a group of politicians and political parties against rival candidates in the general election of 1990, for which they secured funds from Younis Habib. Both the generals expressed their dissatisfaction with the verdict and decided to present their side of the case when it finally came to a trial court. The President then was the supreme commander, armed with Article 58/2/B of the Constitution that could cashier the elected parliament, with the judiciary invariably siding with the troika comprising the President, the prime minister and the army chief. In 2012, the PPP government hardly had the guts to take on the army and try the generals under Article 6 of the Constitution for treason and then ask the army to prosecute them as per its own law.

General Durrani had provided an affidavit, after he left the military, saying he had distributed money among politicians opposing the PPP in the 1990 polls, held after the first PPP government had been thrown out. His former chief, General Beg, thereafter claimed that Durrani's actions had not followed from the orders coming from the GHQ but from the President.

The plot thickened when, in 2018, General Durrani published his book, *Pakistan Adrift: Navigating Troubled Waters*, and wrote a confessional chapter titled 'Mea Culpa'. He said this about his career in the army:

> When I reflect on my past, some of my actions were so outlandish that there must have been an invisible hand that kept pulling me out of all the trouble I got myself into. I entered the corridors of power soon after Zia passed away in August 1988. This was one of the reasons that made me often ponder [on] the role of destiny.[3]

Opportunity without Ethic

Why did General Durrani accept the task of distributing the slush funds to undermine the 1990 elections? From what he writes in his book, his grounds appear to be honestly immoral:

> The fact is that I accepted the task because it was given to me by my former boss, from when I was the DGMI (Director General Military Intelligence), who was also the one who had helped me to acquire the current post as head of the ISI, and perhaps, more important, because I had been witness to the events that led to the dismissal of the Benazir Bhutto government, and

> was therefore not averse to the idea that [she] must be denied another stint in power. That the president, also our Supreme Commander, had taken charge of the entire operation was also a significant factor.

How was General Durrani seen by his contemporaries? One 'insider' ex-bureaucrat, M.A. Siddiqi, wrote an assessment of him in the *Friday Times* of 20 October 2017:

> An intensely political general, considered the intellectual guru of the army officer class, was removed by army chief General Waheed Kakar for his support of elements with extreme Islamist leanings. His removal from service was quite undignified when, while returning from a visit abroad as Commandant National Defence College (now a university), he was informed at the airport of his dismissal from service two years before his retirement. During his ISI days, he had curried favour with Benazir Bhutto who appointed him ambassador to Germany in the good old days[,] when western Europe accepted former army officers as envoys, a facility withdrawn after General Musharraf's takeover in 1999. A vociferous proponent of the military point of view, General Durrani was posted as ambassador to Saudi Arabia by army chief General Musharraf.[4]

General Durrani comes across as a man bereft of all ethics. He is clever, gifted in expression, but opportunistic in the extreme. In his book, he explains his loyalty to General Beg completely in reference to the favours he had received from him while in service. He confesses without thinking how he would appear to his readers:

> General Aslam Beg was an effective Army Chief and a trusting boss. As defence attaché at the embassy, I had organized his visit to Germany when he was the vice-chief of the army, and he was my Corps Commander when I was commanding the

> brigade at Kohat. He got me over to head Military Intelligence (MI) soon after becoming the chief of the army—the position that took most of his attention.
>
> He still found time for the army's traditional role in foreign policy [sic] and his self-assigned charge to guide the nascent democracy of Pakistan. The problem was that[,] though sincere in helping the recruit regime, he wanted things to move on a fast track and was susceptible to bad advice. When Benazir Bhutto appointed a retired General to head the ISI, General Beg started toying with the idea, probably prompted by some of his informal aides, to mobilize the MI to do some political work as well.[5]

Rewarded for Treachery

When General Beg decided to bring down the elected prime minister, Benazir Bhutto, in the middle of 1989, Durrani was more than willing to assist: 'And that is where I faltered. To appease the boss, I volunteered to play ball.'

There was no dearth of the 'mistakes' he went on making. He was, by nature, a reckless man:

> A more serious mistake was to induct a few street-smart operatives into my team[,] who did deliver at the time but subsequently became liabilities. I not only met some politicians to give them the necessary message but also brought some high-profile personalities into contact with Beg. The motion failed, but I had my first lesson in politics, which was that these politicos were just too smart for us naïve soldiers.

Sitting in the middle of the web of a major conspiracy against the people of Pakistan, General Durrani immorally counts the 'benefits' he has reaped:

> General Beg, still in two minds about whether the powers he had inherited from a military dictator struck the right note

> in a democratic order, was nevertheless impressed by my connections in the right places. He made up his mind that once Bhutto was sent packing, I would be the right man to head the ISI. My efforts to get back into the Chief's good books were bearing fruit. Although both Beg and I were to come to regret this power play soon after its success[,] and for years afterwards, at that time, the thought never crossed our minds.

But there is something to be said about the frankness with which he decided to make a clean breast of it:

> Frankly . . . making history was certainly not on my mind. I may not be able to precisely reconstruct my thought process, but I believe it was a combination of some unflattering factors: obliging a regime that had rehabilitated me after my early retirement, the fear of losing another job, and perhaps also a fear of being found guilty of hiding facts from the law.

Is this the specimen of the ideal man that the army professes to nurse to perfection and the nation to admire? He thinks aloud:

> Had I picked up the courage to say a firm 'no' to Beg when he asked me to organize the distribution of funds, I would not have been involved in this unprofitable business. [About betraying Benazir Bhutto] I have rationalized my actions by arguing, as I have done in this book, that I did it out of conviction, having some experience of her many gaffes, but someone more shrewd would have handled the episode better.

Hardened in Felony

After he and General Beg got rid of Bhutto's PPP government, he thought nothing of turning against the new incumbent Nawaz Sharif and going to Bhutto again. A hardened manipulator of his own sense of what is right and wrong, he writes:

> After falling out with Nawaz Sharif, I had no qualms about hobnobbing with Benazir Bhutto, against whom we had all ganged up only a couple of years previously. To justify this somersault, I had made myself believe that she had learnt her lesson—and of course she agreed, and why would she not? It was only much later that it dawned on me that all she had learnt was to posture a little more convincingly.

Then, equally cold-bloodedly, he explains his dismissal:

> Since the new army chief, Asif Nawaz Janjua, was no more a Sharif fan than I was, I actually believed I was on a holy mission. Primed by the PPP leader Farooq Leghari, who said my word would be more effective than his, I threw all caution to the wind and called Ms Bhutto from my cellphone when she was in London. When Asif Nawaz died a week later, I lost my immunity. When Bhutto came back to tell the new army chief about our exchanges, I lost my job.

His unrepentant parting shot at the end of the book reads:

> I did not like old-fashioned constraints and suffered from the illusion that I could hold my own against the rest of the world. In fact, the others proved cleverer. They massaged my ego, prodded me to talk more, and were not taken in. We still feel elated when told that ours is a more open society than the Indian [society]. I suggest we make others work hard to read our lips, and harder still to fathom our thoughts.

8

The Sorrows of Identity

The twenty-first century has hardly begun and the great promise of globalization and 'liberal inclusion' of the last century is fading. The world's powerful states, heretofore wedded to internationalism, are turning inward and seeking their primeval identities. The pledge to Adam Smith about free trade has begun to pale and the world economy is being jolted by isolationist sanctions. Nations are seeking identities away from multiculturalism. They wish to protect themselves by banning immigration. Borders are being closed, and those who had crossed them decades earlier as welcome guests are being treated with intolerance.

The US has a conservative Republican President of new isolationist intensity, who will probably win a second term in office because the American economy has done well during his first term. India's Narendra Modi, who seeks Hindutva as an identity for the majority community, has already won his second term in office, even as Muslims, Christians and Dalits in the country fear 'lynchings' on the pretext of cow protection. In Turkey, President Erdogan has overturned Kemalist secularism and used religion to deprive the country of the freedom of expression. In the Islamic world, the struggle for democracy has unleashed an identity-based mayhem. Terrorist organizations seeking the utopia of 'caliphate' have killed men and women belonging to Christianity and Muslim sects such as Yazidis and Shiites.

Francis Fukuyama, an American political scientist, says man is seeking his 'thymos', the deep-rooted primitive sense of identity that excludes others to realize itself. According to him, 'The contemporary Middle East, like the Balkans before it, is an extreme example of out-of-control identity politics and what ultimately happens to countries that do not invest in integrative national identities.'[1] Anthropologist Akbar Ahmed has found the rise of identity politics in Europe interesting enough for him to undertake a journey there and experimentally see if his earlier theses on the subject jibe with what is happening now. His monumental *Journey into Europe: Islam, Immigration and Identity* is a kind of culmination of his earlier examination of 'tribal' identity in his three books.[2]

'Convivencia' versus Identity

Ahmed's latest volume is the fourth in the quartet to study the relationship between Islam and the West. The way he describes it is this:

> The first, *Journey into Islam: The Crisis of Globalization*, published in 2007, was based on fieldwork in nine countries and examined how people in the Muslim world viewed the West and what was occurring in their societies after 9/11. The second study, *Journey into America: The Challenge of Islam*, published in 2010, was concerned with how people in the United States saw Muslims mosques in seventy-five U.S. cities. The third volume in the quartet, published in 2013, was

The Thistle and the Drone: How America's War on Terror Became a Global War on Tribal Islam.[3]

The Thistle and the Drone (2013) made an impact in Pakistan, but Ahmed's anthropological treatment may not have appealed to readers looking for surface causes rather than the deeper phenomenon of 'tribal peoples living in the interstices between states where the U.S.-led war on terror' was being fought. Yet, some of the insights were astounding and could not be ignored: like why almost all members of the group that carried out the 9/11 assault on the US were 'tribals' from Yemen, which led Ahmed back to the first anthropologist, Ibn Khaldun, and his theory of violence-producing asabiya that is now at the root of Europe, which was going back to its tribal roots in 2019.

Ahmed cannot be partisan in any sense because his discipline does not permit it. As he surveys the identity-seeking Europe, he is reminded of the 'inclusive' state of Abdur Rahman in Cordova in al-Andalus (Iberia) in the eight century AD. It was remembered for its *convivencia*, or the idea of different identities living together, which Islam has forsaken today. Rahman was an Umayyad prince born to a Berber woman in Syria and was a descendant of the founder of the dynasty who had married a Christian woman, thus indicating the source of the convivencia in al-Andalus, with the Muslims, Christians and Jews tolerating multiple identities.

Goodbye, Enlightenment

But this convivencia that one associates with a Europe busy forsaking Enlightenment and seeking 'identity' did not last. Ahmed points it out, likening it to what is happening today among most nations. One is reminded of an early Muslim reformer, Jamaluddin Al-Afghani, who opposed Syed Ahmad Khan—an ancestor of Akbar Ahmed—in India but proposed the acceptance of Islam in Europe. Afghani, praised by Pakistan's national poet, Allama Iqbal, in his famous lectures, was a bit of a soldier of fortune, with a lot of traditional learning that eased his entry into the Muslim societies of Turkey, India, Iran and Egypt. But he got his comeuppance in France, where orientalist Ernest Renan, a much-greater mind, told him prophetically that his claim that Muslims would ultimately turn to reason and modernity would never be proved right, as the Muslims would defeat his thinking just as they had rejected Ibn Rushd (Averroes) in the twelfth century for having learned too much of Aristotle. Akbar Ahmed too refers to the unfortunate end of Ibn Rushd in his book.

The BBC programme *In Our Times* told us recently that Aristotle had appeared in a dream of the Abbasid Caliph Al-Mamun, saying that his philosophy confirmed the message of Islam since the Quran called Muslims 'the nation of the middle' as per the Aristotelian ideal of the golden mean and the Quranic rendering of 'justice' through the word *adl*, which means middle.

Too Many Muslims?

President Emmanuel Macron of France, a country that disallows multiculturalism, and the leader of Austria's far-right ruling party, Norbert Hofer, complain of a high birth-rate among immigrant Muslims, which could deprive the Europeans of their status of majority in the future. President Macron said: 'Present me the woman who decided, being perfectly educated, to have seven, eight or nine children.'[4]

Ahmed, meanwhile, wonders:

> In facing this existential challenge, a downward spiral in which Europeans seem to be slowly dying out by failing to reproduce, it seems that Europe has also lost all confidence in its hard-won Enlightenment values, such as personal freedoms, reason and science replacing superstition, and the separation of church and state.

But the book notes that, as destitute refugees, Muslims too 'were not learning lessons'. Is Europe then an arena of populations, rejected by their own states in Africa and the Middle East, refusing to 'integrate' their identities? Already opposed to 'rationality and reason', Muslim multitudes, driven by fellow Muslims fighting on the basis of sub-identities, are confronting a Europe in the act of saying goodbye to Enlightenment and embracing its own primeval tribalism.

'Volk' and 'Heimat'

The terrorist attacks in New York and Washington on 11 September 2001, and the faltering of national economies, not to mention the 'inequality' of incomes and unemployment under capitalism, caused negative attention to turn to asylum-seeking Muslim immigrants. Ahmed's book examines Roman historian Tacitus and his thesis of Germania, the identity that caused exclusion and violence among nations such as England, the Netherlands and the Scandinavian countries because of the variations on the concepts of volk (nation) and *heimat* (homeland).

Ahmed writes in his book that when German-inspired identities intensified, they caused violence:

> French identity incorporates Clovis and Charlemagne, both mighty Germanic warriors of the Frankish tribal confederation that gave France its name; Italy claimed an Aryan identity under Mussolini based on the invasion and rule of Germanic tribes around the time of the fall of Rome; and the Spanish aristocracy long claimed descent from Germanic Visigoths, which they used to define a Spanish identity based on blood lineage.

Of course, Tacitus, belonging to 'a world-dominating military civilization with multiple varieties of people such as the Roman Empire based in the city of Rome', thought the German tribes uncivilized, the same way Europe living under the Enlightenment first perceived Muslim immigrants.

Today, European intolerance of Muslim minorities is a reminder of an early warning by a European genius in a different context. Hannah Arendt (1906–75) in her *The Origin of Totalitarianism* traced the modern state's internal cleansing to its second project, that of conquering other territories and killing off the population there through genocide. It is the imperialism of the modern state that gets internalized when it purges its own population to eliminate those who are 'different'.[5]

Unity First or Faith?

Reading Akbar Ahmed, one is reminded of the motto the founding fathers fashioned for Pakistan: that of unity, faith and discipline, putting unity first to obfuscate the identities of the various communities living in Pakistan. As the state moved away from the British Raj-enforced Enlightenment to an Islamist military dominance, the motto came to be rewritten as faith, unity and discipline, thus clearly embracing an identity that divides, instead of the intended 'assimilation' of all identities. Similarly, the Urdu 'grammatical rule' of writing *marhoom* (blessed) only after the name of the Muslim dead, and disallowing it after the name of a non-Muslim Pakistani citizen, sought exclusion rather than inclusion. In India, the Constitution put together by Bhimrao Ramji Ambedkar, leader of the Dalits, charted the assimilation of all identities in secular integration; but today the new consensus reflected in the electoral victory of the BJP seeks to follow the path traced by the state of Pakistan. Outside Hindutva, all identities are 'impure', just as the non-Muslims of Pakistan have to live under laws that victimize them.[6]

Ahmed writes about 'tribal' Europe:

> Yet the aggressive promotion of German tribalism is far from finished. The emergence of Far Right political movements

> such as Pegida (Patriotic Europeans against the Islamization of the West) and Alternative for Germany (AfD), the attacks on foreigners and Muslims, refugee shelters, and mosques, and the disturbing re-emergence of anti-Semitism reflect a deep-seated hostility to all that is 'impure'.

Expat Jihad for the ISIS

When around 5000 Muslims from Europe went to Syria to fight as soldiers of ISIS, the largest number came from France. The reason was not difficult to understand: France had laws forbidding display of their culture. In 2004, during an earlier outbreak of 'Muslim violence' in France, *The Economist* (on 16 December 2004) had this to say:

> Liberal multiculturalists have long said that secular France is too intolerant to religious minorities, especially its 5 million Muslims (the biggest Muslim population in Europe). It is accused of being too rigid in denying religious freedoms in public institutions, and too suspicious of goings-on in mosques. The French ban on the headscarf in state schools was widely condemned in America, Britain and the Netherlands.[7]

The France of today is a far cry from what it was in 1798–1801, when Napoleon went to Egypt and 'wore Arab robes, honoured the scholars of al-Azhar, declared his admiration for the Quran and the Prophet (Peace Be upon Him) . . . Praised the social and civil clauses of shariah law, and promised to introduce them to France'.

The second-largest batch of Muslim boys and girls who went to Syria to join ISIS was from the United Kingdom. Here, communication technology played a part even in cases where the families were deemed to be 'secular', 'modern' and 'integrated'. Sitting in front of their computers, or in bed with their cell phones, the 'jihad' warriors yielded to the persuasion of the ISIS propaganda. The book examines the case of Aqsa Mahmood from Glasgow, who at the age of nineteen 'left her modernist family in the pursuit of literalist Islam' (see Chapter 1). In Syria, the media knew her as 'the bride of ISIS'.

The Scary Case of Aqsa

Aqsa was raised in an affluent Glasgow neighbourhood and attended a prestigious private school before enrolling in university. But after that, her personality was reshaped completely by social media, as she blogged in praise of Abdullah Azzam, who co-founded al-Qaeda in Peshawar; Omar Ibn al-Khattab, the Saudi-born jihadi who fought the Russians in Chechnya; al-Qaeda figure Abu Yahya al-Libi of Libya; Abu Musab l-Zarqawi of Iraq; and Anwar al-Awlaki, who was killed by a US drone in Yemen. Most shocking of all was her hatred of the Shia faith:

> According to Aqsa, the greatest threat to Islam and the Islamic State was the Shia whom she blamed for the deaths of so many Syrians. For example, she shared a photo of a dead Syrian child with the caption 'Shiism is killing us'. She asked: 'The question is, what are you going to do about it?' In other posts she described the Shia as 'filthy,' demons, dogs, crazed apes, crazed animals, and lying deviants.

Aqsa wrote that the Shia were 'the true enemies of Ahlul Sunnah'. Spilling Shia blood, she wrote, was more lawful than spilling wine. She frequently criticized Muslims who spoke of ummah unity with the Shia:

> 'I would rather befriend a pig before go[ing] near that lot for unity.' In more than one post she suggested that 'Shiism is a Jewish sect', and in another she posted a doctored photo of a face that was one-half Israeli prime minister Benjamin Netanyahu

> and one-half Iranian president Mahmoud Ahmadinejad. The caption read: Different Face, Same Agenda.[8]

Ahmed ends his 'journey' with the following message:

> Europe stands at the crossroads: One path leads to tenebrous forests where fearsome beasts lurk, waiting to pounce on the weak and the vulnerable; the other to engagement with and fulfillment of modernity and liberal democracy promising equality and prosperity for all. The second path reflects not only convivencia but also the indomitable spirit of scientific enquiry, space exploration, medical breakthroughs, and technological advancements. There is no denying, however, that if we do not check our aggressiveness and militaristic impulses, we will find it difficult to overcome the real existentialist dangers that confront us—global warming and its devastating effects on the planet, overpopulation, poverty, and religious and racial conflict—and their by-product of terrorism.[9]

9

Peace without Doves

In 2015, former foreign minister Khurshid Mahmud Kasuri served a rich feast of memoir, political tract, theory of diplomacy and anecdotal gloss, with a special focus on India–Pakistan relations, in 840 pages: *Neither a Hawk Nor a Dove: An Insider's Account of Pakistan's Foreign Relations* (including details of the Kashmiri framework).[1] And the book can't be called cloying the way big books tend to be. He wears his middle-of-the-road approach to politics on his sleeve and doesn't care if he is ostracized by the doves on the left and the hawks on the right.

Kasuri says he probably got it from his father, who was supposed to be a Marxist while sincerely practising Islam; he calls it eclecticism, but many would say it is an inability to take a clear stand. He can be called an Aristotelian in a social matrix where textbooks are black-and-white injections into the national psyche. Most Pakistani diplomats, who honed in on unilateral truths that live only in files, would call him wishy-washy, as they flitted over hard solutions that never came.

Clarity, of the kind that most Pakistanis and Indians want, is more absolutist than Kasuri's relativist thinking; therefore, both sides prefer deadlocks as the backdrop in front of which they can dance to their separate audiences for approval. In a region looking for victory, Kasuri offers the non-victory of reconciliation and mutually supported prosperity. Once we finally come out of our zero-sum trance, we will find that his is the only way to go.

Critical Quitting

It is no surprise that Kasuri's decisions are a long way from maturing. He will take the plunge, but only after agonizing over nuances, as he did when he quit the PML (N) after it tabled the Fifteenth Amendment on sharia in parliament; or when he quit again when General Musharraf declared an emergency in the country in 2007, after suspending the Supreme Court and arresting former chief justice Iftikhar Muhammad Chaudhry, whose villainies Kasuri recounts in some detail. He knew that the subsequent lawyers' revolt, which brought General Musharraf down, was intellectually ill-equipped to ponder on the judicial despotism that went on for over a decade.

In Islam, 'adl' means the Aristotelian 'middle' where Kasuri may find himself isolated. As 'senior advisor on political and international affairs' to Imran Khan's PTI, his rare appearance during the dharna in 2014, with downcast eyes, points to his incapacity for heroic absolutes.

Kashmir is the kernel of Kasuri's book. Former prime minister Nawaz Sharif was lucky that he had Atal Behari Vajpayee as his counterpart in India, statesmanlike enough to think out of the box on Kashmir. But when the latter came to Lahore in 1999, the army, led by General Musharraf, tried to torpedo the visit with 'spontaneous' mobs that sought to stop the Indian leader from going to the Minar-e-Pakistan monument in a bid to undermine the Pakistani textbook myth that 'India never accepted Pakistan'. It was after this that General Musharraf unleashed the most mindless post-nuclear adventure on Kargil, as a result of which Pakistan lost whatever global support it had with regard to Kashmir.

The GHQ later claimed that the Kargil adventure was okayed by Sharif, which he denied. Kasuri prefers to remain undecided on the matter, unless you give credit to the story told to Kasuri (which he narrates in his book) by senior bureaucrat Saeed Mehdi, which proves that Sharif had no clue about the Kargil operation that indirectly harmed Pakistan by projecting Hafiz Saeed and the LeT as an adjunct that the army could not do without.[2]

Kasuri was eased into the Musharraf establishment with his 'median' views intact, as Sharif cooled his heels in prison after narrowly missing being hanged. In the 1990s, the Kashmir pantomime between India and Pakistan had thrown up ideas that appealed to some in Pakistan but were never presented in parliament.

The Chenab Chapter

One such idea was the Chenab formula, conceived by India in a series of meetings with late foreign secretary Niaz A. Naik in March 1999, in a hotel in New Delhi where he was staying under an assumed name to keep the Pakistani High Commission out of the loop. The area west of the Chenab River, with mostly Muslims residents, was to go to Pakistan and the area east of the river was to come to India. In Pakistan, the United Jihad Council was immediately out on the roads—like the DPC—fired by editorials in *Nawa-e-Waqt*.

Kasuri doubts, quite realistically, that the Chenab formula would have been cleared in the Indian parliament. He then makes a good case for his own formula that many on both sides of the border thought could have been implemented but which too ran aground. The reasons for this are explained in the chapter titled 'Interrupted Symphony' in his book. Needless to say, it was an out-of-the box solution in the midst of people boxed in by unbending notions of taking on India.

In 2003, while presiding over a UN Security Council session, Kasuri realized that the Pakistani diplomats advising him simply couldn't budge beyond confrontation and that the only feather he could stick in his cap was preventing the deletion of the Kashmir dispute from the UN roster. Luckily, that year his backchannel diplomacy produced the formula: withdraw troops and make both Kashmirs autonomous under an agreed India–Pakistan joint mechanism. Alas, that too did not work.

He is not a hawk when it comes to trade routes passing through Pakistan and carrying Indian goods; he wants the Iran–Pakistan gas pipeline to end up supplying gas to India as well. He is also not a hawk when it comes to regarding the China–Pakistan Economic Corridor (CPEC) as a trade artery which would serve the entire region, an idea that China would definitely appreciate, if not Pakistan. He is not a dove when it comes to India's military action in Kashmir and the growth of a narrow-minded Hindu religiosity, which he saw rising in India during his tenure. His own exit from the government after the Fifteenth Amendment tells us what he thinks of religiosity in Pakistan. Compared to what Pakistan has managed to concoct, the BJP poses less of a threat.

The Army Angle

For a man with Kasuri's way of thinking, one would imagine the Pakistan Army to be a major obstacle. He, in fact, has a big chapter on 'The Pakistan Army and India'. Mercifully, he doesn't bring up what the officers write in the Blue Book and various other 'defence journals', but he realizes that Pakistani nationalism is revisionist and warlike, with the sanction of jihad making furtive references to the ascendancy of the army.

His survey is nuanced, appreciative of the generals' competence and openness to new ideas, although he can't figure out why intellectually gifted General Yaqub Khan thought it fit to go to New Delhi and threaten the then Indian prime minister, Inder Kumar Gujral, even if egged on by the somewhat lesser-rated General Aslam Beg. He says: 'General Pervez Musharraf and General Ashfaq Parvez Kayani . . . were thorough professionals, although, I did find General Aslam Beg to be emotional at times.' One has to take note of just one other general who doesn't get kudos: Former ISI chief General Javed Nasir, 'during whose tenure a strange non-military atmosphere prevailed at the ISI'. Got the hint?

He is not dovish on the 1965 war, but he sure is nuanced enough for us to realize that he doesn't give General Ayub an easy pass, saving himself from the charge of putting it entirely at the door of India by mentioning Operation Gibraltar as a blunder comparable only to the Kargil operation. He realizes how his kind of peace-making will make him a sitting duck for predatory politicians when he considers what Zulfikar Ali Bhutto did to the Tashkent Declaration with India. Bhutto was rewarded with the throne of Islamabad after the fall of Dhaka; by that time, he had scuttled peace twice. Yet Kasuri was the guy who was the beloved of many thinking people in India and the favourite of the Hurriyat leaders of India-administered Kashmir.

Mumbai and McCain

Kasuri recalls in the same chapter how, after the Mumbai attacks in 2008, he was made to endure what he calls the McCain episode. Republican Senator John McCain met him during a dinner at the US Consulate in Lahore—Kasuri was no longer foreign minister then; in fact, his successor Shah Mahmood Qureshi was in India when the carnage was carried out by a group of Pakistanis—to ask him how Pakistan would react if India bombed Hafiz Saeed's headquarters in Muridke, built just outside Lahore by an Arab on the intercession of the al-Qaeda. Obama's advisor Richard Holbrooke was there too, but he kept quiet. The upshot: the LeT, having morphed into JuD, was moved to its new headquarters on Lake Road inside Lahore. McCain surely won't have expected this development after his 'message'.

Kasuri's famous soft touch surges back in this bromide too:

> In an army, as large as the Pakistan Army, it would be surprising not to find some senior officers who had a more hard-line attitude towards India than others. It also depends on a particular period of time that influences and determines attitudes. For example, after and during the Afghan 'Jihad', General Zia ul-Haq did promote officers with a certain bent of mind. After 9/11, Pakistan was compelled to realign its policies in consonance with those of the international community. This led to the promotion of a different type of officers to higher ranks, during the period when President Pervez Musharraf was in charge in his capacity as COAS.[3]

The truth is that General Musharraf's 'Kargilianism' didn't die in all his companion officers. His ISI chief, General Mahmood Ahmad, didn't like the post-9/11 volte-face one bit. There were others who had to be kicked out after Musharraf was nearly killed because the military under him hadn't immediately adjusted to policy change. How can we be sure that Kasuri would have survived with his soft India policy when General Shuja Pasha in the ISI had unleashed his DPC warriors on Zardari, who sought peace with India?

One has to admit that Mian Kasuri did a big thing by landing his 'peace' book in the middle of all this in 2015. Even today, in the days of *zarb-e-azb* (Sword of the Prophet) that have made the Pakistan Army the only really popular institution in the country, he would have had to keep his fire under the bushel amid ministerial 'come-on' challenges to India pledging nuclear escalation.

10

A Sad Surrender

On 27 November 2017, a protest dharna came to an end after the state of Pakistan capitulated to around 2000 followers of a wheelchair-ridden cleric, Allama Khadim Hussain Rizvi—also called pir (saint) by his disciples—and offered the resignation of federal law minister Zahid Hamid. Rizvi had accused the PML (N) government of having insulted the Holy Prophet (Peace Be upon Him) while passing an electoral reform bill in parliament.

For three weeks, the protesting acolytes of Rizvi sat at the Faizabad roundabout and locked down all traffic between Rawalpindi and Islamabad, bringing the capital to a standstill. His followers were well looked-after, with food, tents and beddings, and they seemed to enjoy the challenge they were posing to an apostate government. They were also armed with sticks, slings, and in some cases, firearms and explosives too.

The then minister for interior, Ahsan Iqbal, acted with caution because his conservative PML (N)'s position was not very different from that of the mob with regard to the blasphemy directed at the Prophet (Peace Be upon Him). He brought out the police, the Rangers and finally the army, spending a crore a day on mobilization for three weeks. He also blocked all roads leading from Faizabad to Islamabad to prevent the protesters from reaching the centre of the capital. (The containers he used as obstacles ultimately cost the state Rs 22 crore as rent.) When parleys with Rizvi broke down, he ordered action which was returned with great success by a mostly unemployed underclass of bearded men clearly enjoying the 'outing'.

Iqbal maintained a steady barrage of statements indirectly linking the lockdown to the 2014 dharna of Imran Khan's PTI and the followers of Allama Tahirul Qadri of the normally quietist Barelvi sect of Islam. He also brought out the fact that the earlier dharna against the PML (N) government of Nawaz Sharif was planned and executed by the ISI, as disclosed by PTI insider Javed Hashmi. It had the effect of loosening the jurisdiction of the courts to allow Imran Khan to walk free, despite being issued warrants of arrest. Iqbal's innuendo was that the current dharna was a continuation of the same policy of destabilization.

Solitude of the Scapegoat

The Opposition in parliament didn't side with the besieged government despite the PML (N)'s overtures to the second-largest party in the National Assembly, the PPP. Despite the fact that the PPP government in Sindh was soon to face a similar dharna in Karachi, it allowed the government to bear the punishment alone. Soon, all major cities of Pakistan were brought to a standstill by the Barelvi sect. What was the reason behind this mammoth show of strength by a sect largely given to mysticism?

The rage of the sect—the Barelvis generally being associated with the mausoleums of saints—arose out of a casuistic row over two English words in the oath section of the Election Reforms Amendment Act. The phrase 'I solemnly swear' in the oath-taking text had inadvertently or deliberately been replaced with 'I solemnly affirm'. The culprit was found to be then law minister Zahid Hamid although all the parties in parliament had passed the amendment.

No one in the country paid attention to this picayune matter. TV channels, already divided between support for the government and the army, turned against marooned 'caretaker' Prime Minister Shahid Khaqan Abbasi and regaled his government with angry verbal assaults through a dozen retired generals who appeared on chat shows, castigating the government in unison. The PML (N)–Army feud went back to the Dawn Leaks affair, the scandal that erupted after a newspaper report of October 2016 quoted Prime Minister Sharif accusing the army of subjecting Pakistan to isolation in the region.[1]

The Inimitable Inquisitor

The great dharna leader who was soon to bring the government—and an already unstable state—to its knees was a foul-mouthed pir whose speech in the name of the Prophet (Peace Be upon Him) was occasionally so obscene that it was not reported. Khadim Hussain Rizvi had been an employee of the Punjab government's custodian-of-shrines Department of Aukaf and delivered Friday sermons at Pir Makki Masjid, near Data Darbar in Lahore, till he was fired for demonstrating in support of policeman 'Ghazi Mumtaz Hussain Qadri Shaheed', who had shot Salmaan Taseer, the governor of Punjab, 'with fifteen bullets' in Islamabad for calling the Blasphemy Law 'a black law'. His career took off after that. He refused the gratuity due to him from the Punjab government and was compensated generously by the many custodians of the shrines of Lahore.

On 4 December 2016, the fifth anniversary of the 2011 murder of Governor Taseer, a heretofore unknown Barelvi party Tehreek-e-Labbaik Ya Rasool Allah (TLYRA) laid siege to Lahore's upscale Gulberg–Liberty area, where they thought votaries of Governor Taseer may gather to mourn his death. The clerics and their 25,000-strong following also wanted to showcase their outrage at the hanging of Taseer's killer, policeman Qadri, in February 2016. Rizvi, meanwhile, scored another victory by making a disciple take part in the September 2017 by-election in Lahore, where he won handsomely against the PPP and Jamaat-e-Islami but lost to the PML (N). His candidate's posters showed Qadri triumphant after killing Governor Taseer, something the state pretended not to notice.

Earlier, the Karachi-based Sunni Tehreek, the first Barelvi organization to go violent in the mega-city's criminal underworld, had expressed outrage over the assassin's hanging by effectively besieging Islamabad under directions from their leader, Sarwat Qadri. The group declared killer Qadri a Barelvi saint and a mausoleum was erected over his grave near Islamabad. Sarwat Qadri also helped 'pir' Rizvi spread the dharna to Karachi, thus enhancing his charisma further.

The Barelvi Beast

The Barelvis are the majority subsect of Sunni Pakistan, practising a mystical cult based on the person of Prophet Muhammad (Peace Be upon Him). Because the Wahhabi rulers of Saudi Arabia were opposed to the personality cult of the Prophet, this kept them out of the well-funded covert jihad in Afghanistan and Kashmir in the 1980s under General Zia, and thus 'disempowered' them. The resultant dominance of Deobandis led to the forcible takeover of Barelvi mosques in the big cities, particularly Karachi, where the top Barelvi leadership was killed by a suicide-bomber in 2006, in what is known as Nishtar Park massacre. In 2017, what Pakistan witnessed was the rise of the Barelvi sect as a new and more serious threat than the 'rebellion' of the proxy warriors it sent into Afghanistan to fight the Soviets. The Barelvi wave rising from the obscurity of Pakistan's saintly shrines was likely to be irresistible, as demonstrated by the capitulation of the state at Faizabad.

The pir who had brought the PML (N) to its knees had been through his own trial by fire. In January 2016, when he had been fired and jailed by the Punjab government, he had gone through his 'divine initiation', as recalled by a disciple on the Internet:

> Finally they put Pir Sahib in a dirty cell[,] the condition of which in Pir Sahib's words was uninhabitable even for animals. There were cockroaches in the cell. Pir Sahib informed the cockroaches, 'Do not come near me as you know I am brought here for no crime other than the love of the Holy Prophet Muhammad (Peace and countless blessings of Almighty Allah be upon him).' Thereafter, the cockroaches did not trouble him.[2]

When someone challenged him during the Islamabad dharna, about his obscene language, he trundled out quotes from Allama Iqbal in Persian and Companions of the Prophet in Arabic, saying all of them were obscene but 'permitted'. Encouraged by him, another bearded 'saint' harangued the crowd with details of the Prophet's bodily fluids that a normal Muslim would abhor, but which received howls of approval from the Barelvi mob.

The Boots of Capitulation

The great countrywide dharna of the Barelvi sect came to an end on 27 November, barring a few straggling groups that seemed to be liking the power-to-disrupt too much to give up. The army got Rizvi to call off the siege and accept Rs 1000 handouts from the director general of the Punjab Rangers for each of the men arrested and jailed.

The 'peace agreement' said nothing about the policemen captured and tortured by the mob, or the dozens whose heads were hit by glass marbles fired from slings. The ceremony looked even more one-sided when the Urdu-dominated TV channels snarled at the PML (N) government for the 'crime against the

Holy Prophet', as well as failing to meet the challenge of history's most paralyzing dharna. Imran Khan and his party welcomed the triumph of the Barelvis and called for snap elections to set the chaos right.

The terms of surrender, as signed by PML (N)'s interior minister and Rizvi were:

1) Remove Law Minister Zahid Hamid from his position immediately,
2) Issue the report prepared by the Raja Zafarul Haq–led committee on the case in thirty days,
3) Release all protesters arrested since 6 November until the end of the sit-in from across the country, and close all cases against them,
4) An inquiry board will decide what action is to be taken against officials over the operation conducted by security forces against protesters,
5) The federal and provincial governments will determine and compensate for the loss of government and private assets,
6) The points already agreed to concerning the Punjab government will be fully implemented.

Oddly, a judge of the Islamabad High Court at the time, Justice Shaukat Siddiqui, an old Jamaat-e-Islami veteran, who according to the BBC was once rumoured to be an admirer of the killer of Governor Taseer, didn't agree with the surrender. He rejected the army's interference in the matter, which he thought violated the details of the ruling he had given about how the government should go about removing the mullahs from the roads.

Beast or Trojan Horse?

Siddiqui's reaction highlighted the hint dropped earlier by several PML (N) spokesmen about how the army was acting against the government behind the scenes, starting with the 2014 dharna of

Imran Khan and Allama Tahirul Qadri. Big money was spent then; big money was in evidence this time too. The intelligence agencies kept mum and walked gingerly through the rubble of the state, pretending not to know. One source quoted Rizvi as saying that the army would not harm his great dharna 'because we are doing the army's job,' a likely reference to the army's kidnapping of blaspheming bloggers, whom it tortured and let go on the pledge of keeping mum.[3]

The law minister was laid off and the nation briefly mourned the death of the state facilitated by the army. The then Punjab chief minister, Shahbaz Sharif, who sensed that the Faizabad build-up by the Barelvis was yet another assault on his brother Nawaz Sharif's party, recommended flexibility, an advice his brother interpreted as betrayal. Shahbaz thought things had gone too far and that any further confrontation with an establishment unwilling to take on the dharna would be too risky. He then favoured the law minister's ouster to allay the forces behind the dharna.

At first unwilling to kowtow like then interior minister Ahsan Iqbal, Zahid Hamid flew to Lahore to sound the chief minister in person and resigned after meeting him. Shahbaz's friend Chaudhry Nisar Ali Khan—now without his interior portfolio—accused his replacement (Iqbal) of 'lying', putting on notice his disagreement with Nawaz's policy of defiance yet again. Ominously, half a dozen PML (N) members of parliament and provincial assembly announced that they were leaving the party, even as Imran Khan tweeted in favour of immediate elections.

The Challenge of Maximalism

When already cashiered prime minister Nawaz Sharif, who returned from London to face his various trials at the National Accountability Bureau (NAB) court, saw the edifice of his politics falling apart, he didn't like it one bit. He publicly rebuked the decision taken by 'caretaker' Prime Minister Abbasi to get the army to sort out the Barelvi beast, and he disagreed with the 'surrender' he saw in the resignation of the law minister.[4]

This meant that he was still in his 'rebellious' mood and wanted to continue taking on the army against the advice of his brother. His daughter, Mariam, backed him in this stance, which all political observers saw as fatal to his career, and maybe even his life. She must have been aware, however, that her husband, an ex-army man whom she married out of love, was ploughing a different furrow, that of Pir Khadim Hussain Rizvi and the Barelvi beast now challenging the state of Pakistan.

The state of Pakistan is reaping more than it sowed in the rise of the Barelvis as challengers of state governance. The Deobandis, who fought the covert Afghan and Kashmir wars, jumped ship and joined al-Qaeda and, later, the ISIS, squeezing the writ out of the state. In 2014, the Barelvis were called in to force the ruling PML (N) to vacate Islamabad, a move that reached its high point of fruition after three years. But it is the ideological state that is emerging as the loser by becoming ungovernable in the face of its maximalist challengers.

11

Sorting Out the State

After the 25 July 2018 polls, in a national address declaring victory for his PTI, Imran Khan dilated on some aspects of Pakistan's security and foreign policy. Recognizing that they affected the country's economic well-being, he was mellow about India and the US—one a big power in the region and the other a major power at the global level—as the country's most critical foreign policy roadblocks. He said he wouldn't indulge in the witch-hunting of his political opponents to slake the thirst for revenge in his party, despite the strong language he had used against them in the past. The originator of extreme discourse in Pakistan in recent times, Khan was conciliatory on coming to power.

During 2013–14, Pakistan first broke the low-growth pattern of the past decade, but only to succumb to economic collapse again because of Khan's campaign against the incumbent PML (N). As he pledged punishment to the Sharifs for their corruption, he pointed to the good job of governance his government had done in Khyber Pakhtunkhwa. In fact, after the elections, his party had put out a 100-day programme of action that detailed how the PTI government would proceed to set things right in an almost-bankrupt Pakistan.

Economy's Nasty Nettle

If the 100-day programme was an indication of how Prime Minister Khan would proceed, one could only marvel at the enormity of the challenge in the six domains of action that would be undertaken:

1) Transforming governance,
2) Strengthening the federation,
3) Revitalizing economic growth,
4) Uplifting agriculture and conserving water,
5) Revolutionizing the social sector,
6) Ensuring national security.

Shuja Nawaz, in an article, had quoted Pakistani economist Rashid Amjad as saying:

> A severe foreign exchange crisis threatens significantly the recent economic upturn when GDP growth had crept back up to near 6 per cent annually. Pakistan faces a $25 billion financing deficit to meet its imports and repay external debts that are coming due in 2018. This is roughly 8 per cent of the country's GDP. Foreign exchange reserves have been declining and currently are only enough for two months of imports.[1]

Even if Khan abstained from opponent-bashing and focused on the economy, he would have found the going dangerously destabilizing. His pro-people efforts would have actually upset the peace of the country. For instance, what if he were to sort out the two messed-up public sector undertakings his predecessors couldn't do much about: Pakistan Steel Mills and Pakistan International Airlines (PIA)? Going after the black hole of the 'circular debt' may have actually endangered his government in the first hundred days of his rescue package. His economic adviser may have advised him to stay away from such immediate 'rescue' measures as rapid privatization and a steep hiking of the interest rate, but that would have been needed if his 100-day programme was to get off the ground. He would have had to cut subsidies, which would mean a hike in energy prices and leasing out the Water & Power Development Authority's (WAPDA) production, distribution and collection functions to the private sector. There was no alternative to stamping down on imports and increasing incentives for exports by eschewing the old habit of holding back on duty paybacks to exporters.

State Sector Sorrows

There is no doubt that the PTI enjoys the support of Pakistani expats, but would this community be persuaded to invest their money back in the country? One should note that more than half of the remittances come from the Middle East, where Pakistanis mostly work in the labour sector and send money back to their deeply impoverished families. As for Pakistanis living in Europe and America, so far the trend has been to sell assets in Pakistan and take the proceeds abroad to 'safe' economies through what is called money laundering. The amnesty scheme for bringing back money stashed abroad, initiated by the PML (N) government in its dying days, would have worked if the PTI overcame its political bias and allowed it to proceed.

Any 100-day policy may become hamstrung if the other 'implied' policy of 'accountability' is allowed to proceed in tandem. If the 'promised' reforms, such as the elimination of the private sector's 'expensive' schools to create 'one nation', were allowed to proceed, the result would not have been as beneficial as many Pakistani politicians had projected. The education sector in Pakistan can't be rescued because it is greatly influenced by the ideology of the state. Elimination of the sector where expensive 'English-medium' schools are seen as hostile to the 'idea of Pakistan' would only drag the country further away from the transfer of technology Pakistan needs in its industrial sector.

Pakistan's failure to indigenize technology showed up clearly in the election commission's failure to collect voting data effectively through a new computer software. Its auto industry had already failed to bring into effect the transfer of technology implied in allowing foreign cars to be produced in Pakistan. In India, not only is the mammoth five-yearly general election conducted through self-produced software, its automobile industry has completely indigenized the production of foreign cars. In Pakistan, however, ideology has intervened to divert education from its primary task of developing the mind of the youth.

PTI's expert on the economy, Asad Umar, has conceded that Pakistan would have to approach the International Monetary Fund (IMF) for the foreign exchange it needs to avoid default on earlier loans and current payments. In Pakistan, the IMF is regarded as a hostile institution run by its enemies intent on making the people of Pakistan suffer. Unfortunately, Pakistan has reached the nadir of its resistance to IMF because of its abysmal tax collection and a sharply declining export sector. Also, its wastrel state-owned organizations have let it down.

Pining in the Policy Prison

It is in the realm of security and foreign policy that the PTI government was likely to feel handicapped. These were the 'textbook' roadblocks where Pakistani nationalism had been nurtured over the decades. India had been permanently defined in textbooks as the 'regional enemy' and the US was projected by the media as the 'global enemy', forcing 85 per cent of Pakistanis to define the US as such in Gallup polls in the best of times—even when Pakistan was pocketing generous handouts from

Washington. This has led to the foreign office becoming the most non-innovative institution in the country, forcing a prime minister intent on breaking new ground to run without a foreign minister.

Imran Khan's post-election address pledged 'normalization' with both the 'enemies' within the known formula: with India, any peace would have to include the solution of the dispute of Kashmir; and with the US, nothing would move without 'equality'. Both the innuendos were unpragmatic. In the Indo–Pak bilateral dialogue under the Simla Agreement, Kashmir could have been postponed and normalization allowed with free trade, without giving up on the Pakistani claim; but Kashmir was frontloaded and the talks were allowed to drag and fizzle out amid mutual name-calling.

Today, however, the opinion in India has hardened among all classes of people, and the statesmanlike Vajpayee has been replaced by a Chanakya-follower, the high-performing Modi. Seeking 'equality' with the US seems apparently redundant given Pakistan's bedraggled economy and internal disorder. 'Equality' actually points to a refusal to 'do more', despite the outlawed Taliban freely publishing their official journal *Shariat* in Karachi since 2012; and the JeM publishing *Al-Kalam* for the benefit of Indian journalists who 'inform' the FATF that is currently adjudicating a 'grey-listed' Pakistan's case in Paris. Pakistan's caretaker government has 'mainstreamed' some more groups that still bother close friends like China and Saudi Arabia.

Sorrows of Solitude

It is a good sign that Kabul moved quickly to communicate with Imran Khan after the PTI's victory. President Ashraf Ghani wanted easing of tensions and Khan recommended open borders with Afghanistan. But the latter position will have to be squared with the state's reaction to the presence of India in its neighbouring state. Despite the fact that there are other actors in Afghanistan who target Quetta, Pakistan continues to think that India is somehow involved—which is not an unrealistic conjecture—but it is a foreign policy hiccup Khan will need to overcome.

Pakistan also needs to 'normalize' its relationship with Iran so that the Iran–Pakistan gas pipeline project may be completed. Pakistan is already under punitive contractual conditions for delaying its completion. But in this case too India has stolen a march and sewn up important gas contracts with Iran, despite growls from its ally, the US. Pakistan's geostrategic importance has also been watered down by the construction of a new Arabian Sea port in Chabahar by India, which might just persuade Pakistan to place a negative gloss on relations with Iran. At the current juncture, India tends to decide Pakistan's thinking; but there is also the Saudi factor that impedes Pakistani thinking in breaking out of its regional isolation.

Khan will have to take another look at the regional–strategic importance of the CPEC, and China's advice to include India in it. It means, once again, normalization of relations with India through trade. He will also be required to take another look at Kabul's request for a two-way trade corridor to India, which is what some foreign policy experts in Pakistan recommend too: Let there be an east–west corridor in parallel with the north–south CPEC and fulfil Pakistan's geostrategic destiny, forever changing its national security state status with dangerously revisionist thinking.

Khan's most vociferous support has come from the expat community. While Pakistanis working in the Middle East are important in terms of their share in the remittances, it is the community in the US and the European Union (EU) that is politically important. And that will require Pakistan to change its policy course from proud defiance to pragmatic caution. It is not only that Pakistan's trade is overwhelmingly concentrated in the two regions; Pakistan must act with more flexibility and pragmatism in the face of changing global values and the decline of the pluralist nature of international affairs. When the big changes come in Europe and the US, Pakistanis living there must not be exposed to discrimination.

In 2009, addressing a lawyers' gathering at the Rawalpindi Bar Association, Khan belaboured a certain section of society called the liberals—'who fly in the face of national emotion and hurt the state of Pakistan'—and condemned their interpretation of the phenomenon of the Taliban while 'obediently following the dictation of the United States'.[2] He blamed them for causing the Lal Masjid massacre in 2007 by pressuring the General Musharraf regime into taking brutal action against its 'innocent' seminarians. He has been 'pragmatic' in his dealings with the Taliban and their madrasas; he must be equally pragmatic in paying heed to the 'double-crossing' liberals who continue their hapless advocacy of the rights of women and the minorities.

12

The Begum We Bypassed

The story of Begum Ra'ana Liaquat Ali Khan is a romance that few in Pakistan are aware of. After 1947, the state quickly metamorphosed away from the dream she had shared with her husband, Pakistan's first prime minister, Liaquat Ali Khan, and Pakistan's first governor general, Muhammad Ali Jinnah. Starting with the Objectives Resolution, adopted in 1949 after Jinnah's death, the dream catapulted into a differently imagined utopia that the two founders had not thought of.

Liaquat Ali Khan had no idea what he was getting into when passing the Objectives Resolution—a constitutional blueprint of an Islamic state. He died too soon, assassinated in 1953, to see what he had done. The story is told in the biography titled *The Begum: A Portrait of Ra'ana Liaquat Ali Khan, Pakistan's Pioneering First Lady* by Deepa Agarwal and Tahmina Aziz Ayub.[1]

Ra'ana Liaquat Ali Khan was born as Irene Ruth Margaret on 13 February 1905, in a Brahmin clan whose founder,

Taradutt Pant, her grandfather, had turned Christian, dooming his offspring to lifelong ostracism by the Hindu upper-caste community. Pushing back against this legacy, Irene grew up as a fiercely independent person unafraid of accepting challenges. The Pants lived in the Himalayas of northern India, part of the proud population of Almora in the Kumaon region, wedded to Christian ideals and close to the Methodist Church.

Pretty and Precocious

Irene, a pretty young girl, initially went to Wellesley High School of the Methodist Episcopal Mission, but moved to Lal Bagh High School in Lucknow after passing fifth standard as a boarder because her father, Daniel Pant, a civil servant had to switch between the seat of government in Calcutta and the mountains. The school was founded by Isabella Thoburn, an American missionary of the Methodist Episcopal Church. Irene passed school standing first in her class and moved to college, Isabella Thoburn College, where independent thinking was encouraged.

In Lucknow, she was in the company of some outstanding female students who later became famous for their rebellious and unorthodox thinking: Ismat Chughtai, Qurratulain Hyder, Rashid Jahan and Attia Hosain. (Jahan, a leading light of the Progressive Writers' Movement, was one of the first Muslim women to study medicine at Lady Hardinge College in Delhi and later join the Provincial Medical Services. Chughtai's Urdu fiction often took her to the courts as it was regarded as 'obscene'.)

Irene passed BA in first class and joined MA Economics, for which she had to move to Lucknow University where her thesis on 'Women's Labour in Agriculture in the United Provinces' was adjudged the best in the university, earning her a very high grade. After MA, she entered the Diocesan College in Calcutta for the Graduate Teachers' Training Course. Here too, she stood first, both in the theory and practice of teaching in the Licentiate of Teaching Examination of the Calcutta University. After that, in

1930, she got appointed as a lecturer of economics at Indraprastha College for Women, Delhi, at a salary of Rs 200.

That was the year she met and married Liaquat Ali Khan.

Irene becomes Ra'ana

'Nawabzada' Liaquat Ali Khan, son of Nawab Rustam Ali Khan and Mahmuda Begum, was born in 1895 at his ancestral home in the city of Karnal, now in the Indian state of Haryana. The couple's second son, he was born into a family of nawabs who owned many landed properties both in Punjab and the UP. His father believed in the Western style of education and donated large sums of money to many centres of learning, something that Liaquat Ali continued to do. His father sent him to Muhammadan Anglo-Oriental College in Aligarh, now called Aligarh Muslim University, where he completed his BA in 1918 before marrying Jahanara Begum and becoming the father of Wilayat Ali Khan in 1919. In Aligarh, Liaquat Ali took part in sports (he was the captain of the cricket team), learned music and was the monitor of his hostel.

He went to England in 1920 to study at Exeter College, Oxford, and completed his bachelor's in jurisprudence in 1921. Thereafter, he went to study in London and was called to the Bar at Inner Temple in 1922. While at Oxford, he unsurprisingly gravitated to politics and became a good debater, being elected treasurer of Oxford Majlis, a debating society. On his return in 1922, he took a plunge into politics, pushed by the communal riots that had flared up in Karnal. He joined the Muslim League, in natural preference to the Congress, although the League was riven by dissensions created by the Khilafat Movement. Liaquat Ali attended the Lahore session of the Muslim League in 1924, where attempts were on to revive it.

In 1926, he was elected to the Uttar Pradesh (UP) legislative council as an independent candidate from Muzaffarnagar, a 'reserve' seat for Muslims, which was part of his family estate.

Irene first saw him when he made his fiery speech in the UP assembly against the Simon Commission that proposed provincial autonomy in India but rejected parliamentary responsibility at the centre. Well-spoken and articulate in English, he was already popular with the students; but his sincerity and fervour touched a chord in Irene too.

At that point, there were floods in Bihar and the students had arranged a play to collect funds for the flood victims. Irene went to the assembly and knocked on the door of Liaquat Ali's room, 'by chance', as she said later. She asked him to buy a ticket for the play, which he did, but then she asked him to buy another, which he did too. 'Bring someone to see the show with you,' she said. He replied saying he didn't know anyone he could bring. To this she quickly said: 'I promise I will find a companion for you; if not, I will sit with you myself.'

Before long, Liaquat Ali was elected deputy president of the UP legislative council, giving Irene an opportunity to get in touch with him again. She wrote to congratulate him, to which he replied: 'It is a delightful surprise to know that you are in Delhi, because it is close to Karnal, my hometown, and since I pass it on my way to Lucknow, I hope you will have tea with me at Wenger's Restaurant.' That sealed the deal.

Irene then resigned from her teaching job and moved to a room in Maidens Hotel in Delhi. Liaquat Ali, lonely after his 1928 separation from his first wife, married Irene in 1933, after she converted and took the name he gave her, Gul-e-Ra'ana. This was also the name of the stately residence in which the couple lived at 8 Hardinge Road (Tilak Road now), Delhi. In 1947, the Liaquat Alis, instead of selling the house, willed it to Pakistan as the permanent ambassadorial residence, now called Pakistan House. The couple moved with their young sons, Ashraf and Akbar, from 8 Hardinge Road, New Delhi, to 10 Victoria Road, Karachi. Jinnah, meanwhile, sold his luxurious residence at 10 Aurangzeb Road (A.P.J. Abdul Kalam Road now) to Ramakrishna Dalmia for Rs 3 lakh!

The Jinnah–Liaquat partnership

Liaquat Ali Khan and Jinnah were close to each other. Jinnah trusted him and had appointed him the secretary-general of the All-India Muslim League in 1936, publicly declaring him to be his 'right hand' as early as 1942. In 1947, soon after the formation of Pakistan, Liaquat Ali Khan became the country's first prime minister. It all began with Jinnah, as the leader of the Muslim League, falling out with the great Hindu leader Mahatma Gandhi over the Khilafat Movement supporting the Ottoman emperor against the British. This movement, the greatest-ever in the life of Indian Muslims, buttressed Hindu–Muslim unity for some years, but put-off a staunchly secular Jinnah who protested but was shouted down at the 1920 Nagpur session of the Congress. Disgusted, he left for London with his sister, Fatima, and started his legal practice, determined to be there for the rest of his life.

Then came the little-noticed milestone in the history of South Asia. In the summer of 1933, Liaquat Ali and Ra'ana journeyed to London and met Jinnah in his home in Hampstead, appealing to him to return to India. (Historian Sunil Khilnani, writing about Jinnah in London, mentions that he became the epitome of the successful London barrister: chambers in the city, a mansion in Hampstead and a chauffeured Bentley in the driveway.) The persuasion—emphasized by the charm of Ra'ana whom Jinnah liked—worked, and created, fourteen years later, the independent state of Pakistan.

Jinnah was known to be cold and distant, but he was not so formal when he visited Liaquat Ali and Ra'ana, both great bridge players and an amazing tabla-and-guitar duo, in Delhi. (Liaquat Ali was a great singer and equally skilled at playing the piano.)

He once referred to Jinnah's loneliness and proposed that he marry, to which Jinnah replied saying that he would do so if found another Ra'ana. When the first son of the Liaquat Alis was born, it was Jinnah who gave him his name, Ashraf, overriding the nawab clan's preferred 'Akbar', which was then passed on to the next son.

Religion Invades the New State

In Pakistan, things got off to a bad start. On 11 August 1947, Jinnah sought to clear the Muslim mind about what kind of state Pakistan was going to be, despite his past references to Islam. He told the Constituent Assembly: 'You are free; you are free to go to your temples, you are free to go to your mosques, or to any other place of worship in this State of Pakistan. You may belong to any religion or caste or creed—that has nothing to do with the business of the State.'[2] This shook the house, if not Prime Minister Liaquat Khan who had to bend to the dominant religious trend after Jinnah's death in 1948, to get the Objectives Resolution passed from the same Constituent Assembly.

The full story of the Objectives Resolution has been told by lawyer Hamid Khan in his monumental book *Constitutional and Political History of Pakistan* (2001).[3] Prime Minister Liaquat Ali Khan introduced the resolution that quaintly referred to Allah as 'God Almighty' (later, this more generic name was changed to Allah) and strangely set up the Ottoman Empire as the model Pakistan was to follow in its treatment of non-Muslims. The Ottoman Empire was the most secular order in Islamic history, especially towards the end of its life, it was said. Liaquat Ali Khan also said the usual things about Islam being a progressive force, which treated the minorities better than how Christian Europe had treated the Jews.

Khan definitely had a 'liberal' dispensation in mind when referring to a 'truly liberal government' in Pakistan. Unsurprisingly, the non-Muslim reaction came in the speech of Prem Hari Barma, who sought time so that he and his friends could scrutinize the text of the resolution. He pointed out that when he had left East Pakistan for Karachi, no one among his group had any idea that this resolution would be tabled.

General Zia, who Islamized Pakistan in the 1980s, far to the right of Jinnah and Liaquat both, was to inaugurate the dangerous phase of cross-border clandestine jihad, finally putting the Objectives Resolution inside the Constitution as its preface.

After Jinnah's death, Prime Minister Liaquat Ali Khan was left to take care of a broken state with no money in the kitty. He himself was reduced to poverty as, unlike Jinnah, he had no properties in Pakistan. Later, when the law of 'claims' was passed, Ra'ana was given a piece of land in Lahore to compensate for what her husband had lost in Karnal. Her son tried to settle on this piece of agricultural acreage but had to give up soon enough. After Liaquat Ali was assassinated, Ra'ana didn't have enough money to run the house and educate her boys.

Riding over Bad Times

Ashraf was sent to Aitchison College in Lahore when his father, then the prime minister, was still alive. But on his first leave home, Ashraf told his father that he felt embarrassed that all his classmates had personal servants from home to take care of their needs and he had nobody. To this, his father retorted: 'Then come back home and study here as we have enough servants here.' And thus Ashraf had to join a school in Karachi. Born in 1937, he was fourteen, and his younger brother, Akbar, born in 1941, was barely eleven. Ra'ana's youngest brother, George Pant, worried about her, joined her in Karachi, converted to Islam and took the name Jamil Parvez to live as a Pakistani citizen.

After Liaquat Ali's death, Ra'ana threw herself into social work and created the All Pakistan Women's Association (APWA) in 1969 with the help of noted social worker Begum Shahnawaz. Its office was on Jail Road, Lahore, on a property previously owned by the great builder of the city, Sir Ganga Ram. As economist of the All-India Muslim League (appointed by Jinnah), she knew the nitty-gritty of running organizations and was indefatigably devoted to the upliftment of women in Pakistan. Her husband, the late prime minister, had left her precious little to survive on. Jamsheed Marker, in his book *Cover Point: Impressions of Leadership in Pakistan* (2016), wrote: 'Born and bred in the luxury of ancestral nobility, Liaquat died a virtual pauper.'[4]

One reason Ra'ana was somewhat neglected after her husband's death was her scrap with Fatima Jinnah during a dinner, when Ra'ana refused to sit next to her saying someone 'more worthy should be selected to sit next to her'. This had led to a temporary split between the founder of the state and the prime minister. Later, Jinnah, by refusing to accept Liaquat Ali's resignation, put the matter to rest; but a kind of 'national' indifference to Ra'ana set in after that. For instance, there have been comments appearing in the press in recent times.[5]

The Scrap with Fatima Jinnah

Former chief secretary (Punjab), S.K. Mehmood, told the daily *Pakistan* (on 27 August 2004) that former Prime Minister Liaquat Ali Khan was having problems with governor general Jinnah after 1947 on the question of settling refugees from India. He said there was an overall policy for settling them that had been agreed to, but Khan wanted his own constituency carved out in Karachi by giving them special attention. The Constituent Assembly constituencies were mostly located in India. Because of these bad relations, Jinnah was not looked after when he travelled from Balochistan to Karachi and died on a road.

The Liaquat–Jinnah 'conflict' appears often on the margins of official history in Pakistan. Increasingly, individual accounts keep hinting at an intense difference of opinion that led to the death-by-neglect of the Quaid-e-Azam. There is an equal amount of personal witnessing of the treatment meted out to Fatima Jinnah after the death of her brother.

Writing in monthly magazine *Naya Zamana* (on 1 September 2004), politician Naseer Ali Shah stated that 'relations between the Quaid and Liaquat Ali Khan were not good.' He referred to the autobiography of Amir Abdullah Khan Rokhri, *Mein aur Mera Pakistan*, and quoted that Liaquat Ali Khan's wife (Ra'ana) was very uppity and her attitude had put off the Quaid and Fatima Jinnah. Ra'ana, he said, even besmirched the name of the Quaid. She got Hector Bolitho to write in his book on Jinnah that the Quaid was attracted to her. 'The truth was that the Quaid was a cold person who could not have fallen for the charms of Ra'ana Liaquat Ali Khan,' Shah said.

Muhammad Reza Kazimi, in his biography *Liaquat Ali Khan: His Life and Work* (2003), wrote:

> On Christmas Eve, Liaquat hosted a birthday party [f]or the Quaid-e-Azam, at the end of which some unpleasantness took place. A question of formal precedence between Miss Fatima Jinnah and Begum Ra'ana Liaquat took place during which Jinnah personally upbraided Liaquat's wife. On 17 December 1947, the Prime Minister sent in his resignation to the Governor-General . . . In 1947, Jinnah rejected his resignation but their ties had snapped. In the atmosphere of mistrust that was created, there is no reason to doubt—or edit—the Quaid-e-Azam's suspicion that his Prime Minister had not come to Ziarat to enquire after his health but to see how long he would last.[6]

President Ayub Khan, opposed politically by Fatima Jinnah, wanted Ra'ana to be on his side to defeat Fatima in the polls, but she refused. She, however, persuaded President Khan to promulgate the Muslim Family Law Ordinance (1961) that lingers on as a more pro-women legislation than a clerically dominated Islamic state can stomach, and is more often violated in practice than observed. She also set up the Ra'ana Liaquat Ali Khan College of Home Economics in Karachi and, later, the University of Home Economics in Lahore. She procured a substantial amount of funding from the Ford Foundation for these institutions and was able to get Eleanor Roosevelt, once the US's First Lady, to come to Pakistan to lay the foundation stone. The third Home Economics college was set up in Dacca, now Dhaka, a few years later.

A Brilliant Diplomat

In 1954, Begum Ra'ana Liaquat Ali Khan was sent to The Hague as Pakistan's first ambassador to Holland, where she was to spend two tenures lasting six years before being sent to Italy on her second posting. This allowed her sons Ashraf and Akbar to be sent to school in England, where Ashraf nevertheless had to work during the day to meet the educational expenses, despite Pakistan setting aside a monthly fund of 50 pounds for the brothers till the age of twenty-one.

Back in Pakistan after her diplomatic stint, Ra'ana was made governor of Sindh and the chancellor of Karachi University in 1973 by Prime Minister Zulfikar Ali Bhutto. In 1980, she fell and suffered a hip fracture while travelling abroad and never recovered her health after that. This didn't stop General Zia from suspending her monthly official support of Rs 2000, which compounded her problems. She witnessed the Islamization of Pakistan in the years that followed and was able to comment on it (quoted in *The Begum*) before she died in 1990, to be buried alongside Liaquat Ali Khan next to the mausoleum of the Quaid-e-Azam in Karachi:

> The idea of Pakistan when it first started was completely different from what we see today. There was no question of religion coming into politics. Everybody was free to follow their worship as they pleased, nobody interfered; it was between you and your God. We never talked of religion: there were Shias and Sunnis, we didn't know who was who; we were just working together. Quaid-e-Azam himself said the basis was religious but Pakistan was visualized as secular and democratic.

Way back in 1950 she has had clarified in New York's Town Hall:

> In Pakistan, we attach a great deal of importance to religion. And we want to build up our country as an Islamic state. I must explain that we are not going in for any sort of domination by priests or fanaticism or intolerance. What we wish to emphasize are the basic Islamic principles of equality, brotherhood, and social and economic justice.[7]

This is what she steadfastly believed in. And that's why the textbooks in Pakistan have bypassed her.

13

In Marker's Memory

There is no better description for Jamsheed Marker than the foreword penned by historian Stanley Wolpert for the former diplomat's autobiography, *Quiet Diplomacy: Memoirs of an Ambassador of Pakistan*:

> One of Pakistan's wisest diplomats, whose career as its most brilliant Ambassador started in 1964, ending with the Security Council of the United Nations in 1994.[1]

Jamsheed Kaikobad Ardeshir Marker (1922–2018), who died at his home in Karachi on 21 June at the age of ninety-five, served Pakistan for three decades in countries that ranged from Ghana to Romania and Bulgaria, the USSR and Finland, Canada, Germany, Ireland, Japan, France and the US. The multilingual diplomat—he spoke six languages—was honoured for his service with Pakistan's second-highest civilian award, the Hilal-i-Imtiaz, in 2003. However, it would not be an exaggeration to say that Pakistan recognized his skills and talent only after realizing how greatly admired he was among the international community. In 1997, the then UN secretary general, Kofi Annan, tapped him to head a campaign to persuade Indonesia to do the legal thing by East Timor and allow it to become independent. Marker was instrumental in the success of that mission, as outlined in his second book, *East Timor: A Memoir of the Negotiations for Independence*.[2]

Zoroastrian Zeal

Born on 24 November 1922, Marker was from a distinguished Parsi family of Quetta. He rose to prominence in the 1950s as a radio cricket commentator alongside Omar Kureishi. The diplomatic career that defined the rest of his life began in 1964 when Aziz Ahmed, the foreign secretary under President Ayub Khan, offered him an ambassador's post in Africa. As detailed in his memoirs, Marker picked Ghana for his post because he hoped to witness and get to know Kwame Nkrumah, the Ghanaian revolutionary who led his nation to independence from Britain.

In his 1997 book *Pakistan: A Dream Gone Sour*, Roedad Khan,[3] Marker's friend and one-time co-author, says that they were both attracted to Marxism while studying at Lahore's Forman Christian College. If this was the case, Marker's disenchantment from that political philosophy likely began in Ghana and filled the years that followed, culminating in the career of Zulfikar Ali Bhutto. His views on the Ghana founder can be applied to a lot of socialist leaders that he also got to observe, and of course Bhutto in Pakistan, whom he would serve later:

> Nkrumah's policies, an amalgam of dynamic idealism, vainglorious self-promotion and ruthless repression, constituted a vivid enigma whose early impact continues to resonate on the African continent.

Charisma accompanied the autocratic enforcement of socialist utopia tipped with nationalization and state sector dominance, eventually resulting in the perfect mix for dictatorship. Marker could see the crisis that could result from replacing capitalism with socialism without adequate planning and told Nkrumah that Ghana was a rich country with poor people.

There is wisdom in this remark. The post-colonial presumption was that the resources exploited by colonial states would now be fully available to the liberated nations and that, by replacing capitalism with socialism, these would enrich the people. Marker appeared to realize that they were wrong on both counts. Without making too much of a point of it, he outlined the crises facing Pakistan in his survey of the foreign office led by Bhutto:

> My third observation was that the policy orientation of the Foreign Ministry was more than a few points to the left of the center, and that it was being pushed further in that direction by Bhutto, despite Ayub's reluctance and disinclination, and notwithstanding the undisguised suspicion of the Americans.

A Short-lived Enchantment

Marker's disenchantment with socialism was perhaps also linked to his career trajectory, which saw him represent Pakistan in many states that were trying to distance themselves from capitalism. After Ghana, he was sent to the Socialist Republic of Romania, which was followed by his first major mission in Moscow in 1969. The following year, election results prompted East Pakistan to succumb to a national campaign for independence. The global community reluctantly sided with the people of the newly minted Bangladesh. Moscow also backed India's support for the new nation on the basis of a mutual defence treaty in 1972. Pakistan's struggling democracy was perhaps summed up best by American diplomat Henry Kissinger, who told Marker: 'Everywhere else in the world elections help to solve problems; in Pakistan they seem to create them.'

While Marker's autobiography is full of insights worth reading in full, the chapters on the USSR are particularly interesting. They show the former diplomat in his true colours under pressure, standing up to the wrath of the Soviet leadership and defending a dictator at home who had mishandled the uprising in East Pakistan. It is apparent that this was not to Marker's liking, but he was nonetheless the best ambassador Islamabad could have had in Moscow after losing East Pakistan. He was well-liked despite his tit-for-tat meetings with Soviet ministers. His circle of diplomatic friends was wide and his personal conduct immaculate, complete with an undying admiration for Russian literature and music. Everybody in the embassy thought he would be drummed out as a non grata ambassador, but just the opposite happened. When he left the Soviet Union in 1972 for a post in Canada, he was made a permanent citizen of Moscow by a visibly moved Soviet bureaucracy.

The Tragic Trio

Marker, by now his nose for character quite developed, thought East Pakistan fell because of three men:

> Mujibur Rehman, Zulfikar Ali Bhutto, and Yahya Khan, the first two because the compulsions of their fascist character precluded the compromise and sharing of power implicit in a democratic polity; and the third because he completely lost his earlier political acumen, and committed strategic blunders of the highest magnitude.

Marker did not win the battle for East Pakistan in Moscow, but he benefited in the shape of the friends he made in the world of diplomacy: the Western world sent its best men as envoys to the USSR. His friends Gunnar Jarring and Javier Pérez de Cuéllar both played their roles at the UN. By then, Pakistan had also recognized that he was a good man to have for matters of multilateral diplomacy and began asking him to attend important sessions at the UN.

After a decade spent at postings in Tokyo, Geneva and Germany, Marker found himself in France in 1982. It was during this tenure that Shahnawaz Bhutto was found dead in Nice. Recalling the incident in his book, he says:

> The final report, conveyed to me verbally by [French official] de Grossouvre after about six weeks, was that the incident had commenced in a restaurant in Nice, where the immediate Bhutto family, comprising Begum Nusrat, Benazir, Sanam, Murtaza, and Shahnawaz, together with their wives, had gathered for dinner. There was a heated conversation, reportedly over money matters, and the brothers came to blows.

He goes on:

> The party then broke up, and Shahnawaz and his wife, after returning to their hotel room, were followed by Murtaza, and another altercation took place between the brothers. The French police, when they arrived at the scene a little later found that Shahnawaz was dead and accordingly arrested his wife and Murtaza. The latter was released on production of a Syrian diplomatic passport and immediately fled the country. Shahnawaz's wife was charged under a French law that imposes culpability on any person that fails to assist or call for assistance, in aid of a victim in distress.

He concludes:

> I was told that she had obtained a lawyer and was prepared to defend herself but was dissuaded from doing so by the family, and eventually left the country. Although no autopsy was carried out, the French thought that a drug overdose was the cause of death. I was told that the French Law Minister Robert

> Badinter, who was a friend of the Bhutto family, had helped in bringing the unsavory affair to a close.

Four years later, in 1986, Marker was appointed Pakistan's ambassador to the US, serving in the position for a year that would serve as the climax to his distinguished career. He has been attributed with helping negotiate the Soviet military's withdrawal from Afghanistan, while also dealing with General Zia-ul-Haq's furtive development of nuclear weapons at home. Marker, thanks to his contacts across the world, was just the man to repeatedly postpone the many threats of sanctions facing Pakistan over its uranium enrichment, especially following the passage of the Pressler amendment a year earlier.

An Admired Ambassador

Writing in the *New York Times* in 1989, journalist Robert Pear noted Marker's diplomatic success in the US:

> Jamsheed KA Marker, the Ambassador of Pakistan, is described as tough, shrewd and cultivated by State Department officials and members of Congress. Of all the diplomats in Washington, few work so intimately with the Reagan Administration as Mr. Marker. He has helped forge a joint strategy with the United States in one of the great geopolitical battles of the 1980s, the effort to expel the Soviet army from Afghanistan. In the process he has dramatically strengthened relations between Pakistan and the United States, American officials say.[4]

For his part, Marker loved the then US President Ronald Reagan, and was frequent host to diplomats Henry Kissinger and Zbigniew Brzezinski. He also got along with the intellectually aloof Egyptian diplomat Boutros Boutros-Ghali and enjoyed the company of many US Congressmen. Facilitated by his friend Roedad Khan, Marker also felt comfortable with Zia-ul-Haq and Ghulam Ishaq

Khan. This bonhomie did not continue into the government of Benazir Bhutto, formed after the elections in 1988, despite Marker's brother-in-law Darayus Cyrus Minwalla's enthusiasm for the PPP leader.

As he notes in his memoir, Marker chose to resign rather than continue under potentially trying circumstances:

> In this instance, there were two other factors that motivated my decision. One was my reservations with regard to Benazir's style and management, not to mention the choice of her collaborators as there was a whiff of incompetence and corruption. The other was my conviction that any Pakistani ambassador in Washington must have direct access to, and must possess the confidence of, the head of government. In my case this was clearly not so.

In 1990, after the dismissal of Benazir Bhutto on corruption charges, Marker was appointed Pakistan's permanent representative at the UN. He continued in that role until 1995. Pakistan was part of the UN Security Council at the time, and he presided over its proceedings three times in rotation.

One of Pakistan's elder statesmen, Jamsheed Marker has left a void that might be impossible to fill. Patriotic, principled and fiercely intelligent, he fought to keep the country engaged with the global community even as internal forces backed isolation. We may never see someone like him again.

14

Allama Iqbal: The Name Lives On

Pakistan's ideological journey has reshaped the great poet and philosopher Allama Muhammad Iqbal into a patron of its hardening world view. Reviewing how he has been 'reinterpreted' into an ideological platitude is now hazardous because of his state-approved and clerically backed identity as an orthodox thinker opposed to all modernist revision. At times, secular commentators longing for an identity rollback consign him to the category of 'orthodox' while praising Sir Syed Ahmad Khan as the true modernist. There is, however, steady evidence from his life that defies this orthodox labelling.

The climactic moment in Iqbal's relationship with Pakistan came on 25 December 1986; some forty-eight years after his death. It happened during a national seminar presided over by General Zia-ul-Haq in Karachi on the birth anniversary of Muhammad Ali Jinnah. The topic was: 'What Is the Problem Number One of Pakistan?' Present among the invitees was the son of Allama

Iqbal, then a sitting judge of the Supreme Court of Pakistan. In his speech on the occasion, the late Justice Javed Iqbal explained why his father was opposed to *hudood* (Quranic punishments), which General Zia had promulgated in Pakistan.

The controversial phrasing from the 'sixth lecture' in Allama Iqbal's book, *The Reconstruction of Religious Thought in Islam*, was:

> The Shariat values (*Ahkam*) resulting from this application (e.g. rules relating to penalties for crimes) are in a sense specific to that people; and since their observance is not an end in itself they cannot be strictly enforced in the case of future generations.[2]

The reaction from General Zia was dismissive of Allama Iqbal rather than the hudood he had imposed to appease his vast hinterland of clerical support. He had got into trouble with the clergy when his Federal Shariat Court had decided that since stoning to death (*rijm*) was not mentioned in the Quran, it could not be a *hadd*, that is, a punishment in the penal code. He had to change the court to retain rijm.

But Iqbal was prophetic: Pakistan has not stoned a single woman to death despite rijm being in the statute book, nor has it been able to chop off hands for stealing. The more literalist Iran gave up the ghastly practice of rijm in 2014.

Pakistan is disturbed today by the continuing practice of bank interest after the Federal Shariat Court banned it in 1991 as *riba* (usury) specifically mentioned in the Quran, as also by Aristotle in his *Nicomachean Ethics*. Islamic banking, which actually excludes the taking of riba, does so under a policy of complex self-confessed *heela* (subterfuge).

In his publication *Ilmul Iqtisad* (1904), Iqbal's first book in Urdu as an introduction to how a modern economy worked, he explained and clearly accepted bank interest as the lifeblood of commerce, knowing that it was considered banned by the clerics and accounted for so few Muslims in India's commercial sector.

He did so by accepting Sir Syed's view that interest-banking was not the same as riba.[3]

Hudood and Ijtihad

Iqbal couldn't have found approval in the Pakistan of today, much like Jinnah himself after he declared his preference for the Lockean state on 11 August 1947. To extend the argument, Iqbal was also opposed to the *fiqh* (case law) favouring the Law of Evidence that discriminated against women and the non-Muslim citizens of the state. That he was unhappy with and scared of the traditionalist ulema is testified by his arguments in his lectures; there is also evidence that he was inclined towards a 'liberal' version of Islam in the new state.

Towards the end of his life he was collecting material to write on fiqh and had been corresponding with the traditionalist ulema to elucidate points that he presumably wanted discussed in his new work. He was not a trained scholar (*aalim*) and was not accepted as such by the ulema, but he thought himself qualified to produce a work of *Ijtihad* (reinterpretation).

His son, Justice Javed, wrote: 'The Jinnah-Iqbal correspondence, discussing shariah, points to the establishment of a state based on Islam's welfare legislation; it does not propose that in the new state any laws pertaining to cutting of the hands (for theft) and stoning to death (for fornication) would be enforced.'

According to Javed Iqbal's biography of Allama Iqbal, *Zindarood*, Allama Iqbal read his first thesis on Ijtihad in December 1924 at the Habibya Hall of Islamia College, Lahore.[4] The reaction from the traditionalist ulema was immediate: he was declared a *kafir* (non-believer) for the new thoughts expressed in the paper. Maulavi Abu Muhammad Didar Ali actually handed down a fatwa of his apostasy. In a letter written to a friend, Iqbal opined that the ulema had deserted the movement started by Sir Syed and were now under the influence of the Khilafat Committee from which he (Iqbal) had resigned.

Allama Iqbal's intent in reinterpreting hudood becomes clear when he quotes Maulana Shibli Numani, who had written *Seerat-un-Nabi,* his renowned multi-volume biography of the Holy Prophet: 'It is therefore a good method to pay regard to the habits of society while considering punishments so that the generations that come after the times of the *Imam* are not treated harshly.'

Like No Other

Allama Iqbal was a prodigy. In 1885, he stood first in grade one in Scotch Mission School, Sialkot, and began to be tutored in Persian and Arabic in a mosque. He was in class nine when as a teenager he started writing his juvenile poetry in Urdu. He passed matriculation in first division, winning a medal with scholarship. In his first year at Scotch Mission College, he started versifying under the pen name of Iqbal and was published in literary journals.

He passed his BA exam in first division and won medals in Arabic and English. Three years later, though he passed his MA Philosophy in third division, he was the only one who passed and received the gold medal. He was appointed professor of philosophy at the Government College, Lahore, chosen by Professor Thomas Arnold—the British orientalist who wrote a book proving that Islam was spread in the subcontinent not by the sword but by humanist preaching—who became his patron.

Iqbal was additionally appointed as the Macleod Arabic Reader at Oriental College, Lahore, at a monthly salary of seventy-two rupees and one anna. Later, he took time off from Oriental College to teach English at the Government College. His poems had started showing influence from Spinoza, Hegel, Goethe, Ghalib, Bedil, Emerson, Longfellow and Wordsworth.

He couldn't disagree with Sir Syed, whom he regarded as the Baruch Spinoza (d. 1677) of Islam, rationalizing and demystifying the scriptures. His job description at Oriental College included the teaching of economics to the students of the Bachelor of

Oriental Learning in Urdu, and translating into Urdu works from English and Arabic.

Pioneer of Separation

Lahore lionized Iqbal as the thinker-poet of the city who could spellbind in a mushaira while publishing erudite papers on such mystics as al-Jili, whose concept of *insan al-kamil* was reborn in him with the help of Nietzsche and his 'superman' and 'will to power' but without Nietzsche's rejection of morality—his 'not goodness but strength' slogan. This was before he went to Europe (1905–08) to do his master's and Bar at Cambridge and his PhD with his thesis, 'The Evolution of Metaphysics in Iran' at the Munich University, becoming unbelievably proficient in German within three months.

The period 1908–25, back in Lahore, saw him produce some of his Urdu masterpieces while practising law at the Lahore High Court. Reacting to Hindu revivalist movements, he journeyed from his pluralist view of India to a 'preservative' posture, advocating separate electorates and developing the first geographical map of 'separation' of the Muslim community in the north-east and the south-east within the subcontinent. The All-India Muslim League courted him as the leading Muslim genius and listened to his 'separatist' thesis at its Allahabad session in 1930.

He contended that his idea of an autonomous Muslim state was not original but had been derived from the Arya Samaj Hindu revivalist vision of Lala Lajpat Rai of Punjab, who first recommended 'separating' the Muslims. The view he put forward in his address remained pluralist, which Pakistan neglected in 1949: '. . . [N]or should the Hindus fear that the creation of autonomous Muslim states will mean the introduction of a kind of religious rule in such states'.[5]

As for Iqbal's Nietzschean yearning for self-empowerment, Jinnah was made a practical example of it, as noted oddly by none other than Saadat Hasan Manto in one of his sketches.

Jinnah said this at the 1937 Lucknow session of the Muslim League:

> It does not require political wisdom to realise that all safeguards and settlements would be a scrap of paper, unless they are backed up by power. Politics means power and not relying only on cries of justice or fair-play or goodwill.[6]

It was this separate empowerment of Muslims in the face of such Hindu revivalist movements as *shuddhi* (purification) and *sangathan* (unification) that made Iqbal disagree with the Deobandi scholar Husain Ahmad Madani over the idea of India as a nation state where Muslims and Hindus would live as one nation. Like Lala Lajpat Rai, Dr B.R. Ambedkar wanted the Muslims to be given a separate state and wrote his book *Thoughts on Pakistan* (1941) which was welcomed by Jinnah who then asked everyone to read it to legitimize the league's campaign for Pakistan.

On the Same Page with Jinnah

Iqbal's legally trained mind and his ability to write scholarly tracts quite apart from his ability to write the long poem or *masnavi*—abandoned by most poets of note after him—qualified him for all the three Round Table Conferences in London to present the case of the Muslims. His Allahabad address at the Muslim League conference in 1930 was actually a learned survey of the nature of the modern state, as imagined by such Western philosophers as Rousseau, and could not have been comprehended by most Muslim Leaguers still basking in the afterglow of a doomed Khilafat Movement.

Noting that Pakistan's non-Muslims observe the Independence Day of Pakistan three days earlier, *Dawn* editorialized on 11 August 2017 on how Pakistan first tried to suppress, then set aside, the 11 August 1947 message of the Quaid-e-Azam at the Constituent Assembly: 'You are free . . . You may belong to any religion or caste or creed. That has nothing to do with the business of the state.'[7]

It is not only Jinnah that Pakistan has set aside; it is also the philosopher of the state, Allama Mohammad Iqbal, who has been rejected. Seventy years after its foundation, the state is malfunctioning and religion is a major cause of the shifting of its writ to the non-state actors. Denigrated are human rights—of the minorities and women—on the basis of a coercive interpretation of religion. So much so, that the faith-based but unexamined constitutional provisions in Articles 62/63 have finally destabilized governance by causing conflict between state institutions.

Justice Javed Iqbal[8]

Justice (retd) Javed Iqbal died in Lahore on 3 October 2015 after living for ninety years in the shadow of his great father, Allama Dr Muhammad Iqbal. Did he become stunted in the reflected glory of his father? Did he accept the dubious status of a successor to whom originality was forbidden lest he extend the limits of a great thinker that was his father?

It is possible that people ignored his effort at becoming his own self after docketing him under the larger shelf of a great father. He adhered to his father's legacy, but interpreted him not quite the way the official textbooks did. Javed Iqbal was original and walked a little bit ahead of his father, not minding that the state had to thrust him into obscurity in order to save its ideology from being modified.

In his book *Islam and Pakistan's Ideology*,[9] he accepts the fact that his father imagined an Islamic state but is at pains to clarify that he did not envision what Pakistan finally became after 1947. He asks that if Islam was the basis of Pakistan, then which interpretation of Islam was its inspiration? Why were most ulema opposed to its creation? Especially when the earlier Islamic movements had failed in India, why did the one opposed by the ulema succeed? He further asks the framers of the Constitution if

Pakistan is an Islamic state in the conventional sense of an Islamic state as envisaged by Iqbal and Jinnah? And why doesn't the expression 'Islamic state' appear in the Quran and Hadith? Even the expression 'Darul Islam' doesn't appear in the Quran but was coined by later jurists.

Ill-fitting with Ideology

One can guess why Javed was sidelined, if one reads his thoughts on Islam and Pakistan. He said that Pakistan was established on a reconstructive view of Islam and was opposed by the ulema because it was not established on the basis of conventional Islam that would not gibe with modern conditions. Whenever the Muslims of India were derailed from workaday pragmatism by the emotionalism of the ulema, they suffered grievously. The problem is compounded by the fact that an Islamic state had never been formed before, and the one that was formed by the Holy Prophet in Medina is not acceptable today because his 'constitution', called Mithaq-e-Madina, conferring equality of citizenship on the non-Muslims is not acceptable to the orthodoxy.

Javed had a tough childhood because his father's marriage to his mother went through a period of upheaval. In fact, the matrimonial life of the national poet was a bit of a shipwreck. He knew that his father was great and guarded Allama Iqbal's originality without scaling down his genuine admiration for him. He studied philosophy and was habitually a thinker like his father who definitely passed on some of his DNA to him.

Convivial Confessions

His memoir *Apna Gareban Chaak*[10] recalls Rousseau's *Confessions.* He was unworshipful of his great father without seeking to build himself up at his expense. His story begins with his acting as the prodigal son, unheedful of his father's last advice against extravagance, and ends in Javed meeting his father's expectations of him. He stood first in MA Philosophy in Punjab and received a gold medal from Governor Mudie before leaving for Cambridge for higher studies. When he was sailing to London in 1949, he noted that, passing the Saudi peninsula, he was not overcome by any feeling of desolation at not being 'called' to Hijaz as his father was during his voyage.

What he did during his sea voyage was flirt like crazy, as revealed in his book *Jahan-e-Javid*.[11] His diary reveals that, on the first day on the deck of Celicia, he attitudinized brazenly, pretending to write his first novel, *I Am a Muslim*, in his room after dancing all evening on deck. He was soon noticed by a forty-year old lady—to his twenty-five—and a relationship developed. She was rich and beautiful and quickly graduated from 'aunty' to an object of envy for other women.

A Playboy Puritan

Ironically, after all these little affairs on the ship, he was to meet his future wife, Justice (retd) Nasira Iqbal, in London. But his playfulness soon resulted in him losing his first three terms at Cambridge without a clue about what he had come there for. Professor Arberry found that his lack of knowledge of Arabic, Greek, and Latin disqualified him for research into Imam Ghazali and Imam Abu Hanifa. He subsequently plumped for an investigation into the theory of the Islamic state and got his PhD in it. As a result, he has written more clearly about the Islamic state and has done a better job of confronting the clerics than his father who must have been pleased to know that he was no dud.

Perhaps the most important book Javed ever wrote was the voluminous biography of his father, titled *Zindarud*, in 2004, carefully recording facts without fluffing some of the warts that a conventional son would have discreetly left out. The book remains the best explanation of why his father was a great man. It is available for free on the Internet as an e-book.

Taking about the General

Javed took on Pakistan's most transformational military dictator, General Zia-ul-Haq, while being a sitting judge of the Supreme Court, and did something at a meeting that our bearded judges can't even think of doing. It happened during the seminar presided over by General Zia in Karachi on 25 December 1986. Javed told the general that Allama Iqbal was opposed to punishments like the cutting of hands in modern times. He was referring to the sixth lecture in the volume titled *The Reconstruction of Religious Thought in Islam*,[12] which has become the second document of national embarrassment after the 11 August 1947 speech of Jinnah saying Pakistan was to be a secular state. Zia told Javed in the conference: 'If that is the case, then we have to set Allama Iqbal aside.'

In 2008, Javed wrote his interpretation of his father's lectures in the face of a studied neglect of the poet's take on the Islamic state. In *Khutbaat-e-Iqbal: Tas-heel-o-Tafheem* (Iqbal's Lectures: Facilitation and Comprehension), he explained to the conservative critics of his father what the 'sixth lecture' had really tried to communicate. The crux of the argument was whether the Allama was overstepping the boundaries of 'reinterpretation' set by the classical jurists of Islam.

Javed Iqbal defended his father against the fundamentalist upsurge peaking by the end of the twentieth century. Ground reality gives the lie to those who want Islamic punishments retained under one pretext or the other. Iran stones people to death under 'rijm', killing mostly women, which has been possible under a draconian system based on coercion. The Taliban too promised such a system in Pakistan with the help of a vast madrasa network.

The Hassle of Hudood

The 'real' hudood, that is, cutting of hands, bore no fruit in Sudan. A colony of crippled Sudanese men with their hands cut had to be looked after by a German charity. In Kohat, the Taliban similarly crippled two men. Pakistan is still unable officially to cut the hands of its thieves although these punishments have been awarded by the lower courts. It has still to stone its first woman to death.[13]

Javed spoke from his experience as a judge when he found fault with the *diyat* (blood money) law favouring the rich and encouraging planned homicide.

On the night of 7 March 2011 Javed Iqbal was interviewed on a TV channel on the nature of the Pakistani state. He said Pakistan, as envisaged by Jinnah, was to be a secular state: 'Hard Islam was not the project of Jinnah: the Islam of hudood and blasphemy laws was imposed by General Zia.'

15

Deeds of a Doomed State

In the first week of September 2018, Prime Minister Imran Khan set up an Economic Advisory Council (EAC) to get Pakistan out of its economic emergency. He chose eleven well-regarded economists from the private sector to help the country bolster its fast-depleting foreign exchange reserves and boost a collapsing balance of payments. The then information minister Fawad Chaudhry came on TV to defend the inclusion of one of the appointees, Dr Atif R. Mian of Princeton University's Department of Economics and the Woodrow Wilson School of Public Policy, who was also a member of the Ahmadi religious sect that had constitutionally been declared non-Muslim by Pakistan.

Chaudhry said the constitution gave to its non-Muslim minorities a status equal to that of its Muslim citizens. He asserted that if there was protest against this appointment, his government would stand firm on its decision because Dr Mian was rated among the top twenty-five economists of the world. A day later, however, his government decided to ask Dr Mian to leave the EAC, which he did. There is speculation that the ruling PTI itself was convulsed with protest, apart from the 'reported' outrage felt in Pakistan's muscular religious organizations that Imran Khan avoids offending.

A Nervous 'New' State

The liberal section of the social media, having heaped kudos on Khan for appointing Dr Mian, not caring for the extremists, couldn't take the retreat kindly. Yet their outrage counted for nothing and became predictably muffled in the face of a backlash they too wanted to avoid. No reference to the Constitution, already defiled by apostatization, would secure their position on Dr Mian who was graceful in his farewell message:

> For the sake of the stability of the Government of Pakistan, I have resigned from the Economic Advisory Council, as the Government was facing a lot of adverse pressure regarding my appointment from the Mullahs (Muslim clerics) and their supporters. Nevertheless, I will always be ready to serve Pakistan as it is the country in which I was raised and which I love a great deal. Serving my country is an inherent part of my faith and will always be my heartfelt desire. Moving forward, I now hope and pray that the Economic Advisory Council is able to fulfill its mandate in the very best way so that the Pakistani people and nation can prosper and flourish. My prayers will always be with Pakistan and I will always be ready to help it in any way that is required.'[1]

The same day, Dr Asim Ijaz Khwaja, professor of international finance and development at the Harvard Kennedy School, walked out of the EAC in protest. He was followed by Imran Rasul, professor of economics at University College London. No Pakistan-based members protested publicly or resigned, case-hardened by what Pakistan routinely does to its Ahmadis. Notable was Imran Khan's ex-wife, Jemima's, tweet on the subject:

> Indefensible & v disappointing. New Pak gov asks renowned & respected Prof of economics to stand down because of his faith. NB: The founder of Pakistan 'Quaid-i-Azam' appointed an Ahmadi as his Foreign Minister.[2]

Collapse of Conscience

The PML (N) kept quiet at the ouster of Dr Mian because its leader, Nawaz Sharif, was in jail after failing to appease his detractors by removing the name of Dr Abdus Salam, Pakistan's Ahmadi Nobel laureate, from the signboard of the physics department of the Islamabad Quaid-e-Azam University. The PPP, now 'liberal' under Chairman Bilawal Bhutto-Zardari, also remained non-committal, perhaps remembering that its own government had inserted the Second Amendment in the Constitution that declared the Ahmadi community non-Muslim. One of its leaders, a former prime minister, now under inquiry for corruption, had said in 2016:

> No one has been able to compete with [the] Pakistan People's Party. If someone has served Islam, only the Government of 'martyr' Zulfikar Ali Bhutto has. It solved the 90-year-old problem, the problem of Qadianis [Ahmadis] who challenged the Prophethood of Prophet Muhammad (Peace Be upon Him). The PPP shut them up, broke their neck and buried the [Ahmadi] problem.[3]

A Tainted Constitution

The 'apostatizing' Second Amendment passed in 1974 by a 'socialist-liberal' government led to the following insertions in the Pakistan Penal Code: the Ahmadi community cannot call their places of worship 'masjid' (mosque) and cannot give the call to prayer (azan). Section 298-C says the Ahmadis cannot pose as Muslims, directly or indirectly. This led to the extremely touching incident of an Ahmadi being hauled up for the *kalima* (oath of Islam) being inscribed on the house that he had just bought; he was hauled up again, for desecration, when he tried to wipe it off!

The Constitution declares the Ahmadis non-Muslim and places them in the category of minorities that have equal rights under its own articles. Islamizing dictator General Zia introduced separate electorates in Pakistan, not allowing non-Muslims to vote with the Muslims. When this abuse of human rights was corrected and separate electorates removed from the Constitution, all non-Muslims got back their right to vote with the Muslims, except the Ahmadis, thus implying that they are not accepted even as a minority in Pakistan. Subliminally, they remain apostates and, under Islamic law, they deserve death. Few Pakistanis realize what message they are sending out to the world by treating the Ahmadis the way they do. By remaining passive, the state allows the extremist elements to 'enforce' this law.

A Calendar of Calumny

In May 2010, two Ahmadi mosques—which can't be called mosques under the law—were attacked in Lahore during the Friday namaz (prayer)—which can't be called namaz under the law. When the attack was over, ninety-five graves were dug in Rabwa (a high or raised place)—which can't be called Rabwa under the law—to receive the Ahmadis killed. (Rabwa is now Chenab Nagar.)

The deed was done by six or seven suicide bombers armed with Kalashnikovs and hand grenades. The Punjabi Taliban claimed responsibility. The then Punjab law minister Rana Sanaullah revealed on TV that the attackers had come from south Punjab after being trained in the tribal territory of Waziristan. A terrorist captured alive revealed that the attackers were brought to Lahore nine days earlier in a group from Bannu, kept in various mosques, including the Tablighi centre at Raiwind, and were driven to the two targeted locations. He said their handlers were waiting in back-up vehicles, ready to kill and replace any attacker who tried to run away instead of killing the Ahmadis.

The killers were clearly terrorists who routinely killed Pakistani troops, but the state blinked away their adventure as a part of its hidden promise to exterminate the Ahmadi community. The then federal interior minister Rehman Malik was more revealing. According to him, the attackers in Lahore belonged to the JeM and the LeJ.[4]

The then chief minister Shahbaz Sharif was greatly upset but announced no compensation for the dead. He also did not make an appearance at the two targeted locations. The TV channels tried to discuss the issue, but the anchors were bemused by the legal implications of discussing the Ahmadis without attracting the mischief of the anti-Ahmadi laws. The reporters had already committed the blunder of referring to the 'mosque', 'juma', 'khutba' (sermon) and 'namaz' before being corrected.

Fomented by Foreign Foes

The daily *Jang*, on 29 May 2010, carried a front-page report communicating a message from the intelligence agencies of Pakistan. It said that the Qadianis were being killed in accordance with the plots hatched by the United States, India, Afghanistan and Israel to defame Pakistan. These four countries, opposed to Islamic jihad, were determined to damage the image of Pakistan in the international community, and India sought in it a justification for clamping down on the Deobandi madrasas in India. The report added that Indian intelligence agents had contacted a Qadiani—a pejorative for Ahmadi—representative in Kapurthala in east Punjab to tell him that his community would be targeted in Lahore. Commissioner Lahore Khusrau Parvez was quoted in the same report as saying that R&AW agents had penetrated

Lahore and killed the Ahmadis to avenge Youm-e-Takbir—the anniversary of the day Pakistan tested its nuclear devices in 1998—because through Youm-e-Takbir Pakistan had become secure against India. He did not explain, but it was assumed that after the Ahmadi massacre Pakistan would start worrying about its international image and stop celebrating the historic achievement of becoming a nuclear state.

The then US defence secretary Robert Gates in the May–June 2010 issue of *Foreign Affairs* wrote:

> In the decades to come, the most lethal threats to the United States' safety and security are likely to emanate from states that cannot adequately govern themselves or secure their own territory. Dealing with such fractured or failing states is, in many ways, the main security challenge of our time.[5]

Exclusion and Expiry

In the case of Pakistan, it is a weak state stricken with the additional palsy of 'exclusion' that may be forced to apostatize the Shias—then killed like flies in cities along the road from Kohat to Kurram—and the Ismailis too. With the killing of the Ahmadis in Lahore, Pakistan's pariah status in the world became more consolidated, giving rise to more xenophobia—expressed through its commissioners and senior police officers—and leading to more killings at home.

Most Pakistanis think the minorities enjoy complete freedom in Pakistan. They are shocked when international institutions such as the Human Rights Council object to Pakistan's conduct, and not India's, forgetful of the rule that only maltreatment emanating from legislation is blamed on the state. Most Pakistanis don't count the Ahmadis as Muslims but then they don't treat them as a protected minority either.

Statistics on the human rights performance of Pakistan are available but are rejected as lies. The NGOs who undertake to publicize these numbers are angrily condemned as foreign-funded institutions carrying out foreign agendas in Pakistan. When organizations like Amnesty International reveal Pakistan's negative record, they are rejected; but when they reveal India's negative record, their findings are gleefully highlighted.

Dr Mian should know that persecution of Ahmadis has not ceased. A TV channel caused the death of three Ahmadis in Sindh in 2008 after a discussion programme called them insulters of the Holy Prophet. From April 1984 to December 1999, as many as 753 Ahmadis had been arrested for displaying the kalima and another 379 for posing as Muslims. Now they take persecution silently and hate to be noticed by hypocritical Muslims feeling the rare twinge of conscience. More than 250 members of the Ahmadi sect have been killed since 1984, not including those under death sentence after being accused of blasphemy.

The Habit of Exclusion[6]

According to a recent assessment of state persecution in Pakistan, the excommunicated Ahmadi community lost thirty-nine members through murder in three years (2012–15). Forty Ahmadis were injured after assault and six were kidnapped. Eight Ahmadi graveyards were desecrated, ten 'places of worship' damaged, while harassment occurred in eleven cases.

States at times practise exclusion, 'the majority considering the minority sections to be an intolerable deficit in the purity of the national whole'.[7] They do it through impunity or manifest legal devices; but Pakistan did it by excommunicating the Ahmadi community through the Second Amendment of the Constitution. In his remarkably even-handed book *The Ahmadis and the Politics of Religious Exclusion in Pakistan*,[8] Ali Usman Qasmi, assistant professor of humanities and social sciences at Lahore University of Management Sciences (LUMS), has told the story of how it happened.

It is fascinating how Pakistan's Islamic teleology evolved as it distanced itself from the secular 'afterglow' of British Raj and zeroed in to what looks like a precursor phase of an al-Qaeda and Islamic State world view in the twenty-first century. In 1953, when the riots against the Ahmadi community first led to the setting up of a judicial commission, the Grundnorm of the Objectives Resolution of 1949 had not yet been internalized, and the judges ended up delivering a humane verdict in favour of the victim community.

The Internal Trigger

All Muslims seem to have an internal trigger making them backslide to Islamic Leviathan. Such a trigger was manifested in 1974 by a parliament dominated by a 'socialist' PPP led by charismatic and secular Zulfikar Ali Bhutto. The author provides evidence of the mystery trigger by narrating how Bhutto never attended the apostatizing sessions of the National Assembly and actually 'reprimanded' his attorney-general, Yahya Bukhtiyar, for unfairly prosecuting the Ahmadis till he was reminded that he had ordered the trial himself.

The 1953 anti-Ahmadi riots had been 'organized' in Punjab by then chief minister M.M. Daultana, who made the most enlightened speech at the judicial commission, saying a community could be converted into a minority only when it asked for such exclusion. Evidence showed that public funds were misused to support newspapers who were agitating the movement.[9] Then prime minister Khwaja Nazimuddin was forced by states aiding Pakistan to abstain from firing his Ahmadi foreign minister, Sir Zafarullah Khan, and said the following in rebuttal of the famous 11 August 1947 speech in which the founder of the state, Jinnah, had pledged a pluralist state in a manifestly Lockean speech separating religion and state before the Constituent Assembly. Nazimuddin is quoted as asserting:

> I do not agree that religion is a private affair of the individual[,] nor do I agree that in an Islamic State every citizen has identical rights, no matter what his caste, creed or faith. The speech of the Quaid-i-Azam must be interpreted in the context in which it was delivered.[10]

There are ironies in this statement that have become manifest only in 2015, when the non-Muslims are under threat of being killed and the community of the founder of the state has been called 'non-Muslim' on TV by the leader of a 'banned' sectarian organization. The book uncannily foreshadows this while reproducing the details of a meeting in which Bhutto's wife actually felt that the apostatization of the Ahmadis would lead to the victimization of her own community, the Shia, in the coming days:

> In this meeting Bhutto's wife Nusrat, a Shiite of Iranian descent, was also visibly perturbed. She expressed apprehension that the exclusion of Ahmadis would be followed by that of Shiites.[11]

In 2015, Pakistan was killing its Shia community, as was being done elsewhere in the Middle East, as 'correction' of the Islamic faith.

Dilemma of Living in Modern Times

The dilemma in 1953 was that the clerics appearing before the Justices Munir-Kiyani Commission, which had been formed to inquire into the Punjab disturbances of 1953, couldn't agree on the definition of a Muslim. If they reduced it to the pronouncement of kalima, the Ahmadis couldn't be indicted as they said it the same way as the 'normal' Muslims. If you insisted on it, however, the Shia could fall into the trap of apostatization as their catechism of faith actually differs. The problem that arose in the post-apostatization period was: How to trap Ahmadis into declaring themselves non-Muslim on identity cards and passports?

General Zia, in the 1980s, 'purified' the state through further Islamization, making Pakistan the pathfinder of what is now going on in the Islamic world. His martial law order imposed the strictest disabilities on the Ahmadis: Curse the founder of the community on ID cards and passports, stop naming the basic instruments of their faith as 'mosque', the 'Quran', 'namaz', etc., on the pain of imprisonment. Ahmadi graves were dug up and removed from Muslim graveyards. The state was reduced to being a silent witness as bloodthirsty collective psychosis took over.

Did Bhutto do it for Saudi money? His reference to the 'solution of a 90-year-old problem'[12] points to the 'trigger' that hides in all Muslims. The Saudi push happened more clearly when in 1980 General Zia took Saudi dictation to impose religious tax of *zakat* on the Shia. The Rabita Alam al Islami (World Islamic League)—the Saudi organization with billions of dollars in its budget—was active in 1974; it was active under General Zia too.

As noted by Vali Nasr in his book *The Shia Revival*,[13] the anti-Shia edicts (fatwas) were 'managed' through a scholar of India, Manzur Numani, then head of Nadwatul Ulema of Lucknow, who compiled anti-Shia fatwas of apostatization from the major seminaries of India and Pakistan in 1986. This compendium of fatwas laid the foundation for Shia massacres in Pakistan. Who is next?

16

UK Muslims: 'The Enemy Within?'

Baroness Sayeeda Warsi is a former chairman of the United Kingdom's Conservative Party and the first Muslim woman to serve in the cabinet from 2004 to 2014. She resigned from ministership after her party's 'morally indefensible' stance on Israel's atrocities in Gaza. As party chairman, she had demanded that the government impose an arms embargo on Israel, claiming that it had killed 2000 people 'in just four weeks'.

She put down her life's narrative and that of her Muslim community in the United Kingdom (UK) in her book *The Enemy Within: A Tale of Muslim Britain* (2018). She is a gifted writer and, reading her book, one is forced to take account of how she gave up her £130,000 salary as a solicitor to stand for parliament, becoming her party's chairman. She brings focus on the anti-Muslim trend in Britain's lawmaking and governance, but not without bringing a similarly critical focus on the state of non-assimilation of her community in a 'multicultural' state, thus arriving at the ironical conclusion that her community is now considered the 'enemy within':

> The Muslims are the latest in a long line of 'others' to be given that label, from those like my parents who sweated and toiled in the mills of Yorkshire half a century ago to successful, integrated British citizens who now make up the growing Muslim middle class; it was a phrase used to describe me in government.[1]

Satanic Seditions

Something happened after the so-called Salman Rushdie affair in 1989, when the Muslims thought the novelist had committed blasphemy in his work of fiction titled *Satanic Verses*. Warsi realizes that it was not only the government that took it wrong but also the Muslims who were not able to comprehend the situation created by the Rushdie book:

> The failure to comprehend and come to terms with the liberal commitment to freedom of speech; and mostly the failure to read the damn book to enable genuinely informed discussion meant that British Muslims spectacularly failed to be heard.[2]

Britain's multiculturalism was likely never understood by the Muslims succumbing to an intensification of identity. It allowed communities to retain their identity without making them sensitive to the needs of 'integrating' with the host community, forgetting how to 'be different and a part of the whole at the same time'. That it happened only to the Muslims and not so much to the Hindus also points to the supra-state 'feeling' that only the Muslims are gifted with as a universal nation, or ummah. This feeling went against 'the promotion of difference, an invitation to experience difference, a commitment to raise awareness of difference and not simply to tolerate but to celebrate difference' that multiculturalism was supposed to inculcate.

Warsi accepts the failure of multiculturalism when she says: 'But multiculturalism can also become a policy of segregation, division and siloing of communities so that each is engaged, supported and accommodated as a section of society rather than as part of a whole. At its best, multiculturalism can create a society in which all feel as if they matter and they belong; at its worst it can leave majority communities feeling "their way of life" is under threat and minority communities feeling ghettoized and left behind. It's why the debate on multiculturalism needs to be informed, evidence-based and conducted in language which explains in detail exactly what it is we mean.'

Soon enough, the Conservative Party under David Cameron rejected multiculturalism, citing it as 'a doctrine that tolerated segregated communities behaving in ways that run counter to our values' and what Cameron called 'muscular liberalism', an approach Warsi thought sounded like a 'we-need-war-to-find-peace' doctrine. In 2005, Prime Minister Tony Blair too ditched multiculturalism in favour of 'integration'. This was triggered by 7 July 2005, when a band of Pakistani Muslim terrorists killed fifty-two people of eighteen nationalities in London and injured 700.

The 7/7 trauma

Sidique Khan, who led the suicide attacks, had trained in Pakistan. He was one of the terrorists whose body was allowed to be buried in Pakistan, causing a 'long march' of mourners between Lahore and Gujranwala. Some of the 'reverse gifts' were bequeathed later by the UK to Pakistan in the form of Hizbut Tahrir and Al-Muhajiroun, boys who shouted extremist slogans in cockney accents. London was gestating something known nowhere else as Muslim but something that was catching on in a growingly middle-class Pakistan. Warsi's comparison of these movements with Irish terrorism don't seem compatible. She has described and analysed all the Muslim organizations in Britain. She herself has a Barelvi background and is clearly critical of them just as much, if not more, as her debunking of the British 'preventive' policy towards Muslims. She finds outfits as Quilliam under Maajid Nawaz ineffective because he lost the support of fellow Muslims after his exit from Hizbut Tahrir, as if him giving up Islamism was something the Muslims didn't like.

She is critical of the way London dragged its feet over the advocates of London-based terrorism like Abu Hamza al-Masri, Omar Bakri, Abu Qatada and Anjem Chowdary, as they poisoned Muslim minds. London also watched an earlier nursery of dangerous minds that other scholars before Warsi had noted, even as fallout-recipient France across the channel called Britain Londonistan. She writes of Chowdary: 'The son of a market trader who failed even his first year at university because of his preoccupation with drugs, drink and porn, he pronounced on live TV that I was not a Muslim because I didn't dress like one, and believes that a Muslim takeover is possible.'

Radical Conversions

French scholar Gilles Kepel, in his book *Allah in the West: Islamic Movements in America and Europe*, had already seen what was coming in Britain.[3] According to him, communalization rather than integration suited the UK because it could then farm out the menial jobs to a community formed especially for them. Workers' mosques came up in the 1950s in the industrial areas of the UK, as opposed to France where this trend started only in the 1970s. Out of the fifty-five mosques serving the 85,000 Muslims of Birmingham in 1985, nearly half were set up before 1970.

Warsi takes account of this dividing-through-mosques process which began in the 1950s and 1960s. Separated along sectarian and even ethnic divides, different mosques catered to Barelvis, Deobandis, Pathans, Punjabis, Mirpuris, Bengalis and Gujaratis. The first central mosque in Birmingham was built in 1971, two years later, one Barelvi Pir Maroof Shah built a number of mosques for his followers in Bradford, founding the World Islamic Mission.

Sufi Abdullah built himself a similar Barelvi empire in the area in the early 1980s. The Bradford Council of Mosques in the 1980s was already 'separating' the community on such questions as halal food and girls' education. The Labour Party was the popular party among the Muslims. Then came the Rushdie affair which almost coincided with the explosion caused by the Islamic scarf affair in France. The protest that was organized against Rushdie's *Satanic Verses* united the fragmented Muslim community in the UK, toppling its less educated leaders in favour of the Anglophone radical ones inspired by the Islamic Revolution of Imam Khomeini in Iran.

Goodbye Integration

With the passage of time—and the rise of the Deobandi warriors in Pakistan—Warsi's Barelvi community went into decline, their mosques increasingly manned by Deobandi clerics close to the Ahle Hadith who attracted funds from Arabs, especially Saudi Arabia. Disturbing news kept trickling in about the growing lack of integration among the Pakistanis in the UK. In particular, a 2001 study by Professor Muhammad Anwar of the University of Warwick[4] set out findings that could only spell trouble in the days to follow. The Pakistanis living in the UK were 700,000, a majority of them Kashmiris.

According to this study, Pakistanis were concentrated in four regions: 30 per cent in and around London, 22 per cent (100,000) in Birmingham, 20 per cent (65,000) in Bradford, 20,000 in Manchester and 15,000 in Glasgow. The figure of 700,000 had grown from 5000 in 1951. Because of high birth rate, fully 47 per cent of them were under the age of sixteen, as compared to 17 per cent for whites. They had the highest unemployment rate, five times the British average; and the rate was higher among them than in any other community. As many as 2 per cent of the prisoners rotting in British jails were Pakistanis, the highest for any one community.

And then a Pakistani ex-journalist happened to Britain. Kalim Siddiqi, of Jamaat Islami background, set up his Muslim Parliament in 1989 and issued what was termed the Muslim Manifesto, a year later, actually challenging the British system. This caused Labour politician Roy Jenkins, who had described the British policy of integration as equal opportunities with cultural diversity in 1965, to say in 1989 that the policy had failed to effect any integration of the Muslim culture and religion within the British society.

Letting Londonistan Live

As Warsi notes, London looked at Kalim Siddiqi as some kind of a crazy person and ignored him. It ignored others like Abu Hamza Al Masri and Umar Bakri too, even as the Muslims retreated further from British society. The climax of this failure to integrate came in the shape of the conversion of the British mosque to Deobandi and Ahle Hadith identity during the 1990s.

Kepel noted that the Finsbury Mosque cell of al-Qaeda was run by Abu Hamza Al-Masri, an Egyptian who had lost an arm and an eye fighting in Afghanistan, whose journal *al-Ansar* glamorized the murderous GIA (from the French Groupe Islamique Armé) in Algeria, and who got his son to abduct British tourists in Yemen for the sake of jihad. Another Egyptian, Yasser al Sirri, headed the London-based Islamic Media Observatory, the news agency that provided letters of accreditation to a pair of suicide-bombers posing as journalists who killed Ahmad Shah Massoud in Afghanistan three days before 9/11.

London turned a deaf ear to protests made about its export of radical British youth into Pakistan and other regions of the world. It turned its face away equally from protests against its policy of giving out visas to people in Pakistan (ex-ISI chiefs included) and elsewhere known for inciting violent reactions among Muslim communities in the West. Author Warsi takes account of all this, intellectually connected as she is to the UK, her home, while being emotionally moored in the faith undergoing its most stultified phase in the twenty-first century. Whose side is she on, one might ask? Perhaps the emotional one, in favour of her community; and that could be a reaction too to how the state in the UK will behave towards her no matter how rational and objective she is about her identity.

Islamophobia is a term condemning the trend of hating Islam in the West. Intellectuals all over the world denounce it as a disease inside states evolved as highly tolerant and humane societies. Expatriate Muslims suffer at the hands of local miscreants who have embraced Islamophobia against their own law. Huntington's thesis 'Clash of Civilizations' is seen by some as unfolding in Europe and America as extreme-right politics that bids fair to triumph.

Muslim Islamophobia

But there is another Islamophobia to consider and that is the Muslims' own fear of Islam as terrorist organizations such as the al-Qaeda and the ISIS rally hundreds of gangs of Muslim killers under their flag and threaten Muslim states in the name of Islam. Looked at from this angle of internecine intolerance, Islamophobia looks like a Muslim phenomenon which is likely to grow.

The kind of Islamophobia suffered in Pakistan—despite Pakistan's effort at pinning this carnage on someone else—is also being experienced in Afghanistan, Iraq, Syria, Libya, Nigeria, Yemen and Somalia. Many sects under Islam, heretofore tolerated, walk in fear as the trend of apostatization gathers strength inside unstable states. Whereas in the West Islamophobia tends to unite the nation, in the Islamic world self-hating populations inside a state feel less and less like a nation.

Thankfully, in the UK, Muslims will not be able to do such harm to one another and Warsi should be thankful for that.

There are Shias and Ahmadis living in peace there without fear of radical Islam harming them. Ahmadis are accepted as Muslims and their rights are protected, although there are incidents of criminal assault—by fellow Muslims—against them occasionally. There are Shias living in Quetta and Parachinar who remain uncertain of their survival on a daily basis inside the Islamic state of Pakistan that discriminates against women and the non-Muslims under law. At least Pakistanis can't repeat in Britain what they have done to their community in Pakistan.

But, to conclude, there is the native UK's own future to consider. From the 1968 'Rivers of Blood' speech[5] of a racist member of parliament, Enoch Powell, the UK has travelled to the crossroads of Brexit in 2016; and the hidden message in this 'verdict of the people' is against immigration and immigrants who now live in the UK without assimilation under a policy of failed multiculturalism. But it is the Muslims—and not so much the non-Muslims—living in the UK who will face the brunt of this new inward-looking state because of their own religious intensity and inability to become integrated with the native community.

17

Strongwomen of South Asia

It is a great compliment for a writer if you say that his/her latest book is their best. In the case of Anna Suvorova, one is compelled to say that her book *Widows and Daughters: Gender, Kinship, and Power in South Asia*[1] is a kind of climax to her earlier books on Muslim saints, Benazir Bhutto, Lahore and the poetic genre of masnavi. A bestselling author, Suvorova has been awarded the Sitara-e-Imtiaz from Pakistan and heads the Department of Asian Literature at the Institute of Oriental Studies (Russian Academy of Sciences) in Moscow.

Her book tries to make sense of the women who ruled—and suffered, if not died in the process—over countries of South Asia where patriarchal misogyny refuses to die. She writes in arresting detail about Indira Gandhi (1917–84) in India, Benazir Bhutto (1953–2007) in Pakistan, Khaleda Zia (b. 1945) and Hasina Wajed (b. 1947) in Bangladesh, and Sirimavo Bandaranaike (1916–2000) and her daughter Chandrika Kumaratunga (b. 1945) in Sri Lanka. All of these women belong to elite ruling families whose male leaders had established the personality cult before dying or being martyred.

Suvorova's Specifications

Suvorova notes the violence that created the niches where these women could establish themselves:

> Of all these women leaders, only Indira's father (Jawaharlal Nehru) and husband (Feroze Gandhi) died a natural death (i.e., they were not assassinated). Nevertheless, Indira lost both of her sons: Sanjay died in a plane crash in 1980 during her second term as prime minister, while she did not live to see Rajiv assassinated in 1991.[2]

A Buddhist monk killed Solomon Bandaranaike, the prime minister of Sri Lanka in 1959, leaving behind his widow Sirimavo with three children. Bandaranaike was not a Buddhist by birth but later converted from Christianity. Sirimavo was often called 'the weeping widow'—a pun on 'weeping willow'—by her ill-wishers. Her daughter, Chandrika, also became a widow when her husband, actor Vijaya Kumaratunga, was killed by a Sinhalese extremist in 1988.

Given the instinctive public reverence of the assassinated leaders, death established the dynasties that let these women climb to the top. Sheikh Hasina Wajed, daughter of the 'founder' of Bangladesh, Sheikh Mujibur Rahman (1920–75), had to survive the assassination of her father, mother, brothers, sisters-in-law, and nephews (twenty people altogether) in August 1975 by a group of officers of the Bangladesh Army, which was then led by General Ziaur Rahman. The founder of the PPP, Zulfikar Ali Bhutto, was overthrown by the army in 1977 and killed by General Zia-ul-Haq. Bangladesh saw a shortlived coup-atop-a-coup the same year, led by General Khaled Mosharraf. But after just three days, Mosharraf was taken down and killed by General Ziaur Rahman who then survived twenty-one attempted coups between 1977 and 1980. In 1981, General Zia, who had become the President, was killed in Chittagong.

A Case History of Cruelty

Hasina survived because she and her sister, Rehana, were on a private visit to west Germany, to meet Hasina's husband, Wajed Miah (not Mian, and Wajed pronounced as Wazed). Khaleda Zia, the wife of General Ziaur Rahman, was also widowed meanwhile with two teenage sons. The rumour that General Zia had a hand in killing Sheikh Mujib has never died. Ziaur Rahman was in turn killed by General Ershad. Thus the two women have stood face-to-face claiming legitimacy of rule, while Bangladesh got neatly divided into two kinds of nationalisms: Bengali, championed by Hasina and supported by India, and Bangladeshi, embraced by Khaleda and backed by Pakistan, adding venom to the national divide.

In 1977, the then prime minister Zulfikar Ali Bhutto (1928–79) of Pakistan was toppled by a military coup staged by his chosen army chief General Zia-ul-Haq. A servile judiciary—self-confessing its perfidy in later years—allowed the general to hang Bhutto in 1979. Bhutto had sent his two sons, Murtaza and Shahnawaz, out of the country, thus leaving the onus of his charisma to fall on his daughter, Benazir. The unspoken dynastic rule of routine made an exception in her case. She too was killed by a suicide bomber in 2007 while General Musharraf ruled Pakistan. In India, Indira Gandhi too had been killed but her father, former prime minister Jawaharlal Nehru, had died a natural death.

Sonia Gandhi (b. 1946), an Italian by birth, had to face a region getting more sinister by the day. She was to be one of the widows that came to power indirectly in South Asia. Her husband, the dynastic heir of the Nehru family, former prime minister Rajiv Gandhi, died in 1991 at the hands of a Tamil terrorist. But the transfer of dynastic charisma got her party, the Congress, to win the elections despite malicious opposition against the fact that she was a 'foreigner'.

Matching Male Muscle

In the case of Pakistan, the plot thickens. It can be called the path-breaking dynasty-killing state of the region. Normal rule gave way to charismatic leadership after 1970. The personality cult of Zulfikar Ali Bhutto was erected on socialism as hero-worshipped by the masses, mixed with Islam as enshrined in the constitution by the Objectives Resolution of 1949. The chief architect of the Indian Constitution, Dr B.R. Ambedkar, had warned in 1949, and no one had listened:

> There is nothing wrong in being grateful to great men who have rendered lifelong services to the country. But there are limits to gratefulness. Bhakti in religion may be a road to the salvation of the soul. But in politics, Bhakti or hero-worship is a sure road to degradation and to eventual dictatorship.[3]

In the patriarchal world of South Asia, women have to act tough or risk being toppled by men. In a sense it applies universally, as former British prime minister Margaret Thatcher was often said to be 'the only man in the cabinet'. Sheikh Hasina Wajed is authoritarian and harsh. She got her father's killers hanged, vanquished the Opposition, with the army under her thumb, the Constitution giving her unlimited power with a majority in parliament touching two-thirds. Sirimavo Bandaranaike too had to act tough despite being a Buddhist. After her election as prime minister, she made Sinhalese the official language of the country (in place of English), which alienated the Tamil minority who then embraced violence.

Why do women rulers act tough? Suvorova has this diagnostic:

> The male majority considered women to be inherently apolitical, passive, easily swayed, eager for compromise,

> incompetent, subject to the influence of their male entourage, and in a word, marionettes controlled by puppeteers present among advisors in the party hierarchy or cabinet.[4]

The toughness actually comes from how the males view them. The capacity to bear pain and survive is the hallmark of the human female species since 'the [Biblical] Fall'.

A Roll-Call of Women Warriors

What happened to Chandrika, the daughter who took over after Sirimavo, could have happened to Benazir too had her brothers been around when Zulfikar Ali Bhutto was hanged. Chandrika had a brother, Anura, who felt cheated and, in 1994, joined the Opposition, as he 'believed that his sister had stolen his political heritage'. In the 1980s, as Khaleda Zia ruled in Bangladesh, her two sons came of age but neither Tarique Rahman (b. 1967) nor his brother Arafat (1970–2015) had any political experience. They were arrested on charges of corruption—and money-laundering—and fled the country after their mother lost power. Khaleda had no one from her family around her even though Tarique continued to wage her propaganda campaigns from London.

Were all these widows and daughters 'accidental' rulers? Suvorova gives us a survey of some of the 'leading' women in the region: Pratibha Patil (former President of India, 2007–12) and chief ministers of Indian states: Jayaram Jayalalithaa (Tamil Nadu), Vasundhara Scindia (Rajasthan), Mamata Banerjee (West Bengal) and Anandiben Patel (Gujarat). Sushma Swaraj (1952–2019) acted as the powerful minister of external affairs in the government of Narendra Modi; Pakistan and Bangladesh once had Hina Rabbani Khar and Dipu Moni, respectively, in the job.

The book takes account of other women toughened by their circumstances into becoming 'great', from Shahjahan Begum (the ruler of Bhopal) to the adventuresome Begum Samru whose life can be called a study of the tyranny of circumstance. Men were to demonstrate their love for India by calling it mother but such was the tyranny of events that 'Vande Matram' (honour the mother),[5] the song that was supposed to unite, ended up dividing India.

Enter the 'Weeping Widow'

The Supreme Court in Sri Lanka found Sirimavo guilty of abuses in 1980. She was stripped of her parliamentary seat and prohibited from engaging in political activities for seven years. Before she had taken over, Colombo's army had 60 per cent Catholics in the officer corps, which made it easier for the Bandaranaikes to rule. She reformed the country to bring in some normality, but the ostracism imposed on her by the court insulted a woman who had been considered for two decades as the 'Mother of the Nation'. She was however allowed to return to politics in 1986.

Things got rougher after the defeat in the 1989 elections. She had to flee an electoral meeting in Colombo after three bombs exploded in the crowd, her earlier magnetism a thing of the past. But she received support from her daughter, Chandrika, who took over the party and became the fifth President of Sri Lanka the same year, only to face opposition from Anura.

Was Sirimavo Bandaranaike then the role model for the future women rulers? No, it had to be Indira Gandhi (1917–84), the Durga, the deity who made it possible to break up Pakistan in 1971. The gift of the current paradigm of politics in South Asia is her gift to the region and men dutifully bow to it. Unconsciously, Benazir was to follow Indira's early route to power by being educated in the West. (Chandrika too was in Paris for five years studying political science.) Indira had married a Parsi—as Jinnah had earlier—which made Maneka, her son Sanjay's wife, declare in court that her mother-in-law could not inherit a third of the property of Sanjay because she had ceased to be a Hindu after marrying a Parsi.

After Jinnah, Fatima Jinnah

Jinnah had turned into a Twelver Shia from the Ismaili sect to be able to bequeath his property to his sister Fatima through a will. After he died in 1948, it was necessary for his Fatima to declare him a Shia in order to inherit his property as per his will. (Sunni law partially rejects a will, while Shia law does not.) The grand-nephew of Jinnah, Liaquat H. Merchant, in his book *Jinnah: A Judicial Verdict*, wrote:

> She filed an affidavit, jointly signed with the Prime Minister of Pakistan Liaquat Ali Khan, at the Sindh High Court, describing Jinnah as 'Shia Khoja Mohamedan' and praying that his will may be disposed of under Shia inheritance law. The court accepted the petition.[6]

Jinnah's comment on his sister is reproduced by Suvorova: 'My sister was like a bright ray of light and hope whenever I came back home and met her. Anxieties would have been much greater and my health much worse, but for the restraint imposed by her.' And his will and testament read: 'All shares, stocks, and securities and current accounts now standing in the name of my sister Fatima Jinnah are her absolute property. I have given them all to her by way of gifts during my lifetime, and I confirm the same, and she can dispose of them in any manner she pleases as her absolute property'.[7]

The property was unsuccessfully contested, however, after Fatima's demise by the progeny of her still-Ismaili sisters, Rahemat and Mariam, 'to whom he had left a legacy of 100 rupees per month'. And Fatima Jinnah became the strongwoman of Pakistan when she unsuccessfully challenged General Ayub Khan in the polls in 1965.

In 1967, when Miss Jinnah died, the official cause was a heart attack but many said that she was murdered. Abida Sultaan (1913–2002), heir to the state of Bhopal before it was annexed by India, kept a diary all her life, and sat down and wrote an eminently readable autobiography out of it before she died. In *Abida Sultaan: Memoirs of a Rebel Princess,* she also suspected that Fatima Jinnah was killed:

> I found Miss Jinnah lying surrounded with blocks of ice. There were blue patches on her face, mainly the left eye. There was some blood on the covering sheet but I could not detect whether it had come out from the ear, nose or mouth.[8]

Suvorova writes about the 'Parsi curse' of the Nehru–Jinnah duo:

In 1938, Jinnah's only daughter Dina married Neville Wadia, the son of a rich Bombay Parsi, who was also a textile magnate. The Wadia family was one of the founders of Indian shipbuilding. Jinnah was furious, as he had hoped for a Muslim son-in-law.[9]

In India, Nehru had accepted Feroze Gandhi with his Nehruvian foresight. The possibility of Dina becoming the ready-to-rule charismatic leader in Pakistan after Jinnah's death in 1948 was thus removed:

> She visited Pakistan only twice, the first time in 1948 during her father's funeral and the second time in 2004 together with her son and grandchildren. She came to Jinnah's mausoleum in Karachi, where she wrote in the guestbook, 'This has been very sad and wonderful for me. May his dream for Pakistan come true!' The visit was sad indeed as she felt like a foreigner in the country founded by her father.[10]

Benazir Bhutto of Pakistan and Indira Gandhi of India

Unlike Benazir, who attempted to moderate the 'socialist' excesses of her nationalizing father, Indira was an absolutist, driving socialism forward with great vigour, her party now called Congress-I after her name. A Sikh religious resurgence in Punjab compelled her to take tough action at the Golden Temple in Amritsar, and she couldn't survive it. Her Sikh bodyguards took her life. In October 1984, Beant Singh, who was standing on her left, took out his revolver and fired three shots at her. As she fell to the ground, Satwant Singh shot a volley from a pointblank range with his submachine gun. For this, 3000 Sikhs were to die, and hundreds of Sikh temples, along with thousands of stores and homes, were torched in New Delhi by crowds maddened with grief.

Benazir was to face a similar end. She was incarcerated by General Zia after he got her father, Zulfikar Ali Bhutto, hanged in 1979, and was treated roughly despite being a woman. In bad health, she went into exile and watched as Pakistan tried to digest the 1988 death of General Zia in a plane crash. She had tested the waters while he was still alive by returning in 1986, landing in Lahore to see the city decorated as if it were a national holiday. As her procession moved through the dense human mass, it took ten hours for it to make its way from the airport to the Iqbal Park, which usually takes half an hour by car.

Her charisma became operational and she won the 1988 elections only to see her PPP government dismissed in two years in a kind of merry-go-round of toppling with Nawaz Sharif's Muslim League throughout the 1990s. Much has been written about the corruption that took root in Pakistan during that decade.[11] In 1996, then President Farooq Ahmed Khan Leghari, selected by her own party, officially disbanded the Benazir-led government on charges of corruption and incompetence. Had the Bhutto charisma died on that day? No, it hadn't. She was poised for another comeback when but, in December 2007, a suicide bomber in Rawalpindi killed her.

The Brawling Begums of Bangladesh

In Bangladesh, the post-martyrdom feminine charisma was dealt with less cruelty by the patriarchal grid. Instead, the two women, one a charismatic 'successor' widow and the other a charismatic 'successor' daughter, inflicted defeats on each other as the country proceeded to get divided on their opposed pro-India and pro-Pakistan world views. Just as Benazir's worry-beads helped her conquer the post-Zia Islamization in Pakistan, Hasina Wajed's worry-beads partly got her accepted by a surprisingly Islamized Bangladesh. Finally, what has won is Hasina's policy of friendship with India, despite myriad territorial and water issues. Khaleda was in prison, her poor health not allowing her to sit normally in a chair. She was released in March 2020 on humanitarian grounds to undergo treatment in Dhaka.

The paragraph about the 'widows and daughters' in the epilogue of Suvorova's riveting book is worth reproducing:

> If we combine their life stories into a single narrative, we get a very long martyrology indeed: assassination of the father, mother, brothers, and other members of the family (Hasina Wajed); execution of the father and tragic death of brothers (Benazir); assassination of the father and the husband (Chandrika); assassination of the husband and death of the son (Khaleda Zia); assassination of the husband (Sirimavo); and death of the son in an air-crash (Indira). Indira, Benazir, Hasina, and Khaleda were all subject to imprisonment. Sirimavo, Benazir, Hasina, and Chandrika survived assassination attempts (the latter lost one of her eyes in the process). Finally, Indira and Benazir were killed: the former while in office, and the latter on the eve of elections that she was expected to win.[12]

The strongwomen of South Asia are gone except—with fading haloes—in Bangladesh. India and Pakistan have made a tough male comeback with Narendra Modi and Imran Khan. Charisma is male again, but it has its downside, and its worst trait is the way it shapes the mind of those who follow it.

Democracy by Dynasty

Suvorova's book contains thought-provoking insights about how political dynasties are created in our part of the world.

Two academics, Farida Jalalzai, professor and Hannah Atkins Endowed Chair of Political Science, Oklahoma State University; and Meg Rincker, professor of political science, Purdue University Northwest, have found the following interesting facts about dynasties, including women leaders, compelled to keep the dynastic flag flying:

> Nineteen of the 66 female executives in our sample had familial connections to politics—29 per cent. One hundred of the 963 men we studied—just over 10 per cent—had family ties. This suggests that family ties are particularly important for women to get into politics. In our analysis, the endorsement of a powerful male relative—himself preferably a former President or prime minister—meaningfully helps female politicians establish their credibility with voters and political insiders. Family ties are helpful for men, but in their case there are also other well-trodden paths to power.[13]

Male cult leaders are 'extreme' because of their tragic flaw of overreaching. The party they shape reinforces their hubris and preordains 'over-stretch', which then becomes the very basis of their public acceptance. The excess in their personality is expressed in their pledge of extreme change. They announce drastic change 'because the people want it'. When conditions of life become tough—often because of a mismatch between population and resources—the slogan of gradualist democratic change doesn't work; you have to announce revolution because you can't announce 'violent change' with a straight face. After the comeuppance of the cult male, the fade-away phase may lead a clan strongwoman to take centre stage again.

18

The Sheedi of Sindh

Tanzeela Qambrani won a seat in the Sindh Assembly on a PPP ticket in the July 25 general elections in 2018. She attracted attention because she belongs to the Sheedi community of Sindh, the tribal name 'Sheedi' indicating that she is from Africa. She is no freeloader though, a postgraduate-degree holder in computer science from the University of Sindh, Tanzeela, now forty-one years old, is the first Sheedi to be appointed to the provincial assembly.

No one could have thought of the Sheedis, a gifted but ignored minority group, except Bilawal Bhutto Zardari, the chairman of the PPP, the ruling party of Sindh. She said as much when she was accosted by the media. A mother of three, she was earlier nominated by the party to head the municipal committee in Matli in Badin district, which, it is said, many PPP leaders didn't like too much. One of her detractors actually turned independent and contested against her.

Out of Africa

Tanzeela says her ancestors came to Sindh from Tanzania a century ago. Her sister, in fact, still lives in Tanzania after marriage. Conscious of the neglect and sheer maltreatment of the community, she is defiant as she talks of her routine of wearing jeans and a headscarf to the university. She says Bilawal rescued her from the obscurity that her lawyer father and her headmistress mother had endured.

One comes across the colloquial word 'sheedi' in Sindh, which means a bad person, just as in Punjab 'majha' means hoodlum. Both words, however, have noble origins. 'Majha' originates from 'Mi'raj', a proper noun celebrating the ascension of Prophet Muhammad in the sacred month of Rajab. 'Sahja' is another word that has been added to the list of bad names. This is horrible because it comes from the word 'siraj' (lamp), a name given to the Prophet in the Quran. 'Sheedi', meanwhile, comes from 'sidi'. If you go to Morocco, you will find that the honorific appellation 'Syed' is reduced to 'Sidi', or simply 'Sid'. The usage of the word from honorific to an insult is a journey almost as telling as the one the original Sheedis are believed to have taken to reach Asia from their homes in Africa.

El Cid and Hoshoo Sheedi

In the eleventh century, there was a soldier of fortune in Spain who fought both Christian and Muslim invaders to become the country's national hero. Rodrigo Diaz was called El Cid by the Muslims and El Camprador (the champion) by his countrymen. He was immortalized in European literature when French classical poet Corneille wrote a play titled *Le Cid* based on Spanish writer Guillén de Castro's *Las Mocedades del Cid.*

A few centuries later, in the 1960s, Sindhi nationalism focused on Hoshoo Sheedi, the martyred general of the Talpurs who had fought the British army bravely and was buried in Pakka Qila in

Hyderabad, the traditional castle of the Talpur rulers that is now home to refugees (*muhajir*) from India. After the gravestone of his grave was found in Pakka Qila, the call to resettle the muhajirs was made. Sindhi nationalists wanted the Pakka Qila preserved as a historic site.

Who was Hoshoo Sheedi? Why was he called 'Sheedi'? The original word must have been 'Syedi', which means 'my lord' in Arabic. But why should a Sindhi person be called 'Sheedi'? Helene Basu, associate professor at the Free University in Berlin, is a leading authority on Sheedis. In medieval times, she says, black African slaves were brought to South Asia in large numbers. Medieval Indian history refers to Ethiopian or Abyssinian slaves serving at royal courts or in the armies of imperial and local rulers. They are believed to have ruled even in times of chaos.

Sheedi in South Asia

According to Basu, Sheedis are found in many states in India, but nowhere do they exceed 20,000. The largest community of Sheedis is in Sindh; some years ago, there were 50,000 of them, 'but that number must have trebled.'

She adds:

> Tracing the route is, perhaps, a bit exaggerated. There are quite a few good historical studies about the East African slave trade and its range in the Indian Ocean world, which give some clues about the areas from where slaves were drawn as well as about the geographical shifts of the recruitment areas over time. In the 13th and 14th centuries, slaves were mainly drawn from lower Egypt, Ethiopia, Somalia and Sudan—the Nile area. Many of them ended up being so-called slave-soldiers in the armies of conquerors and Sultans all over the Islamic world.[1]

Mint, on 13 December 2019, published the following note on 'Malik Ambar: A Slave Who Defied the Mughals':

In the 1670s, when the Maratha hero Shivaji commissioned Kavindra Paramananda to produce his epic *Sivabharata*, extraordinary praise was reserved in its verses for a dead Muslim warrior called Malik Ambar. Shivaji's father Shahaji, like his grandfather Maloji, had been a close lieutenant of this man, so much so that in a battle scene, we read how, 'As Kartikeya the gods protected in his battle with Taraka, so did Shahaji and other rajas gather around Malik Ambar.' The general was not only 'as brave as the sun' and 'wondrous in power', according to Shivaji's poet, but also a 'man of most-terrible deeds', before whom enemies quaked in fear. What is not highlighted in this eulogy, however, is another striking detail—that Malik Ambar, who even in death was 'like a brilliant setting sun', was originally a slave, born in Africa.

Though largely forgotten now, African presence in India, in itself, was not unusual. In the 14th century, the traveller Ibn Batuta recorded how they were 'guarantors of safety' for ships that plied the Arabian Sea, with reputations so fierce that 'let there be but one of them on a ship and it will be avoided by . . . pirates'. In the 1230s, queen Raziya of the Delhi Sultanate was accused of being closer than acceptable to Yakut, an African confidant—a pretext used to justify her murder. Unknown, perhaps, to many present-day residents of Uttar Pradesh, there existed for decades in the 15th century a near-sovereign state in Jaunpur founded by an African. Even in Bengal, a coup in 1487 by a group of warriors like Malik Ambar led to a short-lived ruling dynasty. Harems in the Deccan featured *habshi* women—so called after their origins in Abyssinia—and at least two sultans had black begums as consorts.

Ambar, however, remains the greatest of the *habshis* who made history in India. Born in the 1540s into the Oromo tribe in Ethiopia, he was captured and enslaved when still a boy called Chapu. An Arab bought him for 20 ducats; soon after, in Baghdad, Ambar passed into new hands. Yet another transaction followed, and it was his third master who converted him to Islam, gave him the name he would make famous, and eventually brought him to be sold in India. This buyer in the 1570s—by which time Ambar was a trained warrior—was the *peshwa*, or minister, of the sultan of Ahmadnagar, who too, incidentally, was black. It was the launch of a remarkable career. And by the end of it, our slave-soldier would become king in all but name, thwarting the ambitions of such mighty men as Akbar and Jahangir for decades.[2]

Origin and Etymology

To understand how words change over time, it is best to go back to their roots. For Sheedi, the root is 'swd', which means black. It is from this root that we get 'aswad', the adjective we apply to 'hajr al-aswad', the black stone that lies at the centre of the ritual of hajj. Somehow the Quran also uses the word for any collection of things which is called 'sawad'; it is at times used in Urdu to mean people at large. Thickness implies blackness, especially with regard to trees. The Quran denotes wealth and large population by 'sawad'. The leader of a large population is called 'al-sayid', from where 'Syed' (leader) is derived, one who is rich and commands respect. In fact, the majority population is often referred to as 'sawad-e-azam'.

It is therefore not surprising that African slaves brought to Sindh were called sidis. We made 'sheedi' out of that and applied it to hoodlums. Well, some sidis must have taken to bad ways. But the root of 'sidi' does mean 'black'. It is also another way of saying *habshi* (negro).

And Janjira

In India, in times of lax central authority, principalities ruled by Sidis sprang up around the coastline. One such was Sachin in Gujarat, India; another was Janjira, on the Maharashtra coast;

and thereby hangs a tale. The rulers of Janjira traced their origin back to Abyssinia (present-day Ethiopia in East Africa) and they formed a part of the forces of the first Mughal Emperor, Babur. Nawab Ahmad Khan of Janjira (1879–1922) had descended from a Sidi dynasty from Abyssinia. Later, the state of Janjira was under the suzerainty of the Bombay Presidency. The nawab had married into the distinguished Bohra Tyabji family in 1886, his twelve-year-old wife Nazli attracting her sister Atiya Fyzee to her side in the state. Fyzee was a highly cultured lady with an interest in philosophy.

Fyzee and Iqbal

It was an encounter in England—where Fyzee had gone to study—that has left a mark on Pakistan's history. Rafia Zakaria quotes Fyzee in her article in *Dawn*:

> On the first of April 1907, (landlady) Miss Beck sent me a special invitation to meet a very clever man by the name of Mohammad Iqbal, who was specially coming from Cambridge to meet me.

She accepted the invitation and found at the dinner table a 'man of ready wit'. When she asked him why he had come to see her, he said, 'You have become very famous in India and London through your travel diary.' The friendship was to last and is now preserved in their correspondence. The other person of note who was inspired by her was the famous biographer of the Holy Prophet Shibli Numani, who was supported financially in his educational ventures by the state of Janjira.

After the Partition in 1947, Atiya Fyzee moved to Karachi at the request of Muhammad Ali Jinnah and was given land in the new capital of Pakistan. She built a big house there till she was mysteriously made to move into a hotel by the administration.

Sheedi Mela at Mangho Pir

Once Pakistan and India became two nations, the Sheedi of Sindh populated the area of Lyari–Mangho Pir and gave spiritual significance to the crocodiles (*mangho*) by accepting them as their mystical guides (pir) in a throwback to their African origins. Because of their physique, they excelled in the sports events encouraged by the underworld dons who ruled Lyari.

The well-known annual fair at the Mangho Pir reserve is a special Sheedi ritual. It was disrupted and celebrated in 2017 after a gap of seven years because of violence. The Sheedi youth, who earlier organized the festival, had to side with the underworld king Uzair Baloch-led Peoples Amn Committee (PAC) in order to survive in the area. But the fair collapsed after the son of Ghulam Akbar Sheedi, a respected elder, was gunned down in June 2012. Today, Tanzeela Qambrani reminds us that the Sheedi of Pakistan have crossed another barrier to ensure the recognition of their community. Their talent will take them further on this journey of self-realization.

19

A Landscape of Alpha Male Leaders

Some writers have produced a list of 'new leaders' who can be characterized as 'alpha males', like in the animal world, exercising power over their flocks by promising them protection against 'rival' flocks. The alpha male leaders, chosen from the world scene today, are: Narendra Modi in India, Xi Jinping in China, former US President Donald J. Trump, Vladimir Putin in Russia, Recep Tayyip Erdogan in Turkey, Marine Le Pen (sic!) in France and Geert Wilders in the Netherlands.

Modi is particularly lampooned for his boast about his fifty-six-inch chest, but his country posted a high growth rate until a couple of years back, giving him credibility. Xi Jinping too gets counted in this high-growth category. But this doesn't fit all the alphas. Erdogan began with a surplus economy, but his show of muscle in the neighbourhood and against the US-NATO combine has caused him to lose some of the economic sheen. Putin is roaring and pushing his neighbouring statelets around because of the piped gas the European Union gets from Siberia. Others like Marine Le Pen and Geert Wilders are leaders that don't win the polls but claim stature through 'rage': anger that unites people across politics, demanding retrogressive change.

Charms of the Challenger

There is no doubt that Imran Khan of Pakistan is an alpha male leader who, unlike India's Modi, sits on top of a collapsing economy. He won the 2018 election and eclipsed all the 'uncharismatic' leaders of the past. He challenges the leading politicians in the opposition and finds them on the defensive. His formula of success is 'change'—radicalized by his advocacy of collective anger. The theory of collective rage that binds people has been effectively practiced by his party through two years of agitation while out of power, aided by effective financing by party 'electables' and support from the deep state. His organizational theory achieves solidarity through appeal to moral outrage—in his case through condemnation of corruption in an idiom of violence.

Great alpha leaders are not 'transactional', a condition of democracy, but 'transformational', which strongly hints at 'revolution'. Modi relies on the 'outrage' of Hindus over cow slaughter to achieve organizational advantage while his economic achievement dumbs down any credible reaction from the rump of intellectuals still championing secular democracy. Imran Khan's *Naya* (new) Pakistan rests on the pledge of extermination of corruption, mostly persecuting and demeaning Opposition leaders. Meanwhile, the Supreme Court seems to be floating on its own 'judicial populism'. According to Reema Omer, a legal adviser for the International Commission of Jurists:

> Article 184(3) of the Constitution of Pakistan sets out the Supreme Court's original jurisdiction, and enables it to assume jurisdiction in matters involving a question of 'public

> importance' with reference to the 'enforcement of any of the fundamental rights' of Pakistan's citizens.[1]

This article has bestowed Pakistan with another alpha male, this time an alpha chief justice contesting his empire of the suo motu with Khan.

Chavismo and Change

Alpha male leaders are at times labelled 'strong leaders', and they get additional limelight when they emerge in weak, internally troubled states, like Duterte of the Philippines. Who will listen today to a 'liberal' John Stuart Mill who wisely advised people 'not to lay their liberties at the feet of a great man, or to trust him with powers which enable him to subvert their institutions'? The strong man of Mill is in fact the alpha male of today, pledging 'transformation' in a world that has spent several centuries arriving at a much-desired design of an 'inclusive' modern state. What gets him through this early challenge is his reliance on the theory of 'moral outrage'. One early alpha male leader, Hugo Chavez of Venezuela, gave his name to the philosophy of moral outrage: chavismo. Today, one of the world's chief oil-producers, Venezuela is economically belly-up.

President Trump was clearly breaking all norms riding the tide of the white middle-class rage aimed at immigrants and trading rivals that 'take away our jobs'. He could make outrageous statements and send out tweets that no American President would have dreamt of composing. He didn't care that the American media was almost totally hostile to him and the world outside hated him, so secure he was riding the 'American outrage'. Unlike Theresa May of the United Kingdom who didn't know how to direct the subterranean sulfur of British rage against immigrants, Imran Khan has actually manufactured his collective outrage with his historically unprecedented city-by-city campaigns that often declined into violence. His unbuttoned language became the lingua franca of the *homo pakistanicus* and today undermines the discourse of traditionally courteous households.

The Rage of Rizvi

Out of the campaigns of outrage, or dharnas, grew an entire parade of strongmen manufacturing more collective outrage. One such alpha male, of religion, was Khadim Husain Rizvi who was forgiven his obscene language by hand-kissing mobs caring more for protection of the honour of the Holy Prophet (Peace Be upon Him) than corruption and wanted all blasphemers killed. This was an alpha male on a wheelchair who mobilized his warriors on the roads of Lahore and Karachi to inflict brutal violence on innocent passersby. He today cools his alpha-male heels in a jail for widespread barbarity.

There is something apocalyptic about the alpha male leader. He puts an end to an order that existed before his arrival at the scene. For some reason, because of his intellectual 'simplicity' or the 'reductionism' of his understanding of the order he wants to end, the 'new' order doesn't work either. The world sees in him more the end of an order without acknowledging the 'new' order that he has been promising. Looking at what the alpha male leaders are doing to the world, Richard N. Haass has this to say about Europe:

> In what by historical standards constitutes an instant, the future of democracy, prosperity, and peace in Europe has become uncertain. And with the U.S. under President Donald Trump treating its allies like enemies, the continent must confront the growing threats it faces largely on its own.[2]

20

Musings of the Marginalized

Bilal Zahoor and Raza Rumi have put together a volume of 'peripheral' wisdom about Pakistan. Titled *Rethinking Pakistan: A 21st Century Perspective*, it challenges the ideology of misgovernance that keeps Pakistan backward.[1] As Pakistan retraces some aspects of its domestic and foreign policies under pressure from the FATF, this volume might attract positive attention; but it is the dogma of 'permanent' ideology that keeps pulling the institutions of Pakistan back and engenders strange 'identity' problems among its political leaders.

What do the politicians—some of them facing corruption charges—mean when they say they are *nazriati* (ideological)? One supposes it means 'principled'; but why use 'ideological'? Ideology as governance in history brooks no opposition. The word was coined during the French Revolution, which ended up eating its own children. Then the Marxists took it up and an 'ideological' Soviet Union came into being that brooked no opposition to

'The Party' under the constitution. Today, Iran is 'nazriati', has no functioning political parties just like the Soviet Union and thus no opposition in an elected parliament. Pakistan is supposed to be 'nazriati' too, but still has an opposition in parliament—and outside parliament too in the shape of secularists who walk in fear. It can be characterized as an 'incomplete ideological state'.

John Stuart Mill must spin in his grave after hearing that 'liberal' in Pakistan means only morally 'permissive'; and that 'secular' means 'opposed to religion'. (The Soviet Union propagated atheism as a part of its ideology and therefore was not secular in the strictest sense; a secular state tolerates all religions and is opposed to religious discrimination.) Leaders of the ruling party in Pakistan appear on TV to say that those who champion secularism should leave the country; and the prime minister himself has often defined liberalism as a value system he is opposed to.[2]

In 2009, Khan had chastised the liberals and condemned their interpretation of the phenomenon of the Taliban while 'obediently following the dictation of the United States'.[3] He also blamed them for the massacre at Lal Masjid in 2007.

Setting Out with Uncertainty

Bilal Zahoor, editorial director of Folio Books, has this to say to kick off the discussion:

> The Objectives Resolution (1948) influenced all the three constitutions the country adopted during the next twenty-six years. The only constitution that sought to diverge from the Resolution in terms of redefining sovereignty had to capitulate to Islamists and the country had to be abruptly re-named Islamic Republic of Pakistan in less than two years after being denominated Republic of Pakistan in 1962. Over the years, the state kept distancing itself from Jinnah's vision with each dictatorial and political regime introducing its own form of

> appeasement to Islamists. Even the modernist regime of General Ayub Khan had to succumb to the pressure from *ulema* and reinforce all the Islamic provisions of 1956 constitution that Ayub's constitution of 1962 had initially lacked.[4]

Tariq Rahman, a distinguished national professor and dean, social sciences department at Beaconhouse National University, Lahore, speaks of Islamic radicalism and its effects:

> In India, Mawlānā Waḥīduddīn Khān (b. 1925), who was then the President of the Islamic Centre in New Delhi, took the lead in refuting radical Islam. In his brief monograph, *The True Jihad*, written in English to disseminate his ideas outside South Asia, he sums up all he has written earlier. Beginning with the ideological assumption that all Islam's wars were defensive, he chooses the most appropriate hermeneutical devices to interpret the canonical texts. As for the commands in the Qur'an urging Muslims to 'kill them wherever you find them' (2: 191; 9: 5), he uses specification (*takhsīs al-zaman wal makān*) saying: 'such verses relate in a restricted sense, to those who have unilaterally attacked the Muslims' but are not permanent, general commands.[5]

(When Maulana Wahiduddin came to Pakistan to spread his message against radicalism, he was booed out of a gathering in Lahore and left the country in haste.)

Tahir Kamran, historian and former Iqbal fellow at the Centre of South Asian Studies, University of Cambridge, discusses the radicalization of the anti-Deobandi 'Barelvi' sect through its founder to warn against what has become a bloodthirsty Tehreek-e-Labbaik in Pakistan:

> What Ahmad Raza Khan Barelvi failed to guard against was exclusion and *takfir*. In his famous fatwa *Husam al-Haramain ala Manhar al-Kufr wa'l Main* (The Sword of the Haramain

at the Throat of *Kufr* and Falsehood), which was written in 1902 but became public in 1906, Ahmed Raza denounced several individuals in the early twentieth-century India. Mirza Ghulam Ahmad of Qadian was the first on Ahmad Raza's lists of *kafirs* (infidels). He was followed by some eminent *Ulema* from Deoband denomination like Rashid Ahmad Gangohi, Muhammad Qasim Nanautawi, Ashraf Ali Thanvi and Khalil Ahmad Ambethwi whom he described as Wahabis. Among the twelver Shias and the organisation of the *Ulema* known as the Nadwat al-Ulama, he accused some specific people of *kufr*.[6]

Modernism: Met and Mauled

Nadeem Farooq Paracha, a cultural critic, historian and author, talks of the rise and fall of the 'modernist' in Pakistan:

> From 1947 till the mid-1970s, [the] Modernist Muslim project survived. However, after the acrimonious departure of East Pakistan in 1971, the Modernist Muslim project began to erode and was gradually replaced by a new ideological project that was close to the idea of Muslim nationalism of the third, more theocratic, tendency. This created an opening for the once marginalized line of thinking to enter the country's evolving ideological canon. By the 1980s, it had managed to completely overpower the Modernist tendency.[7]

Muhammad Abrahim Zaka, a scholar and an academic, and Fasi Zaka, a political commentator, columnist and TV anchor write:

> The narrative of the fringe mosque is reproducing itself on television, unfiltered and without a scholarly base. In the space of the TV, the Pakistan Electronic Media Regulatory Authority (PEMRA) has taken a lot of steps that could establish some reporting norms; however, the courts have often blocked or reversed those actions. The far-right gets a lot of representation

on television that goes unchallenged. In fact, the airing of adverse or sensationalist remarks is encouraged because, perversely, hate happens to have a commercial value as it makes television-viewing exciting. This far-right influence on the media is one of the reasons why Pakistan, as a country, has been unable to develop a consensus against extremism. The narrative-makers distinguish between pro-Pakistan and anti-Pakistan extremist groups, and the former tends to get a laudatory profile in the media for focusing on Pakistan's neighbors.[8]

Inverting the Identities

Rubina Saigol, an independent researcher in social development, discusses nation-building as psychic violence:

> The process of nation-building by attempting to foist upon people new identities, to which they could not comfortably relate, was a form of psychic violence against the very 'self' of people, who felt threatened by a state overwhelmingly representing the Punjabi identity. Religion was never the sole source of identity of the people; language, culture, ethnicity and other markers of social differentiation were equally strong, if not more. Furthermore, even within religion there has been a vast complexity of sects and sub-sects, with each one eager to transfer its own set of values, beliefs and ideas to its future generations.[9]

According to Charles Amjad-Ali, a founder of the executive committee of the Human Rights Commission of Pakistan (HRCP), and Karamat Ali, founder of the Pakistan Institute of Labour Education and Research (PILER), review Pakistan's labour policies:

> Pakistan has gone through 6 major labour policies: 1955; 1959; 1969; 1972; 2002; and 2018. They were seldom, if ever, followed by requisite legislative and administrative policies

> and reforms. Beginning with the first 1955 labour policy, all the policies contained solemn pledges and assurances of full compliance with the principles of the International Labour Organization (ILO) Conventions. However, the actual laws promulgated—whether by military dictators or 'elected governments'—have continually negated labour and human rights.[10]

A Land of the Landowners

I.A. Rehman of the HRCP surveys the doomed effort at land reforms—forbidden by state ideology—which has filled the country's legislatures with feudal landlords:

> The most powerful legislature in the country, the National Assembly, remains dominated by the landed interest. Out of the 293 new, directly elected MNAs whose profiles were culled from their statements filed with the Election Commission by Free And Fair Election Network (FAFEN), 24 identified themselves as landlords, 79 described themselves as agriculturists and another 19 said they were agriculturists-businessmen. That means 122 MNAs out of 293 belong to the landlord lobby. Similarly, the newly elected provincial assemblies are also dominated by members identifying themselves as landlords, agriculturists, livestock breeders and agriculturists-businessmen. According to FAFEN, the landlord lobby accounts for 49.67% of the directly elected members of the Sindh Assembly. The comparable figures for the Punjab, Khyber Pakhtunkhwa (KP) and Balochistan assemblies are 33.1%, 28.4% and 21% respectively.[11]

Akmal Hussain, distinguished professor and dean, School of Social Sciences and Humanities, Information Technology University, Lahore, surveys the phenomenon of high growth under military rule because, in contrast to civilian rule, it suffers no 'intervention':

> The evidence shows that while during the Ayub–Yahya period (1960–73), there was high economic growth (6.3 per cent annually), during the subsequent Z.A. Bhutto period (1973–77), the growth rate declined to 4.9 per cent annually. Again, in the Zia-ul-Haq period that followed, there was an acceleration in economic growth to 6.6 per cent annually, but was followed once again by the low growth period of the 1990s (about 4 per cent annually). There was another pendulum swing to relatively high economic growth during the Musharraf period (6.3 per cent annually) followed by a decade of slow growth and virtual stagnation of per capita incomes. Over the long run, despite the spurts, economic growth in Pakistan is on a declining trend. This is in sharp contrast to the growth performance of China and India, who have not only achieved sustained high growth but are on a rising trend.[12]

Tariq Banuri, chairperson of Higher Education Commission (HEC), Pakistan, outlines the challenges faced by Pakistan:

> Pakistan has become a water scarce country and needs to invest in water efficiency. It should do so with an eye on the potential for exporting water efficiency technologies and practices to other countries. The government should support industries in developing solutions for exports. One of Pakistan's most dynamic sectors in the recent past has been the livestock and dairy industry. Since it, too, will be affected by climate change, the government should support this industry in finding climate-friendly solutions not only for maintaining its profitability but also, and more importantly, for exporting these solutions to other countries.[13]

Dogma vs Reason

Pervez Amirali Hoodbhoy, distinguished professor of physics and mathematics at Forman Christian College-University, Lahore, says in *Do Not Mix Religion and Science*:

> Demanding that science and faith be tied together has resulted in national bewilderment and intellectual enfeeblement. Massive doses of religion are injected today into the teaching of science, a practice that began under Zia's regime. It was not just school textbooks that were hijacked. In the 1980s, as an applicant to a university teaching position in whichever department, the university's selection committee would first check your faith. The failure of this system is evident. Millions of Pakistanis have studied science subjects in school and then gone on to study technical, science-based subjects in college and university. And yet, most, including science teachers, would flunk if given even the simplest science quiz. Tying faith with science does disservice to both. Science has no need for Pakistan; in the rest of the world it roars ahead. The attempt to create an 'Islamic Science', which began at the time of General Zia-ul-Haq, has never been completely laid to rest and exists in various forms even today.[14]

Reema Omer, a lawyer from Pakistan specializing in public international law, discusses the taboo subject of 'enforced disappearances' by 'you-know-who':

> The Supreme Court first took up the issue of the widespread practice of enforced disappearances in Pakistan in December 2005, when it took *suo motu* notice under Article 184(3) of the Constitution of a news report citing the growing numbers of enforced disappearances in the country. Soon after, the Human Rights Commission of Pakistan (HRCP) petitioned the Supreme Court under Article 184(3) to take notice of more cases of enforced disappearance. The HRCP submitted a list of 148 'missing persons', individuals allegedly subjected to enforced disappearance, to the Supreme Court. During the hearings, the Supreme Court acknowledged evidence, establishing that many of the 'disappeared' were in the custody of the security agencies and summoned high level military

> intelligence officials before the Supreme Court to explain the legal basis of the detention and to physically produce the detainees.[15]

Ascendancy of the Army

Ayesha Siddiqa, a research associate at the School for Oriental and African Studies (SOAS), University of London, discusses the spread of the power of the publicity wing of the army:

> While military, and its civilian supporters like Shireen Mazari, assert that the organization has better accountability systems, others have challenged this claim. It was during this period that the armed forces launched itself in the media industry, financing films and theatre and setting up television and radio channels. The development of a role in the media was done primarily to control the national narrative and change the direction of the discourse. This narrative management was not tactical but strategic, as it catapulted the army into becoming a societal player.[16]

Umar Cheema, an investigative reporter, who was kidnapped and tortured for writing critical stories about the government, talks about the limitations on the freedom of expression in Pakistan:

> In January 2017, in a secret swoop across the country, four prominent social media activists were picked up by security agencies for being critical of [the] state's actions and policies. While all of them were eventually released after weeks of hue and cry in the media, they came out tainted for life with the allegation of having committed blasphemy, a baseless allegation that endangered their lives and forced them to move abroad. In the months that followed, there were two more cases of a similar nature: Gul Bukhari, a columnist for *The Nation* and a commentator on *Waqt TV*, was picked up . . . while the house

> of Marvi Sirmed, a columnist for *Daily Times*, was burgled by mysterious intruders who were only interested in taking away her laptop and passport.[17]

Rafiullah Kakar, a public policy professional and political analyst points to the 'majoritarian' nature of the state:

> With Punjab accounting for 56% of the country's total population, the centralization of power only resulted in the 'Punjabization' of Pakistan. For example, the Punjab had more seats in the National Assembly than all of the other three provinces combined. The upper house, where all provinces had equal representation, had the potential to balance out Punjab's majoritarian influence, but this was prevented by the fact that the upper house (Senate) had lesser powers as compared to the lower house (National Assembly). The Senate had no control over money bills and little influence over matters affecting the federation such as the appointment of high-level executives. Moreover, the indirect election method for the upper house made Senate elections prone to vote-buying practices, especially in Balochistan. In short, Senate hasn't been effective in guarding against the over-bearing power of the Punjab-dominated National Assembly.[18]

Malevolence of the Muslim Male

Afiya S. Zia, a feminist researcher with a doctoral degree in Women and Gender Studies from the University of Toronto observes:

> Piety in Muslim contexts has accelerated because of its embrace by celebrities and women. Against this backdrop, in 2015--16, Pakistan witnessed the mercurial rise of celebrity and social media star, Qandeel Baloch (Fauzia Azeem), who threatened to subvert this pietist trend as she embraced and symbolized sexual impropriety. Apart from posting risqué

> online videos, Qandeel incentivized a victory for Pakistan's national cricket team by promising a strip dance if they beat arch-rivals India. Qandeel's defiant threat-promise sabotaged the male gaze and destabilized sexual politics in the Islamic Republic. But her ingenious impropriety caused confusion and political tension—not just for the pious conservatives but also for feminists and progressives. Also, Veena Malik's case represents a peculiarly Pakistani version of the Madonna-whore complex—one which accepts seductive performances, capitalist enterprises, game shows and other profane ventures, as long as these promise to entice audiences towards piety, rather than self-gratifying pleasure. Such performative piety is simply part of the market that offers Islamic consumerism but depends on the same gender dynamics where the male gaze dominates and objectifies women. In contrast, Qandeel forfeited marriage, undressed, and her performances challenged religious actors and exposed their double-standard hypocrisies. Veena won salvation because she now seduces believers into piety, while Qandeel paid with her life for asserting and encouraging female sexual independence.[19]

Bina Shah, a Karachi-based author of five novels asks *Is Islam Compatible with Feminism*? Her view is:

> Islam embodies many of the principles that feminism fights for: equality, dignity and respect for women. At the time of its birth, Islam was a revolutionary force in terms of the social and personal rights it granted to women. However, in the lands where this religion took hold, patriarchy was the norm. So what we see today, I contend, is a massive distortion of what Islam was meant to be, for women as well as men. But Islam is not to be confused with feminism. Feminism is the mechanism by which women can fight for the rights that have been taken away from them. And, in Pakistan's case, these rights have been usurped by men and in the name

of Islam. For example, if Islam gave women the right to own property, patriarchy in Pakistan makes it difficult—if not impossible—for women to technically and legally administer and maintain the property they own. If Islam gave girls the right to go to school, patriarchy ensures that girls remain without safe and easy access to schools or abandon school in favor of an underage marriage or, if they manage to complete school, abandon higher studies and career aspirations to bear and raise children. In short, Islam and Sharia becomes shorthand for *patriarchy in Muslim countries*. This is the reason why, according to a report published in *The Lancent* journal, Pakistan performs abominably in maternal, adolescent and child health indicators, lagging behind even other Muslim-majority countries such as Iran and Bangladesh.[20]

Foreign Policy Fiascos

Raza Rumi, director of the department of journalism at Ithaca College, New York, talks about the fatal India–Pakistan binary that has hurt only Pakistan:

> Pakistanis and Indians desperately need to revisit the confederal ideas that Jinnah advocated (right until the Cabinet Mission Plan of 1946) for the mutual benefit of their poverty-stricken, ill-governed and violence-torn nuclearized countries. History repeats itself and the course of history is determined by incremental changes made along the way. The populace of India and Pakistan are hostage to the 'national' fallacies that spawn conflict and create further insecurity. This is a grand decolonization project that we need to embark upon. It is not an easy journey, but there is no other choice. Pakistanis and Indians owe it to their freedoms and the million lives lost in Partition to take charge of the present. And the best way to achieve that would be standing up for and selecting peace as the only way forward.[21]

Muhammad Ismail Khan, a researcher at the Pakistan Institute for Peace Studies (PIPS), observes:

> Pakistan needs to expand its foreign policy options. For one, the prism of viewing everything through [an] Indian lens can be revisited in a more sophisticated manner. While no one expects Pakistan–India relations to iron out in a day, overcoming [its] India fixation can help Pakistan ease its ties with Afghanistan and Iran and even put realistic expectations from the US and China. This fixation can partly be overcome by streamlining internal political voices; the knee-jerk reaction of discarding those voices and suspecting their links with India put question marks over the acceptance of major foreign policy decision. Numerous scholars and policy practitioners have concluded that Pakistan's foreign policy largely pivots around India. India's friend is our enemy, and India's enemy is our friend, goes the argument. The centre of gravity for Pakistan, to use military jargon, has been India. A rejectionist response towards India is evident even in societal attitude, so much so that Pakistani nationalism is criticised for being a negation of India, rather than having its own feet to stand on. The remedy to Pakistan's foreign policy is often found in freeing out from the competition with India. As per this thinking, Pakistan should not match India stick by stick and gun by gun, given India's greater size, economy and ambition. Pakistan, otherwise, will be exhausted; instead, it should invest its energies inwards.[22]

Heat for the Heterodox

The heterodox opinions expressed above are not banned in Pakistan but are nevertheless marginalized because they can only be expressed in English. Most Urdu publications would be scared of carrying the message of these writers because Urdu as an agent of state ideology cannot fully accept the logical–sequential discourse of English. Pakistan predominantly expresses itself in

Urdu through the spoken word on television. The printed word is in decline even in Urdu which further queers the pitch for the discourse still available in written English.

TV channels dominate the information market, and the medium of communication is Urdu, with peripheral channels using regional languages like Punjabi, Sindhi, Balochi and Pashto. There are 127 TV channels in Pakistan, out of which thirty-six transmit news. Publication of the English-language newspapers in the country remains minuscule. Urdu as the purveyor of the twin ideological-nationalist knowledge epistemes has replaced the rational discourse of the 'colonial' English language. Ironically, this lack of communication between Urdu and English saves the purveyors of the heresy of 'marginal' discourse from being punished.

21

High or Hybrid?

Nationalism at times curtails more than it adds to human society. In 2018, Pakistan saw Imran Khan win a general election. Among other things, he promised to 'reform' the English-medium schools because they created 'two nations'. Yet, the official legal constitutional text in the country remains English and most judges still write their judgments in English. The question to ask is: Why justice, requiring objectivity and dispassion, is still dispensed in English? The British Raj got us to read and write in the 'language of subjugation', which made Sir Syed Ahmad Khan do something dangerous: distilling rational thought into Urdu. Reacting to British essayist Joseph Addison's discussion in *The Spectator* of Max Weber's *Protestant Ethic*, he wrote:

> Honesty is possible without religion, but religion is not possible without honesty.[1]

In Pakistani Urdu-medium schools in the 1960s, English was taught as a compulsory 'remedial and functional idiom', as if limiting its 'dangerous' discourse to the 'non-logical' and 'non-sequential' to prevent it from trespassing on state ideology. It is still compulsory; so is the official text of the Constitution which is in English. But language-learning ends up getting creative, first giving birth to verse, then descending to the more controversial and demanding prose. This process of the English discourse filtering down to the colonized mind happened in India and is today celebrated in South Asia as 'literature' describing the regional civilization for the world. For those who feel endangered by the sort of 'thinking' English gives rise to, Sir Syed is no longer a part of the Pakistani nationalist pantheon.

Muneeza Shamsie's monumental *Hybrid Tapestries: The Development of Pakistani Literature in English* has brought to light the hidden and neglected 'hybrid' talent of those who wrote in English.[2] She has unearthed the talent of Atiya Fyzee Rahamin (1877–1967), Samuel Fyzee Rahamin (1880–1964), Shahid Suhrawardy (1890–1965), Ahmed Ali (1910–94) and Mumtaz Shahnawaz (1912–48), and made an assessment of their worth as commentators of their times before delving into the more contemporary Shaista Suhrawardy Ikramullah (1915–2000), Zaib-un-Nissa Hamidullah (1921–2000), Zulfikar Ghose, Taufiq Rafat (1927–98), Bapsi Sidhwa, Hanif Kureishi and Sara Suleri.

Even the lesser-known writers have been briefly commented on and listed till the book becomes a kind of directory. Just to test the detail I looked up the index and found Javaid Qazi mentioned with his novels and short-story collections. (Intriguingly, Fakir Syed Aijazuddin's work in eighteen unforgettable volumes could not find a place in this remarkable treasury, although his wife Shahnaz made it to the index with her book.)

Language As Liberator?

Sake Dean Mahomet (1759–1851), a Muslim official in the East India Company settled in Ireland, was the first Indian to use English creatively. He wrote a memoir, *The Travels of Dean Mahomet, a Native of Patna in Bengal, Through Several Parts of India While in the Service of the Honorable East India Company, Written by Himself in a Series of Letters to a Friend* (1794), 'to explain India to his new friends in Britain'. Now our writers are explaining Pakistan to us in English and it looks different from the message we get in Urdu.

Is there a gulf of idioms that divides the writer himself? Does he transform himself according to the idiom he is writing in? Shamsie notes how Bankimchandra Chatterji (1838–94) first wrote the English novel *Rajmohan's Wife*, the story of a sad marriage and unrequited love in middle-class Bengali life, and then wrote the famous novel *Anandamath* in Bengali, which lit the communal fires with its inset song, 'Vande Matram', which the Indian government had to censor before inducting it as a national song. (Members of the BJP today have lamented about only two verses of the song being used.)[3]

The reverse can also happen. The logical–sequential discourse of English at times tilts into a kind of 'globalism' that the Muslim communities simply can't accept, as was the case with Salman Rushdie's *The Satanic Verses*, first published in the United Kingdom in 1988. He, as a Muslim, was accused of blasphemy, and in 1989 Ayatollah Ruhollah Khomeini of Iran issued a fatwa ordering Muslims to kill him. It seems writing in English can get you killed; but this kind of reaction was something Saadat Hasan Manto too had to encounter, whose realism in Urdu carried the unacceptable germs that a more weather-beaten English can pollute us with.

Atiya Fyzee: A Lost Lighthouse

Shamsie's book contains fascinating details of the life of Atiya Fyzee Rahamin (1877–1967) who migrated to Pakistan in 1947. Her family belonged to the Suleimani Bohra community, which had migrated from Cambay (now called Khambat, in Gujarat) to Bombay and acquired English as 'the link language with the country's new rulers'. They also learnt Urdu, which was considered the language of the Muslim elite and of the Muslim identity in India. Atiya Begum and her six siblings were born in Istanbul, but her mother returned to Bombay with her daughters Zehra, Nazli and Atiya. Atiya became known in Pakistan as a friend of Allama Iqbal, Pakistan's national poet.

In 1914, shortly before the outbreak of the First World War, she published her great classic, *Indian Music*, in English under the name of Shahinda (Begum Fyzee Rahamin)[4], with a preface by distinguished British musicologist E. Gilbert Webb and twelve exquisite illustrations by Jewish painter Samuel Fyzee Rahamin, whom she was to marry later. The 'enduring quality of Atiya Begum's prose has long stood the test of time' and also graced the intimate letters she wrote to her friend Allama Iqbal. Her husband, Samuel Rahamin, wrote his novel *Gilded India*[5] in proof of his all-round genius.

Atiya Fyzee met up with Allama Iqbal in London, where he had gone for higher studies and become a toast of social gatherings for his learning and ready wit. He, marrying at eighteen, already had two children when he found in her 'a true companion with whom he could have conversations and discuss literature, art, poetry, and music'. In 1947, shortly before Partition, Atiya published her famous English book *Iqbal*, a collection of memories and letters that is one of the earliest examples of English language 'life-writing' by a South Asian Muslim woman. It reveals 'a very different Iqbal from the clever and carefree young man she knew in London and Heidelberg'.[6] Author Shamsie gives us a comprehensive account of the works of both Atiya and her husband.

Colonial Verse or Worse

The book takes note of the Bengali poet Shahid Suhrawardi whose 1937 *Essays in Verse* 'broke away from the Orientalist traditions of Indo-Anglian poetry and its assertions of Indian-ness'. As a Pakistani in pre-revolutionary Moscow, he could read Bartold in Russian when the great historian was not yet translated into English, and knew more about Russia's 'civilizational' advent into Central Asia than anyone else. He was found among the Pakistani–English poets in *The First Voices* (1965)[7] that featured Taufiq Rafat, Kaleem Omar, and others before writing his *The Art of the Mussalmans of Spain* when posted as the ambassador there.[8] Shamsie marshals all the facts about this early Bengali genius and tells a great story.

What English carried with ease was 'realism', and it came out first in Urdu with the collection *Angarey* (1932). The leading light was Ahmed Ali who was to write his *Twilight in Delhi* in 1940 to become the first major Indian Muslim novelist in English. It became clear by the widespread Muslim protest against *Angarey* that you couldn't say in Urdu what was now being written in English. Manto was to face prosecution for breaking the tyranny of the idiom. The book notes:

> This fuelled the raging post-Independence argument on the 'relevance' of using English, a colonial language, as a creative vehicle in the newly independent countries of India and Pakistan.

Ali's translation of the Quran could be seen as an act of contrition, but he was too much his own man to walk away from the alien discourse. Author Shamsie's verdict was:

> Ahmed Ali's linguistic strategy, his attempts to transpose the language of one culture into that of another, was both innovative and courageous.

Taufiq Rafat: 'First Voice' That Lasted

Zulfiqar Ghose, whose poetry made its first appearance in *First Voices*, had arisen from Sialkot to become a novelist of great merit. The chapter devoted to him is riveting as it explains how Ghose's universalism made him more a Commonwealth kind of writer like

V.S. Naipaul—some of whose work the Indians don't like—who moved away from the 'nationalistic paradigm'. But the next chapter focuses on Taufiq Rafat, another Kashmiri like Ghose and Rushdie, and provides a much-needed assessment of his genius. Taufiq was a poet of wisdom, but he was essentially a pagan who celebrated nature. He was a recognized poet, even writing a play in verse which was directed and staged in Lahore by Farrukh Nigar Aziz in 1969.

Rafat lived in his poems because he was strictly non-judgemental. He stayed close to the senses and let them give their verdict. He was not obsessed with transmitting a message of any kind because that would fall in the category of judgement. He lived a life without final conclusions, creating pathos and beauty by refraining from imposing on us any moral assessment of the object he was looking at. He accepted the flux of time but not the ideologies that tried to arrest it.

Rafat was rewarded for this impartiality of the soul by a freedom that few poets of our time have achieved. His nostalgia for the past was not based on any values that have been robbed by time; he simply noted the passage of a way of life that was no more. What moved him most about transition was death, the death of those he had known, of people who lived without bearing the doubtful burden of being acknowledged by society as great.

Shamsie finishes her best chapter by quoting Waqas Khwaja:

> There are people today who have made somewhat of a name for themselves outside the country as poets, people like Moniza Alvi and Alamgir Hashmi. But Rafat started it all. He's still the standard in many ways of what can be and what needed to be done in the area of English-language poetry in Pakistan to open up the way for succeeding generations of aspiring poets.

Tariq Ali: Advocate Extraordinaire

In 1962, Tariq Ali emerged as the student genius of his time at Government College Lahore, easily emerging as the best debater holding his own against his father, Mazhar Ali Khan, in Old vs Young Ravians debates, reaching his high-water mark with a protest march on Mall Road against the murder of the Congolese leader Patrice Lumumba till his anti-American world view became too much to stomach for General Ayub and he had to take off to the UK 'for higher studies'. It was just as well because his classfellow Salmaan Taseer fell to Pakistan's ideology many years later in 2011.

Ali was a Ravian product of a different order, becoming the founding editor of the newspaper the *Black Dwarf* and the magazine the *Red Mole* in London. He went on to write historical novels, plays and accounts of his own Trotskyite faith which put him at odds with the Soviet Union. Shamsie has done a great job digging up the most important milestones in the life of this extraordinary still-living genius whom Pakistan may never be intellectually able to understand. Connecting him to Atiya Fyzee Rahamin, Syed Ameer Ali and Shahid Suhrawardy, she quotes from his *The Clash of Fundamentalism: Crusades, Jihads, and Modernity* (2002):

> To fight tyranny and oppression by using tyrannical and oppressive means, to combat a single-minded and ruthless fanaticism by becoming equally fanatical and ruthless, will not further the cause of justice or bring about a meaningful democracy. It can only prolong the cycle of violence.[9]

Bapsi Sidhwa to Kamila Shamsie

Bapsi Sidhwa took English-reading Pakistan by storm with her unbuttoned novel *The Crow Eaters* (1979) about the Parsi community. She brought something new to the hybrid legacy of Ahmed Ali and Mumtaz Shahnawaz. She carried on the story of her community with *Ice-Candy-Man* (1988) adding a 'strong feminist consciousness which portrays how the lives of women are circumscribed by social attitudes and ancient rules, regardless of class, country, and religion'. *The Bride* (1982) portrayed the lives of Pakistan's urban poor in contrast to those in the tribal areas, and her experience of the trauma of Partition, when she was only nine, became 'the nucleus of the plot for *Ice-Candy-Man* and some of its characters'. Sidhwa's fiction has to be included in the most significant works of Partition literature in South Asia today.

Shamsie left out her daughter's fiction and other writings for Shobana Bhattarcharji to cover:

> Kamila Shamsie belongs to a literary family, which includes the novelist Attia Hosain and Sahibzada Mahmuduzzafar Khan, co-author of *Angarey* and a co-founder of The Progressive Writers' Movement. Her great-grandmother, grandmother, mother, and sister are also writers. Novelist, freelance journalist, reviewer, a creative writing teacher, Kamila has published five novels since 1998. They have been translated into many languages. Of these, *Burnt Shadows* received the 2010 Anisfield-Wolf Book Award (US) and was also short-listed for the 2009 Orange Fiction Prize (UK). *In the City by the Sea*, *Kartography*, and *Broken Verses* received awards from the Pakistan Academy of Letters and *Broken Verses* was also shortlisted for the 2005 LiBberaturpreis (Germany). *In The City by the Sea*, and *Kartography* were shortlisted in turn for the John Llewellyn Rhys Award. She is on the editorial board of Index on Censorship and has been a judge for several literary awards.

Kureishi's Creative Brood

Shamsie's most fascinating story after Atiya Faizi is Hanif Kureishi's, the first British writer of Pakistani origin 'to win major literary awards on both sides of the Atlantic'. His screenplay *My Beautiful Laundrette* got an Oscar nomination in 1984, before his first novel, *The Buddha of Suburbia*, won the 1990 Whitbread Award in 1991. These works focused on 'the conflicts of, and pressures on, young Asians growing up in Britain'. Kureishi inserted himself in the novel *My Son the Fanatic*, which became a film of that name. His essays beat all rivals in the field in those days.

Born in 1954, Hanif is the son of a Pakistani father and an English mother, brought up in Bromley, Kent, where his maternal grandfather owned three shops. His paternal grandfather was Colonel Kureishi, and thereby hangs a tale told by Shamsie with her usual ferreting skill. Col Kureishi was in the Indian Medical Corps, an Anglophile, which decided the life trajectories of his brood. His son Rafiushan Kureishi, his creativity suppressed, migrated to Britain to study law and married Audrey Buss. Rafiushan could have become a writer on his own, but life forced him to be a half-formed writer, a gap that his son Hanif was to fill so well. But here comes the rest of the story as revealed by author Shamsie. Rafiushan's siblings didn't think of going to Britain but moved to Pakistan at Partition like everyone else. Guess who these siblings were?

They included Omar Kureishi, his uncle, the great cricket commentator that Pakistan will never forget from the days of the radio; Bilquis Nasrullah, the fashion editor; civil servant Enver Kureishi the husband of the more renowned poet Maki Kureishi who appeared on the English poetic horizon of Pakistan with Taufiq Rafat; and Safdar Kureishi, a veteran of the Second World War who joined the Pakistan Air Force. Hanif Kureishi visited Pakistan for the first time in 1983 and said this:

> Am completely fascinated by Pakistan. It has given me time to stop and think about my past, about my roots. Whereas once I thought my place in England could be worked out here, I now realize that it can only be worked out in relation to this country. Think it will also give another dimension to my work.

Hybrid Tapestries is truly a monumental work which only someone like Moneeza Shamsie could have accomplished. The book is truly a keepsake.

22

Syed Babar Ali: Batting till the Last Ball

(In December 2019, the twenty-second Sustainable Development Conference, organized by the Sustainable Development Policy Institute [SDPI], paid tribute to renowned Pakistani businessman Syed Babar Ali. The ninety-three-year-old business tycoon is the founder of Packages Limited, Nestlé Pakistan Limited and Lahore University of Management Sciences [LUMS], and also served as a caretaker finance minister of Pakistan in 1993. He has also been awarded the Order or the British Empire [OBE].)

Say Babar Ali and people in Pakistan will immediately think of the sprawling Packages Ltd beyond Kot Lakhpat and LUMS in Lahore's Defence Housing Authority. For some reason, whenever I heard my mother say 'Milkpak', I thought of Syed Yawar Ali, the chairman of Nestle Pakistan, not Babar Ali, who spent most of his life tending to Packages Ltd because of his behind-the-scenes nature. And now that he has written his memoir *Learning from Others: The Autobiography of Syed Babar Ali*, I know why.[1]

He recalls that he had once told me that he didn't want to be remembered. Should he be embarrassed now that he has finally indulged himself and recorded his life? I think he should realize that while wishing not to be remembered, he never vowed against remembering others. The book celebrates the people he has treasured, and self-reference is his way of explaining what they helped bring about. The trick is to latch on to people you sincerely rate as your superiors. You may call it 'learning from others', resulting in your own rise 'by association' rather than 'by competition'. Ordinary mortals see self-promotion only in being surrounded by lesser people, but not Babar Ali. A back-of-the-book couplet from Saadi says:

> My companions' virtues elevated me/Otherwise I am the same humble creature that I was.[2]

But there are other secrets attached to this self-effacing empire-builder.

Starting Small

In the post-Mutiny period, the British Raj, which replaced the East India Company, arrived in India and needed massive provisioning for troops on the move. Babar Ali's grandfather, Syed Wazir Ali, ran a shop in Rang Mahal in Lahore's Walled City and expanded in 1858 to the Lahore Cantonment, selling 'food, clothing, furniture, and household goods, combined with a business as contractors for individual regiments of the British Army'. The key passage in the book is:

> My grandfather developed a reputation as a reliable businessman . . . this enabled him to own the property where the shop was located and the adjoining house. He also made money from property in Ferozepur that was rented out to the British Army.[3]

Francis Fukuyama would exclaim that this was the first chemistry of 'trust' felt by a Lahore shopkeeper, which had transformed Europe after Protestantism thought 'ethic' was linked only to 'work', and Luther invented the word 'vocation' for 'profession'. Wazir Ali and his sons comprehended this new work ethic and were recognized as 'reliable'. Was Lahore ready to recognize this epiphany? In front of Lahore's Tollington Market, where his father Syed Muratib Ali had his big shop, the local elite called them 'sons of a contractor'—in Urdu, the word for 'contractor' is strangely more demeaning—and made them feel bad. It hardly mattered that they held their own among the 'sons of the chiefs' at Aitchison College.

There is consolation here for those who think their hero-worshipping nature will somehow hold them back. Babar hero-worshipped his elder brothers, Syed Amjad Ali and Syed Wajid Ali, and kept at it even after becoming a tycoon on his own. This admission of others' superiority never harmed him. In fact, the folded-hands reverence he shows in his book to his Aitchisonian class-fellow Harcharan and the Swedish inventor of Tetra Pack, Ruben Rausing, seems only to lift him above his contemporaries. Did this self-subordination prevent him from scoring the highest marks in class and winning the college blazer for swimming, hockey and riding? In fact, he kept up with his polo matches till age caught up with him.

Syed Amjad Ali was clearly the first flash of brilliance which took the 'shopkeeper' family out of its low social rung. While in the Punjab Assembly with the Unionists, he had developed an interest in 'industrial production', partnering with a fellow-member of the Assembly, Sir William Roberts—who was to be the first principal of Lyallpur Agriculture College and a very successful cotton grower from Khanewal with business contacts in Lancashire—in setting up a textile mill in Bahawalpur. After that got going, they persuaded the Lever Brothers of Bombay to join them in setting up a 'vegetable ghee factory, as well as a soap factory' in the state with the nawab as a shareholder. Syed Amjad Ali constantly gave Babar the leg-up he needed, including his marriage to his cousin

Perwin in 1955, when Amjad Ali was Pakistan's ambassador in Washington DC. The personal triumph for Babar Ali, twenty-nine at the time, was getting 'reluctant' Perwin to overcome her fear that he had been a bit of a playboy during his Karachi days—'my father disapproved of my lifestyle'. They were married in DC, with then vice president Richard Nixon attending.

The Faqir Connection

Syed Wazir Ali had got his son Maratab Ali to marry Syeda Mubarak Begum, the daughter of the distinguished Faqirkhana family of Lahore, the erstwhile distinguished courtiers of Maharaja Ranjit Singh of Punjab. Faqir Syed Iftikharuddin was no ordinary man. He was from the Indian Political Service, had a posting as the resident in Tonk state (Rajasthan) and was attached to the Amir of Afghanistan when the latter toured India. He was also posted as the British agent in Kabul, from 1907 to 1910, with the special credential that his mother was from the Afghan royal family. He ended up bagging the title of CIE (Commander of the Indian Empire). Thus began the gene pool that was to give rise to one of the most respectable entrepreneur families of Punjab. In early 2015, Babar's niece, Syeda Abida Husain, a member of the National Assembly, ambassador to the US and the wife of the former speaker of the National Assembly Syed Fakhar Imam, Babar's nephew, published her own political and diplomatic memoir and caused quite a stir.

Babar Ali was twenty, out of Government College Lahore, when he decided to go to Massachusetts Institute of Technology (MIT) in the United States for a business and engineering programme. He had a B.Sc. degree from the government college that finally got him admitted to the University of Michigan at Ann Arbor instead, the alma mater where his children, Henna and Hyder, too were to get their degrees. But it was 1945, he was unmarried, and Pakistan was still in the offing. The family was friends with all the Indian leaders—Amjad Ali could walk into Jinnah's Bombay residence anytime without prior permission—

but the Muslim cause was close to the heart, just as Shiism was always the font of non-demonstrative spirituality mixed generously with charity, giving rise to Babar Ali's almost secular world view. His enlightenment was probably triggered by his gradual disenchantment with the 'Islamic republic' of Pakistan. His best friend from his Aitchison days remained Harcharan Singh Brar, the horse-breeding Sikh who finally rose to be the chief minister of Indian Punjab. As a student in Ann Arbor, 'Ali Barbar' was reported in the local press as an ardent supporter of Pakistan before the partition of India.

Owning a lot of real estate—from Ferozepur to Bhopal to Bombay and Karachi—came in handy when the Alis went into industry and needed acreage to build on. Babar Ali touched base with the Lever Brothers in Massachusetts for his brother Amjad Ali, in addition to joining the first Pakistani delegation to the United Nations under Chaudhry Zafarullah Khan in 1948. Looking after ghee and soap factories spread over Punjab and Sindh, Babar Ali was based in Karachi, thinking he would be there for good, linking up with Ford Motors that was to result in the well-known Ali Automobiles.

From manufacturing soap in Hyderabad to making blades in partnership with Treet of America was another step typical of Babar Ali. (Babar Ali and Treet blades is difficult to imagine today!) His four years at the Bunder Road office gave him invaluable experience supporting the industrial units in Hyderabad and the textile mill at Rahim Yar Khan, while importing textiles and exporting cotton and oil cake, his biggest buyer being the Soviet Union! But the game-changer move was to come just then. He had built his house in Karachi, but he was advised to buy the furniture for it from Finland. This was to change his life.

Treet Blades to Packages

It was 1954 and he had to go to Finland through Sweden to buy his furniture, and he thought he could also look up Akerlund &

Rausing, a packaging company in Stockholm that had offered him packaging material for his Treet razor blade plant in Hyderabad. Talking to the managers of the company, he made his move: Why not get together on setting up a packaging plant in Pakistan? Barring Ali Automobiles, all of his family's business was outside of Lahore, their home city. Thus was born the idea of Packages Limited, the near-monopoly whose product Milkpak has become part of household conversation without the realization that it is a brand name.

Admiring people who are superior to you is the wisest way of ridding yourself of envy, which normally gives us our much-needed instinct of competiveness. At twenty-eight, Babar Ali admired Ruben Rausing—'he took me under his wings'—the founder of the company, in his sixties. He listened to Rausing as he told him why he put up the plant in a small city which had a university. He said, 'All the brains are here.' That was why Packages Ltd was located in Lahore: to be near the universities. Maybe it also gradually also dawned on him that what Lahore offered as academia was below par. A new institution matching global standards was needed.

Then came the Zulfikar Ali Bhutto interregnum and the economy was nationalized in Pakistan. Bhutto soon sensed the destruction involved in PPP's ideological takeovers and offered Babar Ali the chairmanship of the nationalized fertilizers sector. Babar, at fifty, didn't want it but was advised by friends not to rebuff socialism's revengeful captain and took up the job for the stipulated three years. When he called on party ideologue J.A. Rahim and said 'salam' in Urdu, the reply came gruffly in English. Later, Rahim fell afoul of Bhutto and was arrested and tortured by the police, the more gory details of which Babar Ali carefully avoids. Thus was the family's incipient empire saved from total state grab. He was full of energy then, as the *New York Times* noted, calling him 'a huge bear of a man'.[4]

Bhutto was hanged in 1979 by General Zia who offered Babar Ali missions he could politely say no to because he was less scared of the polite dictator; but he did join the general's *shoora*, the beginning of the next luckless pendulum-swing called Islamization that Babar Ali was to decry later in his interviews. Finally it is moot who harmed Pakistan more, Bhutto or Zia, because both scuttled the economy through ideology. Babar Ali noted the slump in efficiency among managers involved in debates over blasphemy and riba and realized that he needed a lot of good professionals if his companies were to survive. It was then that he thought of his own business school.

Wisdom of Spreading Thin

Did Babar Ali spread himself thin because of his hunger for enterprise? The list of peripheral interests he gives us is quite forbidding. Once enriched by the experience of establishing and running LUMS, he was approached by institutions struggling to survive in Pakistan's not-always-friendly environment. Sympathetic to Christians who have selflessly educated Lahore's Muslims—he had himself gone to Lahore's Sacred Heart School—he got 'involved' by joining the Boards of Kinnaird College and F.C. College, later helping out the Lahore School of Economics, and Aitchison College too. He built a beautiful library at Aitchison, planned by architect Nayyar Ali Dada.

The space he gives to World Wildlife Fund (WWF) shows that his involvement with the animal world was passionate, and for once he didn't mind pulling strings to prevent a retired general from harming the WWF from within the cabinet of General Zia—which must have been tough because he had just refused the general's offer of chairmanship of PIA: 'I am running WWF in Pakistan, but your people are hounding me because of General Habibullah.' The next day, General Zia issued instructions: Leave WWF alone.

For headhunting, he went for the low-hanging fruit of the gifted Pakistani youth. Sensing his own future needs, he set up Systems Ltd which later produced the software much in demand, run by Aezaz Hussain, a brilliant scion of Lahore's Baroodkhana family of Mian Amiruddin, later joined by another bright young man who was to rise in the global corporate world, Manzur ul Haq. Then, in 1989, the chemical giant Siemens asked him if he would agree to be the chairman of their company in Pakistan; he agreed 'for the sake of experience'. He had an advisory status with American Express Bank since early 1970, which helped him run his First International Investment Bank Ltd, getting an exceptionally talented person from his mother's tribe as its boss, Fakir Syed Aijazuddin, who 'changed the management style and made the bank pro-active to the needs of the market and increased its activity, previously confined to Karachi, Islamabad and Lahore'.

Babar Ali says his real entrepreneurial bastion is Packages Ltd, where his style of management came into full play. The old style of management was autocratic and it is still impenetrably tyrannical in Pakistan, oriental wisdom saying it works better than the new 'mollycoddling' model popular in the West. Babar Ali is close to the modern 'collegial' model when he writes under the caption of Business Ethics:

> Before regulating your colleagues, you have to discipline yourself. You are not above your colleagues; you are one of them. You have to accept the fact that you are not a privileged person: you cannot break any law, public or private, and whatever the laws and rules of your organization, you have to be the first to conform to them. Only then can you enforce them on others.

The LUMS Climax

Babar Ali was not only looking for companions he could admire, his scent for talent was quite sharp. During a visit to the US in 1984, he ran into Javed Hamid who was to change the identity of Lahore as a laidback non-academic town eating more than thinking. Hamid, an MBA from the Harvard Business School, was once in Islamabad's Planning Commission as an economist but was now with International Finance Corporation in Washington. LUMS was to be Babar's brainchild, midwifed brilliantly by Hamid.

A nothing-to-look-at campus materialized at Lahore's Liberty Market in Gulberg in 1988; but such was the 'trust' inspired by Babar Ali that President Zia visited it and Singapore's founder Lee Kuan Yew had dinner there after speaking to only eighty students. Then he did his fundraising, for the sum of Rs 2.5 million each donor. He definitely had the magic 'touch':

> I went and touched about 100 people, of whom 60 gave me Rs. 2.5 million each. In that group there were people of the stature of Chaudhry Nazar Mohammad, Yusuf Shirazi and Razak Dawood, who all gave generously from their companies.

Of course, he put in the first cheque every time; later, when the big LUMS had come up in Lahore in over 100 acres, and money was needed for the School of Science & Engineering, his first cheque was for Rs 100 million. Incredibly, he later got the Americans, who were giving US$3.2 billion to Pakistan as assistance, to give him a part of it. 'Does US$10 million frighten you?' Ambassador Hinton asked. 'Not really', replied Babar Ali, in an understatement of a lifetime.

If Europe, according to Fukuyama, was built on 'trust' in business, which operates on the basis of uncertainty, Babar Ali's northern European partners responded to his perseverance—which he calls 'batting till the last ball'. (One wonders why he didn't 'touch' southern Europe; and why so much the northernmost Scandinavia?) He was genuinely fond of—if not worshipful of—Ruben Rausing. He suggested to his company in Sweden that he could build an Executive Development Centre at LUMS in his name, but he would need two million dollars for it. The company gave one million; and then the rest when he went to them for the second tranche. Rausing's grand-daughter, Kirsten, 'visited Pakistan and she made a surprise announcement, without telling me, that Tetra Pack would like to give another million dollars'. Now there is a funded library at LUMS named after Rausing's offspring: the Gad and Brigit Rausing Library. About the future of LUMS, he writes:

> I want my family to be involved with LUMS and I hope they will continue to support it from their own resources as well as from my Foundation. I hope they will do well financially and add to what I leave behind as a legacy.

This is what Babar Ali once said to former caretaker prime minister Moeen Qureshi:

> I started work on January 1, 1948, and I have seen a transformation. In many ways, Pakistan was better yesterday than today. At that time, you could get prompt responses from the government, which was keen to push you forward. I have only two options. One is to stay at home and do nothing. The other is to go out and bat to the best of my ability and leave the rest to Providence. This has always been my attitude: to bat till the last ball of the match. I regard it as a physical and personal therapy; you have to stay engaged and do things with passion; you have to get involved. You have to be meticulous about small things. You have to read more than once what you have written, to correct your mistakes. It is a question of habit and discipline.[5]

23

A Life in Watercolours

Fakir Syed Aijazuddin's nineteenth book is another biography. He says: 'One should never write a book, preferably not a biographical study. It merely extends someone else's life, and shortens one's own'.[1]

Sketches from a Howda: Charlotte, Lady Canning's Tours: 1858--1861[2] is another well-produced coffee-table venture generously spread with coloured illustrations. Those of us who enjoy his witticisms in his *Dawn* columns will enjoy the unfailing excellence of his style while bringing to life the gifted, and in some ways obscured, personality of Charlotte Canning, wife of former governor general and then Viceroy of India Lord Canning, who ruled India during the Mutiny of 1857.

Aijazuddin, currently Honorary British Consul for the UK in Lahore, in recognition of which he was awarded the OBE in 1997, after a distinguished career as a chartered accountant, has settled into his overgrown ferreting instinct, digging up facts lying buried in collective amnesia. While still an accountant, he had given evidence of this with his catalogue of miniature paintings from the Punjab Hills. Today he is a recognized art historian, even if you choose to ignore his purely political books, like the one on Henry Kissinger's secret visit to China in July 1971, and another on President Richard Nixon's policy towards Pakistan (1969–74). He has now set his sights on a self-effacing and, in some ways, touching career of Lord Canning's wife as she went around India in his travelling camp, painting the post-Mutiny landscape.

From Charlotte Stuart to Lady Canning

Charlotte Stuart (1817–61) was married at the age of eighteen to Charles Canning, whose father George Canning had served as prime minister for just 119 days (the shortest tenure of any British prime minister). She was herself Lady of the Bedchamber to Queen Victoria while Charles served as postmaster general before being sent to India as governor general in 1855. Actually, in February 1855, Canning had found himself appointed as postmaster general in Lord Palmerston's cabinet, only to discover in June that his name was being proposed as a successor to Lord Dalhousie in India.

Two years on, in India, rebellion began on 10 May 1857 in the form of a mutiny of the 'sepoys' in the garrison town of Meerut, 40 miles north-east of Delhi. It soon spread to the upper Gangetic plains and central India, though incidents of revolt also occurred farther north and east. The rebellion posed a considerable threat to British power in that region and was contained only with the rebels' defeat in Gwalior on 20 June 1858. Canning went through this one-year-long uprising and was not given to revenge after it subsided. ('To his great credit he refused to go along with the bloodthirsty and vengeful atmosphere that prevailed back in Britain in the aftermath.')[3] Although not immune from criticism, Canning, as he appears in Charlotte's letters to the Queen, and to her family back home, creates a good impression, becoming viceroy at the end of the rebellion when the Company rule ended.

Charles, 'cold to the point of arrogance', could never form a warm relationship with his wife, which resulted in her total absorption with painting as she travelled in the post-Mutiny vice-regal caravans 'in her howdah' atop an elephant. Coming to Punjab from Calcutta was a major undertaking in the wake of the disturbances. Canning travelled with a train of 20,000 natives, as well as Europeans, backed by a battery of artillery 'mostly for firing salutes'. The marches were often rigorous—73 miles in one day, from 6 a.m. to 12 midnight, Lady Canning noted. 'It was very tedious and the road decidedly not pucka'. Breakfast would be had mid-morning at the camp, set up by the advance party sent ahead, much like the Mughals marching to Kashmir with fanfare. Only some of the stuff the king carried was typical of their times: 'Then came 200 camels, loaded with silver rupees, and each camel carrying 480 pounds weight of silver; 100 camels loaded with gold coins, each carrying the same weight; 150 camels loaded with nets used in hunting tigers.'

Tame Tenements of Lahore

The arrival in Lahore in February 1860 produced Charlotte's best work.

> Saturday Feb 11: This public entry into Lahore has been the thoughts & plans of all the authorities here for weeks past. Charles left all to their disposal and amiably acquiesced in their arrangements. They were cruel as to length. We were taken on an enormous round along a new road barely smoothed out of the ploughed fields. The concourse of sardars was to be so great that I have thought it best to keep out of the way, and to trot in first in the open carriage with Lady Campbell & Captain Baring. Think they made Charles (Canning) ride 8 miles at foot's pace!

Punjab, run by Lieutenant Governor Sir Robert Montgomery, had been tame during the mutiny of 1857, despite a fraught recent past between the ruling Sikhs and the Company Raj. The soldiers and aristocrats, who could have posed a threat to the stability of the British state in Punjab, after change of policy from Calcutta, had become saviours of the colonial state. Recognizing this pivotal role of Punjab during the war of 1857, Lord Canning remarked that Punjab, 'from being a weakness, had become a source of strength for the British empire'.

Lady Canning's first impression of Lahore was:

> The town is far beyond my expectations. The old walls are like Delhi and the buildings within more raised and various; and I passed some very beautiful trees which are so scarce here. Then we came to Anarkullee, the civil station & after losing ourselves among good roads & bad, meandering for an hour, and being sent wrong deliberately and clearing the camp travelers who saw me after my wrong example, at last we hit upon the rear of our camp street and got in! [Only F.S. Aijazuddin could have deciphered her hieroglyphic handwriting which he gives a sampling of in the book.]

Running into Ranjit Singh

Her visit—on an elephant—to the tomb of Ranjit Singh produced this rare comment:

> Runjeet Singh's tomb and the little knobs round it representing the 11 wives burnt with him was all lighted up and made an excuse for our dismounting. From there we drove safely home. A poor Colonel, swept off his runaway elephant by a branch, was still in bed 2 days after. The good old Sir Robert Montgomery was made very unhappy and no wonder. It was all very sad.

She felt better after visiting a church in the Mianmir cantonment five miles away:

> I never saw a better finished church. Everyone has elephant adventures to tell. Sardars have come from every part of the Punjaub and they must all be received at once.

This detail must have resonated with author F.S. Aijazuddin since his ancestor, Fakir Nuruddin, was the governor of Lahore under the great Sikh ruler Ranjit Singh (who reigned 1792–1839). Nuruddin was the youngest of three brothers associated with the Sikh darbar as senior courtiers, proud to proclaim themselves 'fakir' out of pious humility, as noted in Aijazuddin's *The Resourceful Fakirs*.

On Shalimar Gardens, Lady Canning writes:

> Sir Montgomery was anxious to show me the famous Shalimar Gardens himself. It is a dusty drive by the straight road but not more than 2 miles. The gardens date from Shah Jahan's time and the same family have been gardeners in charge of it for eight generations. They brought us the usual gifts of fruit—all the fountains were playing. It is a grove of mango and orange trees with flowers here and there and long canals full of jets of water. A large square tank surrounded by a terrace and 4 or 5 summer houses. It must be much enjoyable in hot weather. All the fine carved marbles went to the Amritsar temple and Tank. (The last comment refers to Ranjit Singh's policy of embellishing the great Sikh temple of Amritsar with rare items from Lahore.)

About Anarkali, she says:

> The civil station called Anarkullee lies at about halfway and we encamped beyond. These long dull drives are very tiresome. The country is flat except where there are brick kiln mounds,

and no good trees except near the walls. Gardens are good where the ground is well watered, but generally all the only green is young wheat—otherwise dry plains, ravines and the road bordered with young shabby trees. I had to hurry over my difficult sketch to return for an early dinner and at dark we went off to the illuminated gardens—nearly as far as our last encampment. This time no elephants were wanted. All the people walked about or sat in open garden houses. The men are a curious sight not altogether delightful. The city reminded me of Egypt for there are some date palms of great beauty with the contrast of vivid green and the parched soil. I went into the Anarkullee tomb of some old Mussulman and turned to common use by the Sikhs.

Pindi Prevails

On 19 February 1860, Lord Canning decided to march in the direction of Peshawar, which meant visiting Rawalpindi on the way:

> We had 274 miles to go. The first day was 73 miles and we were [on the road] from 6 in the morning to 12 at night getting through it. It was very tedious and the road decidedly not pucka. We have taken leave of most of our escort – only the 7th Hussars (attacking horse regiment) go on with the camp. The 93 Highlanders were marching away to their intended destination Rawalpindee which they take 17 days to reach and we take 3 days with our camels.

At Jhelum, she noted the mound representing the tomb of Alexander's famous horse Bucephalus—today divided into the two towns of Buke and Phalia—as the river passed through the old city, bisecting it:

> We crossed the Jhelum at Jhelum and saw the raised mound said to be the tomb of Bucephalus (the Jhelum is the Hydaspes of

> Alexander)—after crossing the Jhelum the country changes—the view of the snowy range lad been more and more grand every mile. The great mountains of Cashmere and the passes into the valley of Cashmere can be plainly seen but here new ranges appear. The Salt Range from whence the rock salt is brought is in that westerly direction . . . one of the camels of the carriage suddenly broke its leg without even falling. The poor beast had to be left and they settled it was more merciful to shoot it.

Rawalpindi immediately stole her heart in contrast to Lahore—'a very high plain with beautiful mountains only a mile off it is one of the most healthy places in India'. There she saw the Pathans and was clearly impressed:

> I am quite convinced the Pathans or Afghans are the lost tribes. They are the handsomest people I have ever seen—more handsome than Sikhs—exactly like Raphael's Jews, very dark but with model faces and very fine figures. All along the road we have seen them, for these people in the upper half of the Punjaub are Mohametan.

She noted that they called themselves 'children of Israel, dividing lands by lot, managing brothers' wives, taking Jewish names', etc. But she notes the opposing theory too:

> Against this theory there is only the absence of all trace of the Hebrew language – the Pushtoo which they talk is peculiar to themselves and not known elsewhere. Colonel Lumsden who was raised here and knows more about the Afghans than anyone can tell me all I like to ask.

The Jolt in Jalandhar and Kindness of Kartarpur

The Cannings wandered into Jalandhar too, where a cantonment was to be established later, but Lady Canning thought it 'the most hopelessly dull place I have seen'. This established her inclination to feel better as she travelled westwards, most probably as the ethnic map changed in that direction. She was soon to be pulled out of the low impression of Jalandhar as the caravan hit Kartarpur near Sialkot:

> We marched 13 miles to Khurtarpore [Kartarpur]. In the last mile we saw about 6 or 8 very gaily dressed natives riding by in a carriage headed by a very old man on a white horse with the most enormous mane I ever saw. He cantered along quite at his ease dressed in a flowing white and silver robe. He dismounted with his followers & was brought up and presented by the district officer when we arrived. He proved to be the Sikh 'Gooroo'—the head of the Seik religious sect.
>
> All Seik priests are called Gooroos. This man is representative of the family of the founder of the Seik religion rather than a priest himself. Do not think he has any religious office but he has one of the original copies of the Holy book, The GRUNT!! [the Granth Sahib] in his house. He met all the Governors General who had been to see his house & he hoped the present GG would also honour him. So we settled to go there.

High in the Howdah

The cover illustration of the book is a painting depicting Lady Canning sitting atop an elephant, sketching her latest landscape. The 274 miles she travelled from Lahore to Peshawar, she was riding the big elephant at her disposal; or the camel when she had to be in a carriage. For some reason, the horse was not a part of the civilian caravan on the road. The camels were used to pull a 'buggee' in which she was seated through terrain that was less uneven.

On the way, tributes were received as the local grandees called to assert their loyalty. Lady Canning wrote to the Queen:

> When the Maharaja of Cashmere met us at Sealkote, he presented Your Majesty's tribute shawl at his durbar. They are now on their way to England. They are of extraordinary fineness, quite unlike anything made for anyone else. I think the two long white shawls with a quite narrow and irregular borders made in the old fashioned style will please Your Majesty from their extreme lightness and fine texture.

Living in Calcutta, the capital, was not easy given the climate of Bengal. She kept thinking of going to Darjeeling in the northern hills. After she finally managed to dump the hot city, she told Queen Victoria:

> I am about to make another little tour to the hills and to see Darjeeling which ought to be the Sanatorium of Calcutta as it is but 350 miles off—but it is still a tedious journey after crossing the Ganges and above 200 miles of railway there is still at least 3 nights travelling in the most disagreeable of conveyances—a palanquin!

Last Post of Loneliness

Darjeeling was to be the last region she visited, but there was an intimation of the finality in the way she felt as she left Calcutta in November 1861. The official who accompanied her on the way recalled:

> She talked constantly of England, of a house which the Queen had kindly placed at her disposal, and of interesting things she had collected to take home, and she invited us to visit her and see them. On reaching the plains, ignorant of the risk she ran, as the ground was not yet thoroughly dry, she ordered the palanquin to be set down in the fog, while she took one last sketch of the distant mountains.

It is likely that Lady Charlotte Canning was aware of her deteriorating health upon her return to Calcutta. A doctor checked her out and her condition appeared to be stable, but then suddenly it took a turn for the worse. Lord Canning remained by her bedside, 'aware that she was slipping away'. She died on 22 November 1861. Lord Canning described her burial at Barrackpore within hours of her death, admitting that in Calcutta, 'there is no burial place for the Governor-General or his Family, and the Cemeteries at Calcutta are odious in many ways'. Barrackpore was 15 miles from Calcutta, 'a beautiful spot looking upon that reach of the grand river which she was so fond of drawing—shaded from the glare of the sun by high trees, and amongst the bright shrubs and flowers in which she had so much pleasure.'

On his departure from India after being replaced by Lord Elgin, Lord Canning looked like a defeated man to Sir Richard Temple:

> Canning looked pale, wan, toil-worn and grief-stricken; the brow and forehead had, indeed, their inseparable dignity; but the complexion had become sallow, losing those hues which so often lighted up his aspect on occasions of state ceremony.

If Charlotte was looking down on the man she had failed to relate with, she must have been generous:

> The legacy left by Lord Canning is well-known: his temperate handling of the 1857 crisis, his abolition of the dreaded doctrine of lapse by which rulers forfeited their states if they died childless, his palliative Durbars across the country, his defense of income tax and tobacco tax, the encouragement of tea plantations in the hills, his selection of competent subordinates, and above all his imprint as the first Viceroy of a substantially expanded British India.

The 'temperate handling' bit should be tempered with the observation that British officers lost in the Mutiny numbered 2392, while 10 million Indians were killed over ten years, beginning in 1857.

Her verdict on her paintings belied the confidence she lacked in her own abilities:

> I think my drawings are ugly, but I daresay you will think they give an idea of this strange and grand country, and I shall be glad to possess them. I somehow never did exactly what others admire most; one always sees something at an inconvenient moment, and hopes the halting-place will do as well. The rough places in the beds of rivers, amongst rocks and trees, with enormous mountains and precipices, would make the best pictures; but a ten-minute's sketch of such things, which all artists would give a fortnight to do, is useless. And then one may see fifty such scenes in a day's march, and there is no particular reason for stopping at one more than another, so they do not get done.

24

Romila Thapar Answers

(Romila Thapar is an Indian historian whose principal area of study is ancient India. She is the author of several books, including the popular volume *A History of India*. She is also professor emerita at Jawaharlal Nehru University in New Delhi.

Most recently, Thapar is the author of *The Past as Present: Forging Contemporary Identities through History*. She declined the Padma Bhushan, India's third-highest civilian award, in 2005 and was the co-winner, in 2008, of the Kluge Prize for the Study of Humanity. She spoke at the Lahore Literary Festival 2018.)

This chapter presents excerpts from an interview with her.

Napoleon said history is the version of past events that people have decided to agree upon. Does one have to agree with the narrative or the interpretation of it?

No doubt Napoleon had good reason to think, or even to fear, that history is the version of the past that people have decided to agree upon. Today, such a statement would be unacceptable to historians as much has happened in the discipline of history during the last two hundred years. The historian is a narrator, but implicit in the narrative is the interpretation of the data. The viability of both is dependent on three steps in the process of writing history. Information on a subject is collected from as many sources that can provide it, and the reliability of this information has to be checked. This is essential or else all kinds of fantasies can be passed off as data. It is then analysed through the answers that a historian gives to a range of questions that are asked. This shades into the third step, which is interpreting the data. Needless to say, the third step implies that whatever generalizations are made should be based on reasonable and logical argument. Examining the cause of an action is the basis of historical analysis and understanding.

Because history is no longer only a narrative of events but requires an interpretation of these, there can be differences of interpretation. The reliability of the data can be questioned. Agreement or disagreement depends on the validity of the arguments. Interpretations do vary and can lead to debates. Provided the level of discussion remains intelligent, the debates can be stimulating. Historians do not claim to be giving definitive answers. They are sensitive to the possibility of new sources and fresh interpretations. It is often the general public that wants definitive answers. Since the past cannot be recreated and demonstrated, we can at best try and understand it, and agree on what might be the best understanding—but keeping in mind that even this could change with new evidence and new ways of examining it.

Why do nations need history? What happens to it when nationalism gets attached to it? In his book *Prejudice and Pride: School Histories of the Freedom Struggle in India and Pakistan* (2002), Krishna Kumar took on the subtle task of examining history textbooks in India and Pakistan. He writes: 'Both countries live with the assumption that they know each

other. The "other", after all, is a former aspect of the "self".' History is often a narration of wars. Can it be the 'cause' of war?

All societies have a sense of the past that they represent in various forms. Some have a historical consciousness that we more readily recognize, as it is a more ordered representation of the past as history. But this is different from the use that is made of the past at various times in the history of a community, a society, a country. Nationalist ideologies articulate the aspirations of particular groups in society. They then don't hesitate to use history. This is evident from the way the anti-colonial movement internalized history in the Indian subcontinent, and the way in which religious nationalisms also sprouted. The latter appropriated colonial readings of history to a substantial extent. More recently, historians have been looking at the ideologies of other groups lower down in society. In the twentieth century, the use of a so-called history by fundamentalist religious ideologies of all shades—Hindu, Muslim, Sikh, drawing from colonial interpretations, became quite clear. Insisting on their views can bring them into conflict with historians, as has happened, especially when they insist that there can be only one narrative, which they dictate and which cannot be questioned.

History in post-nationalist times becomes more problematic. For one, there is a difference between the history written by trained historians and that which is essentially ideological propaganda claiming to be history. There is also at this point the demand that a nation's history must include that of more than just the majority groups—however the majority is defined. Nationalism identifies particular groups as prominent but then in post-nationalist times other groups demand recognition and historical accommodation. History is no longer a 'soft' subject about which the opinion of every man and his wife holds true, nor for that matter is it the version of past events that people have decided to agree upon.

As for wars, they are now less central to historical discussion. Wars since early times have not been caused by history, or by

Cleopatra's nose. History discusses the causes of wars but in itself it is not the cause of war. In the recent history of South Asia, it is the political attitudes that are constructed through the way in which history is represented that have been used to fan hostilities. Colonial interpretations deliberately fuelled Hindu–Muslim antagonism, but in recent times historians have questioned these. A discussion on this subject goes into the causes of conflict, where it existed and why. Historians today hesitate to accept the descriptive labels, bracketing large communities said to be thinking and acting conjointly in a uniform way.

There was a time when historians were restricted to physical boundaries. Today they reside abroad in universities where they have tenure. Has that made a difference to history-writing? Does the presumed 'audience' make a difference to history-writing?

Normally there should not be much difference among historians working in their home country or those working in universities abroad. The sources to be consulted are the same. Some are more easily accessible in the home country and others in libraries abroad. The big problem in our countries is getting the up-to-date publications published abroad as they are prohibitively expensive; and also because not all those heading research institutions realize how crucially quality research is dependent on the excellence of libraries. There also has to be an intellectual ambience of asking questions of authorized knowledge for there to be good history-writing. In our countries we can be heavily abused if we question conservative opinion or the propagandist versions of history that come from fundamentalist ideologies. It takes more than normal courage to assert intellectual freedom.

Obviously, not every university in our countries is going to produce a state-of-the-art historian, but a critical mass is what is required to bring in change. The brighter students go in for studies that are glamorous and well-paid, which is fair enough.

We shall have to convince them that the more rooted disciplines have a value of a different kind and are equally necessary. As for the 'presumed' audience, it is primarily an academic audience of one's peers in the field, and of students hopefully with new ideas. Our societies lack the 'middleman', the person who understands the ideas being discussed at the research level and knows how to make them intelligently popular. As far as the public is concerned, there is still too great a reliance on hearsay and gossip rather than on serious reading.

As far as general audiences go, societies abroad are not too interested in the history of South Asia—unless one is addressing a population of non-resident Indians and Pakistanis. The ideas that many in such groups have about their history are frequently dated and often extremely conservative and virtually fundamentalist. Their problems of living in an alien culture lead to their using the past as an agency of self-confidence and to endorse their earlier identity. These ideologies are not absent in the homeland, but they do have to contend with larger numbers of those who hold secular positions. In the homeland, the ripples of a rigorous history go out much further.

India and Pakistan are politically so far apart and culturally and geographically so close that there is no room for an epistemic space between them. Yet there is a deep 'enmity of the civilizationally related' between them, which Freud put so neatly in his phrase 'the narcissism of small differences', and their diplomats best represent it. How can the historian help?

The historian can help. If history is important to the creation of a nation, as it seems to have been, then implicit in this idea is that it can give some insights into the kind of society that the nation may want. History is after all not just a narrative. In its interpretative aspects it can provide a commentary on past societies together with critiquing or applauding some of their facets. It can draw attention to comparable situations in other countries and what that resulted in. But historians cannot force citizens and their representatives to choose a form of society, nor do they control social change. I don't believe that there is necessarily a deep enmity of the civilizationally related, nor is there alternatively, an automatically deep friendship. Relationships are determined by circumstances, but at the same time need to be insightfully understood, nurtured and cultivated. History can provide some of that insight by watching closely what the premises of the relationship are and how they change. And, as in all relationships, there is the narcissism of small differences. The historian can help to keep the difference small and to be watchful of a difference becoming threatening. This is done not through propagating a particular ideology but by showing where society is at, and what its destination could be.

25

NAB: The Wrong Road Taken

Fake News One: After hearing that Amazon, which is valued at nearly $800 billion, had paid nothing in federal taxes even though it had almost doubled its North America profits from $5.6 billion to $11.2 billion between 2017 and 2018, the US National Accountability Bureau (NAB) arrested Amazon founder Jeff Bezos and denied him bail until such time as he proved himself 'not guilty', also disallowing his family and lawyers to meet him in prison.

Fake News Two: British–Pakistani businessman Zameer Choudrey, CEO of Bestway Group, which is the tenth largest privately owned business in the UK, was appointed Commander of the Order of the British Empire (CBE) in 2016 for creating jobs and running a big charity. After rumours of fraud, however, the UK National Accountability Bureau arrested him and put him in prison on the pain of proving himself 'not guilty'. The Queen took away his knighthood and recommended Class C prison for him until he submitted to a plea bargain, which is an admission of guilt and a deemed conviction.

A Deeply Troubled Economy

In 2019, Pakistan was deep in economic trouble. It had to submit to doctor's orders from the IMF to cure its financial maladies, to collect taxes which it didn't because of the corruption it couldn't uproot, to make itself attractive to foreign investors which it didn't because of war and the rip-offs the state subjected investors to, and to cut the red tape to make it easy for investors to work in an environment friendly to economic activity of any sort.

The problem of corruption has hounded Pakistan for a long time. But it couldn't be more perilous than what the investors faced while trying to undertake permissible risk, borrow money and set up industries needed to create employment, thus enabling the state to collect from a larger tax-paying base. But Pakistan read the signs. It created the Ehtesab Bureau in 1997 that morphed into a weaponized National Accountability Bureau (NAB) in 1999, armed with powers that militated against democratic governance and economic administration, exempting it from the requirement of proving the accused guilty by shifting this legal onus on to them.

The NAB is hardly exempt from the moral turpitude rampant in society. Manned by minimally presentable officers, it seems unaware of the economic damage its pursuit of businessmen is doing to the economy. It is focused on the satisfaction of an uninformed public passion instead of responding to the subtle requirements of internal and external trust on which today's capitalism depends.

Hounding the 'Trouble-Takers'

Abdul Hafeez Shaikh, economic adviser to the prime minister, objected to what the NAB was doing to investors, saying they should not be hounded by the process of 'accountability' unleashed in Pakistan. No distinction was made between the holders of public office under scrutiny, doing their usual hanky-panky, and men of business who had to suffer red tape and consequent extortion while putting up new projects.

Shaikh must have taken account of the recent observation made by the chief justice of Pakistan that accountability was slipping into 'political engineering' rather than providing justice.[1] The ruling PTI is also rumoured to be working on an amendment of the NAB law to 'protect businessmen'. The NAB chairman has announced that he will not go after businessmen on charges of tax evasion.

Nabbing the Entrepreneur

And yet, the most outrageous example of Pakistan's economic myopia was the arrest on 4 September 2019 of Iqbal Z. Ahmed of the Associated Group, which was noted with concern in the national media. In 2016, Ahmed's company had set up Pakistan's second Liquefied National Gas (LNG) import terminal with foreign expertise and investment, substantially from Norway and China, totalling $500 million. According to the Ministry of Energy, the project yields annual foreign exchange savings of an estimated $1.5 billion through fuel substitution in electricity production.

People who continued to read alarmist reports about how big business was ripping off the nation hardly noticed that Pakistan had been trying to set up an LNG terminal for decades without much success. The delay could have been caused by politicians wanting their 'pound of flesh' through graft; but Ahmed managed to set up a terminal, thus opening the door finally for global investment into Pakistan. He was arrested outside his office half an hour before his scheduled meeting with foreign investors to set up another LNG import terminal for gas-starved Pakistan.

The NAB picked up Ahmed for money-laundering of Rs 112 billion[2] and, as usual, was not required to prove anything before it arrested him and treated him like a convict. His media trial continued, and his family has refrained from issuing any public statement. The campaign against him is ugly to anyone looking objectively at Pakistan's process of justice.

Apart from the normal risk-taking, for which capitalism rewards its entrepreneurs, Ahmed, in his mid-seventies with four stents in his heart, has had to face persecution to satisfy the partisan lust of the rulers masquerading as champions of 'accountability'. No one can visit him in his NAB prison, not even his lawyers, and the NAB is taking its time framing the money-laundering charges derived from reading his company's bank statements.

NAB: The Sinister Side

There is no bail provision in case the NAB is revealed to be mishandling the case; and the infamous 'remand' (keeping someone in jail without giving reason) can go on for ninety days, and may be 'renewable'. Ahmed can be incarcerated for years and still come out un-sentenced—if he lives—without the NAB being answerable for it. In Pakistan, a judge can rescind international contracts for which the state ends up coughing up billions of dollars as penalty, without the judge being lynched for it.

The common enthusiast who wants to 'uproot corruption' in quick time appears satisfied by the 'emergency' measures taken by the NAB. If you plead that the methodology of uprooting corruption without due process looks ugly, he in turn pleads that the 'correct' process of proving the wrongdoer guilty has been forever damaged by corruption; and therefore leapfrogging due process was the only course left.

But deep down there is an almost medieval resistance to accepting the demands of modern economy and the place in it of the risk-taking business community. There is a deep-seated resistance to looking objectively at what the state has done to projects in the public sector now withering on the political vine, with Prime Minister Imran Khan unwilling to privatize them.

A Murky Past[3]

Investigation into the past of accountability in Pakistan shows that on 14 January 1949, the then premier Liaquat Ali Khan had promulgated the Public Representative Office Disqualification Act (PRODA) to check graft and misuse of authority.

The Act was passed in 1949, but with effect from 14 August 1947, and politicians could be disqualified for as long as ten years. His political foes had slated PRODA saying it was aimed at protecting the corruption of the ruling Muslim League and targeting whistle-blowers in the opposite camps. Proceedings under PRODA were also initiated against then Punjab chief minister Nawab Iftikhar Hussain Mamdot and his lawyer and the future Pakistani Premier Hussain Shaheed Suhrawardy.

In 1949, the Mamdot government in Punjab was sent packing and administration of the province was taken over by the then West Punjab Governor Sir Francis Mudie. Critics argue that Governor General Khawaja Nazimuddin had shown Mamdot the door at the behest of Liaquat Ali Khan.

Liaquat Ali Khan had also initiated legal proceedings against the then chief minister of Sindh Pir Ilahi Bukhsh and got him disqualified for six years on charges of corruption, resulting in the appointment of Yusuf Haroon as the new constitutional head of Sindh province. Similarly, East Pakistan's chief minister, Abul Kasem Fazlul Huq (A.K. Fazlul Haq), was dismissed in May 1954 by Governor General Ghulam Muhammad. In 1954, Liaquat Ali Khan's Public Representative Offices Disqualification Act was denounced as incompatible with democratic politics and was hence repealed, but not before it had claimed a few well-known victims.

In March 1959, General Ayub Khan replaced PRODA with a new law called the Public Offices Disqualification Order (PODO) and later substituted it with the Elective Bodies Disqualification Order (EBDO). Under this law, not fewer than seventy-five senior politicians were charged tainted with corruption charges.

These formidable politicians included the likes of Qayyum Khan and Hussain Shaheed Suhrawardy. They were disqualified from contesting elections till the end of 1966. However, they were never tried and convicted.

The Case of Iqbal Z Ahmed[4]

A press release in *Profit* magazine by *Pakistan Today* on 7 November 2019, discussed the following case pertaining to a Pakistani entrepreneur:

> A senior member of the Associated Group Limited has shown extreme concern that it has been over 60 days since Mr Iqbal Z. Ahmed, Chairman of Associated Group (AG), was arrested by NAB in a dramatic manner on September 4. No formal charges framed against him to date and Mr Ahmed's liberty has not been restored. After 47 days in NAB custody, Mr Ahmed was transferred to judicial custody on October 21, 2019.

The Sindh High Court, through its order of 15 October 2019, directed the NAB to provide a questionnaire to him, which till the filing of this report had not been furnished to the accused.

Furthermore, the NAB chairman recently revealed that 'no concrete evidence has emerged' in the inquiry against Mr Ahmed. In fact, it appears that the NAB opted to arrest Mr Ahmed without any cogent evidence, while also being absolutely unclear about the precise nature of the allegations it seeks to level against him.

During the court proceedings on 2 November, the NAB investigation officer in the case submitted a progress report which 'contains several false statements', according to a legal counsel of Mr Ahmed, M.N. Beg.

The counsel also asserted that 'in the fifth NAB progress report, the investigation officer has not been able to link Mr Ahmed to any specific money laundering charge', which was the purported grounds for arrest.

A heart and diabetes patient, Mr Ahmed is known for having demonstrated a risk-taking appetite for large-scale energy infrastructure projects in Pakistan with pioneering initiatives in LPG and LNG sectors. Jamshoro Joint Venture Limited (JJVL), which commenced operations in 2005, has saved 'an estimated US$727 million in foreign currency by replacement of LPG imports by local product,' according to a company handout. Operated and maintained by Exterran, an NYSE-listed company, the JJVL plant at present has a replacement value estimated at the $200 million.

Under a Supreme Court order in December 2018, Sui Southern Gas Company (SSGC) and JJVL work together to maximize value for SSGC pipelines by extracting the liquids so that pipelines are not choked and the extracted condensates form part of the value-chain in the country gas infrastructure. 'Having set-up a world-class LPG production company in one of the country's remotest parts, Deh Shah Bokhari, Sindh, has won JJVL international recognition including by Platts Businessweek Awards for operational and industrial excellence in the energy sector,' an AG statement said.

'In the fifth progress report, all matters and affairs the investigation officer refers to are taken from the audited balance sheets of the Company and are fully justifiable,' AG commented.

'The transactions conducted from the official accounts of the companies were bona fide business transactions, inter alia pertaining to deposits of sale receipts, disbursement and repayment of loans, interbank transfers and equity inflows. The receipts and documents pertaining to all such transactions are available in the record of the companies,' the statement by AG further elaborated.

In a marked departure from the standard operating procedure of the NAB, wherein a questionnaire is issued, an inquiry is held, summons are sent and so on, in Mr Ahmed's case, none of the steps were taken, which is in contravention of the NAB's standard operating terms.

That a private businessman, who has been one of the country's highest taxpayers and has undertaken large domestic investments, including a recently-signed EPC contract with a Chinese state-company, Xinjian Petroleum and Engineering Company (XPE), of around US$100 million for setting up of a LNG terminal, be meted such treatment is a setback to the business sentiment in the country and particularly affects the already beleaguered LNG sector, which was till a year ago one of the most promising new sectors in Pakistan for foreign investors.

It is worth noting that without involving any government guarantees for offtake or purchase of LNG, Mr Ahmed signed with a Chinese government-owned company a contract which allows credit to Pakistan without any financial instrument from either the government or any banks.

State Suicide through NAB

After Ahmed was dramatically and suddenly arrested by the NAB, *Express Tribune* noted:

> Two top global LNG suppliers have stayed away from participating in the bid to procure 200 million cubic feet per day, following a case taken by NAB on LNG terminal and imports from Qatar.[5]

Ahmed had been appearing at international energy conferences abroad making the case for the economy, talking up the investment climate and emphasizing that Pakistan is open for business. The foreign investors who were left waiting in his conference room in Lahore on the day of his arrest got to see just how inclement the business environment really is.

The newspaper *Dawn*, on 23 October 2019, reported from the NAB that the case against Ahmed was deliberated upon. Both cases are still under investigation.

The sources said that the NAB chairman also held a separate meeting with experts about the case since, so far, no 'concrete evidence' has emerged against Ahmed.[6]

A Broken Bureaucracy

The NAB continues cannibalizing Pakistan's politics. It is empowered to arrest its victims on suspicion and is not required to prove the arrested guilty; those who get picked up and rot in NAB's prisons, and don't have bail, have to prove themselves not guilty.[7] The NAB is meant to hound the Opposition politicians and make them disappear as democracy slinks away from the country with its tail between its legs. It also targets businessmen suspected of siding with politicians on the wrong side of the deep state. Shahid Khaqan Abbasi, the twenty-first prime minister of Pakistan, from August 2017 to May 2018, was imprisoned for years while the NAB looked around for something to pin on him.[8]

The businessmen saw the end coming under the NAB, which had no clue about how the economy runs these days, least of all being cognizant of the fact that fifty-seven billionaires in India not only ran 70 per cent of the Indian economy[9] but were also effecting the kind of transfer of technology that Pakistan was unable to manage because its premier engineering university in Lahore was, till not long ago, being run by LeT chief Hafiz Saeed. (He was teaching Islam in a technology university.) In October 2019, Pakistan's harassed businessmen had a meeting with the army chief;[10] and the NAB thereafter publicly excused itself from subjecting them to its brand of accountability, which meant billionaires rotting in its smelly jails.

Forces of Indecision

The bureaucracy wanted to protest too, more suitably to the army chief, because the NAB was nabbing top civil servants in charge of taking big decisions, and keeping them in the doghouse till they pleaded guilty. At the National Institute of Public Policy, Lahore, two civil servants, Shahid Rahim Sheikh and Saifullah Khalid, prepared a study explaining why civil servants had stopped helping the elected government in the implementation of public projects. Titled 'Bureaucratic Decision-making amid Multiple Accountability', the study begins with:[11]

> Turbulent political developments also destabilized the Principal–Agent relationship between politicians and civil servants. This relationship had taken shape over a decade of democratic dispensation (2008–18). In the whirlwind of political upheaval, the civil servants, it appears, also became increasingly insecure, defensive and indecisive. A very strong feeling receiving [of] an unfair deal took root among civil servants. They feel that while political bosses pressurize them into taking difficult and controversial decisions—often informed by political–economy considerations—when it comes to accountability, and when questions are raised regarding the propriety of those decisions, the political bosses disown them, leaving the civil servants high and dry and at the mercy of a scathing accountability process.[12]

Accountability Assault on Integrity

The study took account of the number of anti-corruption hounds the civil servants have to fend against while helping politicians with 'big decisions'. Bureaucrats are answerable to parliamentary scrutiny, and the propriety of their actions and expenditures is subject to statutory audit by the auditor general's office. They also have to defend themselves before the Public Accounts Committees of the National and Provincial Assemblies. With so much punitive scrutiny in operation, is Pakistan doing well economically? Well, the verdict is here: Pakistan ranked 136 out of 190 countries on the Ease of Doing Business Index in 2018. In 2019, it stood at 108.[13]

That, of course, is normal, but it is not the end of the matter. The bureaucrats have to face grilling by additional accountability organizations like 'the National Accountability Bureau (NAB), the Federal Investigation Agency (FIA), and the Provincial Anti-corruption Establishments (PACEs)'. These outfits are used by the politicians in power to punish their opponents and it hardly matters if these organizations are competent and honest or not. 'The ineptitude and incompetence of the staff and agents of the accountability organisations compound the gravity of the difficulty suffered by civil servants', notes the study.[14]

The authors posit that the bureaucratic indecision in Pakistan is due to the impact of four clearly identifiable factors:

1) Multiple accountability organizations,
2) Internal conduct and disciplinary procedures and media trial,
3) Public interest litigation by superior judiciary,
4) Pressures of political economy,
5) The diminishing social respect that bureaucracy has come to receive in society.

A Draconian Birth

It all began with a draconian measure. Political accountability (Ehtesab Commission) was thought up by the caretaker government set up by former President Farooq Leghari in November 1996 after he dismissed the then prime minister, Benazir Bhutto, from office. Revenge was uppermost in the mind of the now deceased Leghari. The draconian NAB earned notoriety when Prime Minister Sharif under his henchman, Saifur Rahman, allegedly used it to chastise his political opponents.[15] Sharif was serving a long sentence for corruption and was ailing. He was eventually allowed to head to London, where he still remains in exile, for medical treatment.

General Musharraf seized power in 1999 and immediately beefed up the NAB to punish his political opponents in the two major parties, PPP and PMLN, reducing accountability to obscenely manifest revenge without transparency and accepted norms of justice. Now, the NAB is taking orders from two quarters to further doom its identity as an instrument of justice. One, of course, is the government of Imran Khan. The other remains unnamed.

Will the NAB Soften in the Face of Law?

In the *News International* of 15 December 2019, Ansar Abbasi wrote that the NAB had begun putting off the judiciary:

> Politicians in particular have started getting relief from the superior judiciary after the courts have started seriously questioning the NAB's disputed use of its authority amid hopes that the senior bureaucrats—both serving and retired—languishing in jails for months and years without any conviction will also start getting justice.[16]

The targeted Opposition politicians began with 'concessions' such as Nawaz Sharif getting bail in two convictions and Shahbaz Sharif, arrested by the NAB in two corruption cases, getting bailed out in both the cases. They were, however, followed by the PPP's Asif Zardari who was let off his from long arrest and allowed to seek cure for his dangerously shrinking brain in Karachi—he had in the past spent fourteen years in a NAB jail without being convicted. The world must have been taken aback by the trespasses of the NAB, but for some strange reason Pakistan, brainwashed by lethal political rhetoric, was not.

The report, however, pointed to the bureaucrats who continued to languish in prisons 'in the same cases'. (Pakistan doesn't stop wondering why its bureaucracy remains supine in the face of crises requiring pre-emptive action.) The report pointed out that, unlike politicians, 'the bureaucrats do not have the elaborate social and political support system' needed for these 'concessions' from a cruel and unjust system:

> It is seen that in many cases like Ashiana, where courts demolished the main cases, the NAB has roped in these officers in assets-beyond-means cases, which is a very vague charge and wherein [the] NAB allegedly counts the entire extended family assets as accused officers 'benami' assets, leaving them to prove it otherwise in protracted trial process.[17]

The NAB accused are denied the statutory bail as directed in the Criminal Procedure Code (CrPC). The CrPC makes it mandatory for courts to grant bail to the accused if their trial is not completed within one year:

> The draconian NAB law ousts this concession available to all other accused in criminal cases. However, some recent decisions of the superior judiciary have brought great hopes for the bureaucrats languishing in jails without any conviction.[18]

One such judgment was handed down by the Islamabad High Court while accepting former managing director of Pakistan State Oil's bail application in the LNG terminal case. In the same case, the NAB prosecutor, while referring to the draconian NAB law, argued that the bail application of the former MD be rejected because the NAB law does not contain the bail provision. To this, the court said:

> The powers to arrest provided under the Ordinance of 1999 are not unfettered nor can they be exercised mechanically and in an arbitrary manner. The ouster of the bail provisions in the ordinance does not deprive the petitioner or any other accused of the constitutionally guaranteed fundamental rights such an inviolability of dignity and freedom of movement provided under Articles 14 and 15 of the Constitution, respectively.[19]

The court also noted that it was implicit in Article 14 that an arbitrary arrest, depending on the facts and circumstances of the case, could amount to torturing an accused for 'extraneous reasons.

ARY News, on 18 December 2019, noted that 'Pakistan People's Party's leader Syed Khursheed Shah [was] released from NAB detention on Wednesday after accountability court granted him bail yesterday in an assets-beyond-means reference. The National Accountability Bureau has challenged the decision of his release in Sindh High Court.'[20]

The NAB seems to be getting divided from the inside in the face of public criticism. Khursheed Shah, in prison since July on 'multiple corruption cases', was allowed out of prison, compelling the NAB boss in Islamabad to go appeal against the release. In 2012, an accountability court had directed the NAB to file a reference against him on a complaint pertaining to 'alleged accumulation of illegitimate assets'. In 2013, the NAB had reopened two corruption cases against Shah under the directives of the Lahore High Court.

Conclusion

Ahmed Bilal Mehboob of Pakistan Institute of Legislative Development wrote in *Dawn* on 10 November 2019:

> Amid the current political turmoil, accountability and the National Accountability Bureau (NAB) figure most prominently. On the one side is a passionate section of the population eager to punish and even 'hang' anyone who, in their opinion, has plundered national wealth. NAB is the prime instrument through which they wish to realise their wishes, as the institution has been at the centre stage of this accountability drive during the past few years. On the other hand is a sizeable and growing lobby which believes the accountability process is not just and even-handed and is turning into a tool of political victimisation.[21]

The then chief justice of Pakistan, Asif Saeed Khosa, added what could be called his verdict on NAB:

> We . . . feel that the growing perception that the process of accountability being pursued in the country at present is lopsided and is a part of political engineering, is a dangerous perception and some remedial steps need to be taken urgently so that the process does not lose credibility. The recovery of stolen wealth of the citizenry is a noble cause and it must be legitimately and legally pursued where it is due, but if in the process the constitutional and legal morality of society and the recognised standards of fairness and impartiality are compromised then retrieval of the lost constitutional and legal morality may pose an even bigger challenge to the society at large in the days to come.[22]

A retired NAB officer said while talking to the *News International* that the bureau took every action strictly according to law. He said the NAB has no personal enmity with anyone, there is no aggression and everything happens according to the rules. The retired officer said all the officers in the NAB work honestly. He even said that a NAB officer can drag any matter if he indulges in personal vendetta, but nothing of this sort happens in the bureau.[23]

According to the officer, priority is being given to recover the looted money after logical conclusion of mega-corruption cases. He said excellent results of the NAB's awareness, prevention and enforcement policy have already started pouring in as prestigious national and international institutions, including Transparency International, Pildat, Mashal Pakistan and International Economic Forum lauded NAB's corruption elimination efforts. According to Gillani and Gallup Survey, he said, 59 per cent people expressed confidence in the NAB as the bureau believes in ensuring self-accountability, transparency and the implementation of law.[24]

26

Was Jinnah Shia or Sunni, or Descended from Ram?

The founder of Pakistan was named Mamedali Jeenabhai Poonja, which he changed to Muhammad Ali Jinnah, the last name referring to the Prophet's (Peace Be upon Him) sacred 'winged' horse appearing proper in vowel-less Urdu. When he was asked to change it to 'Janah' in English, he didn't agree. 'Jeena' in his name referred to the founder of the Jain religion, Mahavira, who was also called Jeena the Victor. Jinnah's family belonged to the Lohana Muslims of Gujarat (India), once dominated by Jainism, and Loh referred to the younger son of Ram, after whom Lahore was named in antiquity. The Lohana community claimed descent from Loh, although some thought that the name referred to 'iron' and their ancient profession as ironmongers.

On 24 September 1948, after the demise of Quaid-e-Azam Muhammad Ali Jinnah, his sister Fatima Jinnah and the then prime minister of Pakistan, Liaquat Ali Khan, submitted a jointly signed petition to the Karachi High Court, describing Jinnah as 'Shia Khoja Mohamedan' and praying that his will may be disposed of under Shia inheritance law. On 6 February 1968, after Mohtarma Fatima Jinnah's demise the previous year, her sister Shirin Bai moved an application claiming Fatima Jinnah's property under the Shia inheritance law on the grounds that the deceased was a Shia.

Family Quarrel over Jinnah's Property

On 29 October 1970, one Hussain Ali Gangji Walji filed a suit at the high court against Shirin Bai, contesting her claim that Fatima Jinnah was a Shia. He sought to prove that Fatima Jinnah was in fact a Sunni, as was Jinnah, and that therefore Shirin Bai was entitled to only half the inheritance under Sunni law, the other half going to the agnate relations, that is, to the offspring of Fatima Jinnah's paternal uncle. Hussain Ali was the son of Gangji Walji, who was in turn the son of Walji Poonja, the paternal uncle of Jinnah and Fatima.

Hussain Ali deposed during the trial that he was himself an Ismaili Shia and not an Isna-Ashari Shia. This takes us back to the question of the adoption of Shia faith by the family of Muhammad Ali Jinnah. According to witness Syed Sharifuddin Pirzada, Jinnah broke away from the Ismaili faith in 1901 after his two sisters, Rehmat Bai and Maryam Bai, were married into Sunni Muslim families. It appears that this happened because the Ismaili community objected to these marriages. It also appears that the conversion to Isna-Ashari Shiism happened in Jinnah's immediate family, and not in the families of his two paternal uncles, Walji and Nathoo.

Ismailism to Shiism

Surprisingly, the case also revealed that Shirin Bai, Jinnah's other sister, too did not convert to Isna-Ashari Shiism but retained

Ismaili faith till Fatima died. It is possible that her husband Jafferbhoy was an Ismaili and therefore her conversion was not possible. She left Bombay after Fatima's death in 1967 and came to Karachi. She gave up her Indian nationality and also embraced Shiism in order to qualify for Fatima's inheritance under Shia law. It thus developed that out of Jinnah's immediate family only he himself and Fatima Jinnah had abandoned the Ismaili faith. In the years that followed, both carefully avoided a sectarian label. Both are on record as saying that they were neither Shia nor Sunni, but 'Mussalman'. The Quaid was at pains to gather the Muslims of India under the banner of a general Muslim faith and not under the divisive sectarian identity.

Liaquat Merchant: The Worthy Son

Out of Jinnah's four sisters, two were married into Sunni families, which should compel one to presume that their offsprings would be Sunni. But it did not happen like that. From the depositions contained in the legal record published by Liaquat H. Merchant in his book *Jinnah: A Judicial Verdict*[1], it is revealed that two granddaughters of Maryam Bai, who was married into a Sunni family, retained the Shia faith. Their names are Gulshan Bai and Zehra Bai, and it appears from the record that both were married to two brothers who were Shia. Merchant, appointed by the Sindh High Court as administrator of the estate of the Quaid-e-Azam, is a civil lawyer in Karachi. He is the grandson of Jinnah's sister Maryam Bai, the wife of Abedin Peerbhai who was Sunni by faith. His mother, Sher Bano, married to Habib Hoosain Merchant, was Maryam Bai's daughter.

The legal record is also silent on the question of Ahmed Ali, Jinnah's other brother. (Bundeh Ali had died early.) During the proceedings, it was not clarified whether Ahmed Ali was buried in a Sunni, Shia or an Ismaili graveyard in Bombay. According to Merchant, Ahmed Ali's daughter Fatima Goepfert is currently a resident of Switzerland. From her married name, Goepfert, one can presume that she had married a non-Muslim. Jinnah's own daughter, Dina Wadia, who lived in the United States, was also married to a non-Muslim.

The Shia Truth

The leading witnesses who appeared for Shirin Bai in 1968 were I.H. Ispahani, a family friend of Jinnah's and his honorary secretary in 1936, and Matloobul Hassan Syed, Jinnah's private secretary from 1940 to 1944. Ispahani revealed that Jinnah had himself told him in 1936 that he and his family had converted to Shiism after his return from England in 1894. He said that Jinnah had married Ruttie Bai according to the Shia ritual, during which she was represented by a Shia scholar of Bombay, and Jinnah was represented by his Shia friend Raja Sahib of Mehmudabad. He however conceded that Jinnah was opposed in the Bombay elections by a Shia Conference candidate. Ispahani was present when Fatima Jinnah died in 1967. He himself arranged the *ghusl* (full-body ritual purification) and *janaza* (Islamic funeral prayer) for her at Mohatta Palace according to the Shia ritual before handing over the body to the state. Her Sunni *namaz-e-janaza* (another term for the Islamic funeral prayer) was held later at Polo Ground, after which she was buried next to Jinnah at a spot chosen by Ispahani inside the mausoleum. Ritualistic Shia *talqin* (last advice to the deceased) was done after her dead body was lowered into the grave. (Jinnah had arranged for the talqin for Ruttie Bai too when she died in 1929).

Matloobul Hassan Syed deposed that he knew Fatima Jinnah to be a Shia. This became clear to him when he accompanied her to Mardan in the NWFP during her election campaign against General Ayub Khan. When the local Shia leaders told her that they had decided to vote for Ayub, she asked Syed to tell them that she could represent them better as she was a Shia. The court found Syed's testimony defective because Shirin Bai had stayed with him after her arrival in Karachi in 1968 and could have been persuaded by him to claim Fatima Jinnah's property under the Shia law. Syed had left his job with Jinnah when he started writing his biography in 1944. His book appeared in 1945 and is still rated as the best account of Jinnah's political career written by a Pakistani. He was away in the United Kingdom at the time of Partition. A court exhibit proved that he had married 'a rich Muslim Leaguer Khoja lady' in Bombay.

Witness Syed Anisul Husnain, a Shia scholar, deposed that he had arranged the ghusl of Jinnah on the instructions of Fatima. He led his namaz-e-janaza in a room of the governor general's House at which luminaries as Yusuf Haroon, Hashim Raza and Aftab Hatim Alvi were present, while Liaquat Ali Khan waited outside the room. After the Shia ritual, the body was handed over to the state and Maulana Shabbir Ahmad Usmani, an alim belonging to the Deoband school of thought, known for its anti-Shia belief, read his janaza according to the Sunni ritual at the ground where the mausoleum was later constructed. Other witnesses confirmed that after the demise of Fatima Jinnah, *alam* and *panja* (two Shia symbols) were discovered from her residence, Mohatta Palace.

The chief witness to appear for Hussain Ali in 1970 was Syed Sharifuddin Pirzada. He had been honorary secretary to Jinnah from 1941 to 1944. He deposed that Jinnah was avowedly non-sectarian and had kept away from Shia politics. He referred to documents which confirmed Jinnah's secular Muslim faith. It appears that Matloobul Hassan Syed and Syed Sharifuddin Pirzada were for some time simultaneously secretaries to Jinnah, one 'honorary' and the other 'private'. When Pirzada supported General Ayub Khan and declared his connection with Jinnah, Fatima Jinnah issued a statement contradicting that he was ever his secretary. Pirzada submitted a press clipping to the court which said that 'Mr Pirzada, the husband of a Bohra lady, had become secretary to the Quaid.'

Justice Abdul Qadir Shaikh delivered the first judgment on 24 February 1970, rejecting Fatima Jinnah's affidavit (co-signed by Liaquat Ali Khan) that Jinnah was a Shia. The honourable judge found that the secular Muslim faith of Jinnah made him neither Shia nor Sunni. He declined to follow the argument put forward by lawyers Liaquat H. Merchant and Aziz Munshi that the court ignore the Shia and Sunni family law and take recourse to Sura Al-Nisa of the Quran, which decreed that one-half of the property go to the descendants of Fatima Jinnah's paternal uncles. The judge contended that this argument would lead to the general renunciation of the Muslim family law and its precedents. The court maintained the succession certificate of Shirin Bai.

Shirin Bai Wins the Case

Justice Zafar Hussain Mirza delivered the second judgment on 23 December 1976, striking down the Walji petition and ruling in favour of Shirin Bai. One Jena Bai, wife of Jan Muhammad Nathoo, had also impleaded herself in the case, meaning that the descendants of the other paternal uncle of Fatima Jinnah, Nathoo Poonja, were included among the contestants of Shirin Bai's claim. Jan Muhammad Nathoo was the father of another Shirin Bai whose grandson, Sikandar Ali, was killed mysteriously in Karachi in police custody in 1998. After this, the Walji case went to the high court Bench presided over by Chief Justice Abdul Hayee Kureshi. On 23 December 1984, the court reversed the earlier judgment(s) and maintained that while the Quaid was definitely not a Shia, the issue of whether Fatima Jinnah was a Shia or not was also now open for further inquiry.

In 1965, Fatima Jinnah had moved from the Quaid's personal residence Flagstaff House (converted to a museum) to Mohatta Palace, an evacuee property which she had acquired in exchange for the Quaid's Bombay house. After her death, her only surviving sister, Shirin Bai, moved into Mohatta Palace. After her death in 1980, a trust created by her took over the property, but once again litigation ensued between the trust and the Waljis, and the palace became deserted and fell into disrepair. In 1993, Sindh governor Mehmood Haroon moved the high court to consider the sale of

Mohatta Palace to the Sindh government. The government paid Rs 61.8 million to the court and took over the property with the intention of converting it into a national monument. The money acquired through the sale was invested by the court and is still contested by the heirs. The federal government has contributed Rs 70 million to the reconstruction and conservation of the property which is being done by architect Habib Fida Ali.

Liaquat H. Merchant, himself a descendant of the Jinnah-Poonja clan, puts it succinctly in his introduction to the book:

> After the demise of Mohtarma Fatima Jinnah, the youngest sister of Quaid-e-Azam Mohamed Ali Jinnah, the question of inheritance surfaced and regretfully became a controversial issue. The entire family was in agreement as regards a settlement of the question of inheritance by mutual consent. Unfortunately, these efforts were pre-empted by the Quaid's only surviving sister, Mst Shirin Bai, who after the demise of Mohtarma Fatima Jinnah, had migrated from India to Pakistan.[2]

A family quarrel led to litigation and the Court was compelled to go into the matter of the sectarian beliefs of two important personages of Pakistan. From the legal record, it becomes quite clear that the court was inclined to repose more trust in the avowed non-sectarian public stance of Jinnah and his sister. Because of the Muslim law of succession and its either/or verdict, the sectarian question had to be considered. It is perhaps in order that the judicial verdict was finally inconclusive: Jinnah was not a Shia; he was also not a Sunni; he was simply a Muslim.

Epilogue

The Future of Follies

F.S. Aijazuddin wrote in *Dawn* on 10 September 2020:

> Pakistan is still a semi-state. It does not fulfil all the qualifying properties of a complete state. Certainly, it has a permanent population (give or take three million Afghan refugees). It has an effective government (albeit splintered into provincial satrapies). It has the sovereign capacity to enter into relations with other states, yet dodges the decisions of international courts. And it would have a 'defined territory' of undisputed borders, if only India and Afghanistan were not so intransigent.[1]

Needless to say, Pakistan continues to wonder what kind of state it wants to be. The founders, under the leadership of Muhammad Ali Jinnah, who himself was suspected of being a secular person, were not clear about this. He announced his 'dubious' motto—Unity, Faith, Discipline—soon after the formation of the state in 1947; but his Muslim League companions were not satisfied with what it meant. Where was Islam in it, the religion of the people who were to live in this new state? If faith was Islam, why was it placed second to unity? In the years that followed, after Jinnah's death, they tinkered with his motto, laying the foundation of self-doubt that continues to haunt the state even in 2020.

Nadeem F. Paracha wrote in *Dawn* on 8 October 2017:

> Zamir Niazi in *The Web of Censorship* quotes Hamid Jalal—a former civil servant and father of the acclaimed historian and author Ayesha Jalal—as saying: 'Jinnah's motto Unity, Faith and Discipline has been presented as Faith, Unity and Discipline. Perhaps our theocrats, clutching at straws, equate the word 'faith' used in the Quaid's motto with Islam. There is evidence to show that for the Quaid, 'faith' [*yaqeen*, not *imaan*] was to be used in the context of the Pakistan Movement.[2]

Paracha adds an interesting coda:

> Once Pakistan had been achieved, the Quaid as Governor General, in his first broadcast from Lahore on August 31 reworded his motto. He said: 'It is up to you to work, work and work and we are bound to succeed and never forget our motto: Unity, Discipline and Faith.'

The Quaid had put faith last!

The journey predictably wandered into the domain of education in September 2020, when Federal Minister of Education Shafqat Mehmood announced the Imran Khan government's resolve to introduce a Single National Curriculum (SNC) in the country. Talking on TV, he did not say what this SNC would achieve, which is always difficult when you discuss education, but he was clear about what it was aimed at removing: pulling down what he called 'educational apartheid' and deriding the 'effete intellectualism' of those who oppose it.

Mehmood's aim was to unite 'a nation divided by perceptual walls', that is 'unable to come up to many challenges that confront us, including poverty, hunger and disease'. The crux of his uniformity-producing educational utopia was contained in the following undertaking to remove English from the system: 'English should be taught as a language, but all other subjects from grade 1 to 5 should be taught either in Urdu or in the mother language.' The minister suppressed a snicker when he conceded that only those whose mother tongue was English could have English as a medium of instruction.[3]

The real problem, which the minister didn't highlight and which would make the removal of English as the medium of instruction meaningless, are the 22.8 million children who don't attend school. Only 2 million do, and the task of putting over 20 million children in school had nothing to do with English. Pakistan spends 2.9 per cent of its Gross Domestic Product (GDP) on education and is haunted by 'ghost schools' and absentee teachers who nonetheless draw salaries; and schools without bathrooms while textbook boards in the provinces produce books not worth looking at. And they are not in English, which is supposed to create 'apartheid'. Some kind of 'unmeasured' religious rift is created by the 40,000 madrasas in the country that belong to at least three internally conflicted sects.

Uniformity of mind is supposed to create 'utopia', but it ends up producing a brainwashed 'dystopia' of an unproductive population given to intolerance of any variant point of view. Thinking of the past, former senator Farhatullah Babar wrote:

> By imposing uniformity, the state not only imposed Urdu on Bengalis but also imposed 'parity' formula to give equal political weight to the majority East Pakistan with the minority West Pakistan . . . Diversity of thought, of religion, of cultures,

> of languages is the soul of a federal structure. Crushing it will crush the soul of the state and society.[4]

In 1947, soon after the creation of Pakistan, the country's first education ministry emphasized the teaching of the sciences, law and economics, whereas religious teaching was to be undertaken privately. In 1959, at the start of the Ayub Khan regime, the Commission on National Education suggested designing the curriculum 'to focus on developing basic skills in reading, writing, and arithmetic, creating a high sense of patriotism as well as a liking for working with one's own hand and additional subjects for specific vocations and careers.'

It is going to be self-damaging to throw English out as the medium of instruction. Its logical–sequential discourse is needed by a people nurtured by religious sermons and a lot of folk and national poetry. If 'rational thought' is the need of the hour in the face of 'moon-sighting' ulema talking of jihad and 130-feet-tall 'young girls' created in the Hereafter for the pleasure of 'good Muslims', then Shafqat Mehmood is walking into a familiar wall. In Punjab, books have started being banned in anticipation and English-medium schools have been instructed to remove a chapter on reproduction from textbooks and purge math books of pictures of piglets.

Article 22(1), obsolete in the eyes of the nazriati (ideological) politicians, says:

> No person attending any educational institution shall be required to receive religious instruction, or take part in any religious ceremony, or attend religious worship, if such instruction, ceremony of worship relates to a religion other than his own.[5]

This law implies that no lesson in any textbook that is compulsory to students of all faiths can contain material specific to any religion. The SNC violates this fundamental right of non-Muslim

Pakistani citizens by prescribing lessons in Urdu and English courses that are already a part of the Islamiat curriculum. Urdu textbooks are asked to start with a *hamd* and a *naat*, and there is invariably a lesson on *Seerat-un-Nabi*, or the life of the Prophet (Peace Be upon Him).

Pakistan's leading educationist A.H. Nayyar points out what happens when this article is violated:

> A lesson on *Seerat-un-Nabi* is prescribed in English textbooks of all grades. When challenged to justify this violation of constitutional right, the officials refused to correct the wrong. Instead they prescribed outlandish ways of avoiding the violation: they want teachers to ask non-Muslim students to leave the class during such lessons (and do what, they do not say). They also prescribe exempting non-Muslim students from answering examination questions relating to such lessons, a risk that few students would want to take since examiners could easily be prejudiced against non-Muslims. They keep insisting on retaining Islamiat lessons in compulsory courses in spite of the fact that these topics are already covered in the exclusive course on Islamiat.[6]

Does all this go back to our rejection of rationality? Paradoxically, Allama Iqbal himself appears to be rejecting *aql* (reason) in favour of a supra-*aql* acceptance of Islam. This he does all the time in his poetry, but it would be untrue to say that he did not do so in his *Lectures*. In fact, when you explore why he liked certain Western thinkers, you reach the conclusion that when not under poetic inspiration he wanted a blend of reason and revelation rather than pure reason. Today, we find Pakistan's physicist Dr Pervez Hoodbhoy arguing with the clergy (without much effect) in favour of the inclusion of science in Pakistan's world view.

The upshot of this is that we are able to deal with emotional moments with great ease. A man who restricts himself to reason will fare badly in such a situation. The unfortunate fact however is that a man who has rejected reason will fare badly when faced by a moment requiring rational thinking. Yet the emotional man has a kind of advantage over the rational man. He can approach a rational moment with emotion, but a rational man is helpless in the face of a highly charged emotional situation. All moments requiring a rational assessment can be confronted with high emotion (*walwala*). There are more tools available in Muslim societies for this walwala than in the West, where reason has suppressed such collectively emotive concepts as nationalism.

What confronts us in the 'uniform curriculum' being handed down by Prime Minister Imran Khan is removal from our children's consciousness the vestiges of rational thinking embodied in the discourse of the English language. Here is how Pakistan's nuclear physicist Dr Pervez Hoodbhoy looked at our 'science' books in an article published in 2016:

> Local biology books are even more schizophrenic and confusing than the physics ones. A 10th-grade book starts off its section on 'Life and its Origins' unctuously quoting one religious verse after another. None of these verses hint towards evolution, and many Muslims believe that evolution is counter-religious. Then, suddenly, a full-page annotated chart hits you in the face. Stolen from some modern biology book written in some other part of the world, it depicts various living organisms evolving into apes and then into modern humans. Ouch![7]

Copyright Acknowledgements

Grateful acknowledgement is made to the *Indian Express* for their kind permission to reprint the following previously published material by Khaled Ahmed. These articles were published originally in the *Indian Express*, and have been reprinted from the *Indian Express* with the permission of The Indian Express (P) Ltd.

Khaled Ahmed, 'Uighur Terrorism Brewing in Pakistan Is Drawing China's Ire', *Indian Express*, 2 November 2019, https://indianexpress.com/article/opinion/columns/pakistan-china-and-a-grey-area-fatf-terror-funding-uighur-terrorism-6098655/.

Khaled Ahmed, 'Al-Baghdadi's Caliphate Was the Most Shameful Phase of Islam Known to History', *Indian Express*, 30 November 2019, https://indianexpress.com/article/opinion/columns/islamic-state-abu-bakr-al-baghdadi-osama-bin-laden-the-reign-of-isis-6143346/.

Khaled Ahmed, 'Could Pakistan Have Stayed Out of US-led Global Campaign after 9/11?', *Indian Express*, 5 October 2019, https://indianexpress.com/article/opinion/columns/what-pakistan-won-and-lost-imran-khan-us-pak-relations-6054141/.

Khaled Ahmed, 'Pakistan Has Compromised Its Internal Sovereignty by Supporting Non-state Actors', *Indian Express*, 28 September 2019, https://indianexpress.com/article/opinion/columns/jihad-al-qaeda-islamic-state-tariq-rahman-book-6035018/.

Khaled Ahmed, 'Self Flagellation in Pakistan', *Indian Express*, 8 August 2019, https://indianexpress.com/article/opinion/columns/kashmir-special-status-article-370-35a-jk-union-territory-imran-khan-5886741/.

Khaled Ahmed, 'The Saga of Hafiz Saeed', *Indian Express*, 5 July 2019, https://indianexpress.com/article/opinion/columns/hafiz-saeed-lashkar-e-taiba-jamaat-ud-dawa-pakistan-sponsored-terrorism-imran-khan-5815658/.

Khaled Ahmed, 'Shuja Nawaz's New Book Explores Differences Between Pakistan Army and Radical Elements', *Indian Express*, 1 February 2020, https://indianexpress.com/article/opinion/columns/khaled-ahmed-pakistan-military-us-india-relations-6244973/?.

Khaled Ahmed, 'Mainstreaming Terror', *Indian Express*, 7 October 2017, https://indianexpress.com/article/opinion/columns/pakistan-hafiz-saeed-military-terror-funding-lashkar-mainstreaming-terror-4878135/.

Khaled Ahmed, 'Afghanistan Polls, Held without a Ceasefire, Do Not Portend Political Stability', *Indian Express*, 19 October 2019, https://indianexpress.com/article/opinion/columns/a-doomed-afghanistan-elections-2019-taliban-isis-al-qaeda-6076648/.

Khaled Ahmed, 'The Return of Hekmatyar', *Indian Express*, 15 October 2016, https://indianexpress.com/article/opinion/

columns/afghanistan-gulbuddin-hekmatyar-hezb-e-islami-ashraf-ghani-pakistan-3083206/?.

Khaled Ahmed, 'Hazards of Identity', *Indian Express*, 13 July 2019, https://indianexpress.com/article/opinion/columns/hazards-of-identity-globalisation-21st-century-identity-politics-5827089/?.

Khaled Ahmed, 'Pakistan's First Lady', *Indian Express*, 24 June 2019, https://indianexpress.com/article/opinion/columns/begum-raana-liaquat-ali-khan-pakistan-first-lady-namita-gokhale-book-pakistans-first-lady-5793889/.

Khaled Ahmed, 'Rule of Violence', *Indian Express*, 4 September 2015, https://indianexpress.com/article/opinion/columns/rule-of-violence-2/.

Khaled Ahmed, 'Defined by Exclusion', *Indian Express*, 22 July 2015, https://indianexpress.com/article/opinion/columns/defined-by-exclusion/.

Khaled Ahmed, 'Integration vs The Ummah', *Indian Express*, 3 November 2018, https://indianexpress.com/article/opinion/columns/integration-vs-the-ummah-britain-radicalisation-of-muslim-community-432052/.

Khaled Ahmed, 'Pakistan's National Accountability Bureau Has Stifled Decision-making', *Indian Express*, 23 November 2019, https://indianexpress.com/article/opinion/columns/pakistan-national-accountability-bureau-nab-6132550/lite/?.

AG Publications (Private) Limited, which produces *Newsweek Pakistan* under license from Newsweek, LLC, New York, has no objections whatsoever to Mr Ahmed's work for *Newsweek Pakistan* being reproduced in the book. Grateful acknowledgement is made to *Newsweek Pakistan* for permission to reprint the following articles:

Khaled Ahmed, 'Difficult to Digest Debacle', *Newsweek Pakistan*, 6 February 2019, https://www.newsweekpakistan.com/difficult-to-digest-debacle/.

Khaled Ahmed, 'The Peace Hawk', *Newsweek Pakistan*, 6 September 2015, https://www.newsweekpakistan.com/the-peace-hawk/.

Khaled Ahmed, 'State's Surrender', *Newsweek Pakistan*, 2 December 2017, https://www.newsweekpakistan.com/states-surrender/.

Khaled Ahmed, Sorting Out the State', *Newsweek Pakistan*, 6 August 2018, https://www.newsweekpakistan.com/sorting-out-the-state/.

Khaled Ahmed, 'The Wonderfully Disobedient Son', *Newsweek Pakistan*, 11 October 2015, https://www.newsweekpakistan.com/the-wonderfully-disobedient-son/.

Khaled Ahmed, 'State Misdeeds', *Newsweek Pakistan*, 11 September 2018, https://www.newsweekpakistan.com/state-misdeeds/.

Khaled Ahmed, 'The "Enemy" Within?', *Newsweek Pakistan*, 4 January 2019, https://www.newsweekpakistan.com/the-enemy-within/.

Khaled Ahmed, 'South Asia's Strongwomen', *Newsweek Pakistan*, 10 May 2019, https://www.newsweekpakistan.com/south-asias-strongwomen/.

Khaled Ahmed, 'The Sheedi of Sindh', *Newsweek Pakistan*, 27 August 2018, https://www.newsweekpakistan.com/the-sheedi-of-sindh/.

Khaled Ahmed, 'The Rise of the Alpha Male', *Newsweek Pakistan*, 31 December 2018, https://www.newsweekpakistan.com/the-rise-of-the-alpha-male/.

Khaled Ahmed, 'Musings of the Marginalized', *Newsweek Pakistan*, 28 May 2019, https://www.newsweekpakistan.com/musings-of-the-marginalized/.

Khaled Ahmed, 'High or Hybrid', *Newsweek Pakistan*, 21 February 2019, https://www.newsweekpakistan.com/high-or-hybrid/.

Khaled Ahmed, 'A Life in Watercolors', *Newsweek Pakistan*, 17 January 2019, https://www.newsweekpakistan.com/a-life-in-watercolors/.

Khaled Ahmed, 'A Sense of History', *Newsweek Pakistan*, 20 February 2015, https://www.newsweekpakistan.com/a-sense-of-history/.

Khaled Ahmed, Marker's Memory', *Newsweek Pakistan*, 25 June 2018, https://www.newsweekpakistan.com/markers-memory/?.

Khaled Ahmed, 'The Sad Saga of Hafiz Saeed', *Newsweek Pakistan*, 17 July 2019, https://www.newsweekpakistan.com/the-sad-saga-of-hafiz-saeed/.

Khaled Ahmed, 'The Ghost of Osama bin Laden', *Newsweek Pakistan*, 28 July 2013, http://newsweekpakistan.com/the-ghost-of-osama-bin-laden/.

Khaled Ahmed, 'The Kargil Clique', *Newsweek Pakistan*, 12 October 2018, https://www.newsweekpakistan.com/the-kargil-clique/.

Khaled Ahmed, 'Bureaucrats' Beef', *Newsweek Pakistan*, 31 December 2019, https://www.newsweekpakistan.com/bureaucrats-beef/.

We are also grateful to the *Friday Times* for granting us permission to reprint the following articles:

Khaled Ahmed, 'Who Sneaked on Osama bin Laden?', *Friday Times*, 20 December 2019, https://www.thefridaytimes.com/who-sneaked-on-osama-bin-laden/.

Khaled Ahmed, 'Batting to the Last Ball', *Friday Times*, 1 May 2020, https://www.thefridaytimes.com/batting-to-the-last-ball/?.

We are grateful to *Dawn*, too, for granting us permission to reprint the following article:

Khaled Ahmed, 'The Name, Not the Philosophy, Lives On', *Dawn*, 9 November 2019, https://www.dawn.com/news/1368130?.

Notes

Introduction: Facing the Fallout

1. Khaled Ahmed, 'Uighur Terrorism Brewing in Pakistan Is Drawing China's Ire', *Indian Express*, 2 November 2019, https://indianexpress.com/article/opinion/columns/pakistan-china-and-a-grey-area-fatf-terror-funding-uighur-terrorism-6098655/.

   Unless mentioned otherwise, the quotes that follow in this section are from the same source.
2. Andrew Small, *The China-Pakistan Axis: Asia's New Geopolitics* (New York: Oxford University Press, 2015).
3. Ahmed Rashid, *Pakistan on the Brink: The Future of America, Pakistan, and Afghanistan* (New York: Viking [Penguin books], 2012).
4. Andrea de Guttry, Francesca Capone and Christopher Paulussen (eds.), *Foreign Fighters under International Law and Beyond* (Springer Books, 2016).

5. Akbar S. Ahmed, *Journey into Europe: Islam, Immigration, and Identity* (Washington D.C.: Brookings Institution Press, 2018).
6. David Brennen, 'U.S.-Pakistan Alliance After 9/11 Was "One of the Biggest Blunders" For the Country, Imran Khan Says', *Newsweek Pakistan*, 24 September 2019, https://www.newsweek.com/us-pakistan-alliance-after-9-11-was-one-biggest-blunders-country-imran-khan-says-1460946.
7. Rana Banerji, 'The Future of Pakistan', Asia Times, 23 October 2019, https://asiatimes.com/2019/10/the-future-of-pakistan/.
8. Khaled Ahmed, 'Could Pakistan Have Stayed Out of US-led Global Campaign After 9/11?', *Indian Express*, 5 October 2019, https://indianexpress.com/article/opinion/columns/what-pakistan-won-and-lost-imran-khan-us-pak-relations-6054141/.
9. 'In New York, Imran Khan Says Pak Shouldn't Have Joined "War on Terror' and Remained "Neutral" with Jihadis', *DNA*, 23 September 2019, https://www.dnaindia.com/world/report-in-new-york-imran-khan-says-pak-shouldn-t-have-joined-war-on-terror-and-remained-neutral-with-jihadis-2791883.
10. Tariq Rahman, *Interpretations of Jihad in South Asia: An Intellectual History* (Walter DeGruyter, 2018).
11. Ibid, p. 258.
12. Julian Borger and Azhar Farooq, 'Imran Khan Warns UN of Potential Nuclear War in Kashmir', *Guardian*, 26 September 2019, https://www.theguardian.com/world/2019/sep/26/imran-khan-warns-un-of-potential-nuclear-war-in-kashmir.
13. 'Facebook Ignored Hate Speech by India's BJP Politicians: Report', Al Jazeera, 15 August 2020, https://www.aljazeera.com/news/2020/8/15/facebook-ignored-hate-speech-by-indias-bjp-politicians-report.
14. James Mackenzie and Martin Howell, 'Pakistan PM Imran Khan Sees Better Chance of Peace Talks with India If BJP Wins Election', Reuters, 9 April 2019, https://www.reuters.com/article/pakistan-politics-khan-idUSKCN1RL265.
15. 'India Tempts Fate in Kashmir, "The Most Dangerous Place in the World"', *New York Times*, 5 August 2019, https://www.nytimes.com/2019/08/05/opinion/kashmir-article-370.html.

Chapter 1: Osama bin Laden in Abbottabad

1. 'Pakistan's Bin Laden Dossier', Al Jazeera, 15 July 2013, https://www.aljazeera.com/indepth/spotlight/binladenfiles/.
2. Khaled Ahmed, *Sleepwalking to Surrender: Dealing with Terrorism in Pakistan* (Viking, Penguin Random House India, 2016).
3. Bruce Riedel, 'The Doha Portent', *Indian Express*, 3 July 2013, http://archive.indianexpress.com/news/the-doha-portent/1136806/0.
4. 'Accounts of Militant Training Camp near bin Laden in Pakistan', *Bangor Daily News*, 22 May 2011, https://bangordailynews.com/2011/05/22/news/accounts-of-militant-training-camp-near-bin-laden-in-pakistan/.
5. Carlotta Gall, Pir Zubair Shah and Eric Schmitt, 'Seized Phone Offers Clues to Bin Laden's Pakistani Links', *New York Times*, 23 June 2011, https://www.nytimes.com/2011/06/24/world/asia/24pakistan.html.
6. Lawrence Sellin, 'From US Perspective, Pervez Musharraf Gets a Well-earned Sentence', Wion, 18 December 2019, https://www.wionews.com/opinions/from-us-perspective-pervez-musharraf-gets-a-well-earned-sentence-268959.
7. 'Ex-ISI Chief Blasts All, Including Musharraf, Agencies, Media', *News International*, 11 July 2013, https://www.thenews.com.pk/archive/print/631659-ex-isi-chief-blasts-all,-including-musharraf,-agencies,-media.
8. Khaled Ahmed, 'Kissing the Hand that Chastises', *Indian Express*, 7 June 2013, http://archive.indianexpress.com/news/kissing-the-hand-that-chastises/1126068/3; AbdulMajeed Abid, 'Book Review: Ye Khamoshi Kahan Tak (Silent No More?) by Lt Gen (Rtd) Shahid Aziz', Brown Pundits, 12 June 2018, https://www.brownpundits.com/2018/06/12/book-review-ye-khamoshi-kahan-tak-silent-no-more-by-lt-gen-rtd-shahid-aziz/.
9. Khaled Ahmed, 'Just Asking, in Pakistan', *Indian Express*, 29 June 2013, http://archive.indianexpress.com/news/just-asking-in-pakistan/1135315/3.

Chapter 2: Who Sneaked on Osama bin Laden?

1. Simon Carswell, 'Seymour Hersh Challenges White House Story of Osama bin Laden's Death', *Irish Times*, 13 May 2015, https://www.irishtimes.com/news/world/us/seymour-hersh-challenges-white-house-story-of-osama-bin-laden-s-death-1.2211505.
2. Amir Mir, 'Brig Usman Khalid Informed CIA of Osama's Presence in Abbottabad', *News International*, 12 May 2015, https://www.thenews.com.pk/print/40040-brig-usman-khalid-informed-cia-of-osamas-presence-in-abbottabad.
3. David Ignatius, 'What Did Pakistan Know About bin Laden?', *Washington Post*, 17 February 2012, https://www.washingtonpost.com/opinions/what-did-pakistan-know-about-bin-laden/2012/02/16/gIQAccLhKR_story.html.
4. 'Ex-ISI Chief Claims Musharraf Hosted Osama in Abbottabad', *News International*, 15 February 2012, https://www.thenews.com.pk/archive/print/620231-ex-isi-chief-claims-musharraf-hosted-osama-in-abbottabad.
5. A.S. Dulat, Aditya Sinha and Asad Durrani, *The Spy Chronicles: RAW, ISI and the Illusion of Peace* (HarperCollins, 2018).
6. 'GHQ Summons Former ISI Chief to Explain Stance on Book Co-authored with Ex-RAW Chief', *Dawn*, 26 May 2018, https://www.dawn.com/news/1409973.
7. Shuja Nawaz, *The Battle for Pakistan: The Bitter US Friendship and a Tough Neighbourhood* (Vintage Books, 2019). All of Shuja Nawaz's quotes are from his book, unless stated otherwise.

Chapter 3: Kargil: High on Low IQ

1. Nasim Zehra, *From Kargil to the Coup: Events that Shook Pakistan* (Pakistan: Sang-e-Meel, 2018). All of Zehra's quotes are from this book, unless stated otherwise.
2. Ibid.
3. Sartaj Aziz, *Between Dreams and Realities: Some Milestones in Pakistan's History* (Karachi: Oxford University Press Pakistan, 2009).

4. Ibid.
5. Mahmud Ahmed, *History of the Indo-Pak War 1965* (Pakistan: Services Book Club, 2006).
6. Riaz Mohammad Khan, *Afghanistan and Pakistan: Conflict, Extremism and Resistance to Modernity* (Johns Hopkins University Press, 2011).
7. Shuja Nawaz, *Crossed Swords: Pakistan, Its Army, and the Wars Within* (Karachi: Oxford University Press Pakistan, 2008).

Chapter 4: The Sad Saga of Hafiz Saeed

1. Mubasher Bukhari, 'Pakistan Announces Terrorism Finance Crackdown on Banned Militant Group', Reuters, 3 July 2019, https://www.reuters.com/article/us-pakistan-terror-financing/pakistan-announces-terrorism-finance-crackdown-on-banned-militant-group-idUSKCN1TY249.
2. Jason M. Breslow, 'The Memoir of an "American Terrorist"', *Frontline*, 21 April 2015, https://www.pbs.org/wgbh/frontline/article/the-memoir-of-an-american-terrorist/.
3. Khaled Ahmed, 'The Cost of Mainstreaming', *Indian Express*, 3 February 2018, https://indianexpress.com/article/opinion/columns/the-cost-of-mainstreaming-hafiz-saeed-jamaat-ud-dawa-5049454/.
4. Paul L. Williams, *Osama's Revenge: The Next 9/11: What the Media and the Government Haven't Told You* (Viva Books, 2005).
5. Khaled Ahmed, *Sleepwalking to Surrender: Dealing with Terrorism in Pakistan* (Viking, Penguin Random House India, 2016).
6. Tariq Rahman, *Interpretations of Jihad in South Asia: An Intellectual History* (Walter DeGruyter, 2018).
7. Declan Walsh, 'Islamic Scholar Attacks Pakistan's Blasphemy Laws', *Guardian*, 20 January 2011, https://www.theguardian.com/world/2011/jan/20/islam-ghamidi-pakistan-blasphemy-laws.
8. Ambreen Agha, 'Pakistan: Cloning Terror', *South Asia Intelligence Review*, 3 April 2012, https://www.satp.org/satporgtp/sair/Archives/sair10/10_46.htm

Chapter 5: The Murder of Syed Saleem Shahzad

1. 'Censors at Work', *Pakistan Today*, 29 December 2019, https://www.pakistantoday.com.pk/2019/12/29/censors-at-work/.
2. Syed Saleem Shahzad, 'Al-Qaeda had Warned of Pakistan Strike', *Express Tribune*, 3 June 2011, https://tribune.com.pk/story/181624/al-qaeda-had-warned-of-pakistan-strike.
3. Ibid.
4. Shuja Nawaz, *The Battle for Pakistan: The Bitter Us Friendship and a Tough Neighbourhood* (Lahore: Liberty Publishing, 2019).
5. Jane Perlez and Eric Schmitt, 'Pakistan's Spies Tied to Slaying of a Journalist', *New York Times*, 4 July 2011, https://www.nytimes.com/2011/07/05/world/asia/05pakistan.html.
6. Nawaz, *The Battle for Pakistan.*
7. Ibid.
8. Syed Saleem Shahzad, *Inside Al-Qaeda and the Taliban: Beyond Bin Laden and 9/11* (Pluto Press, 2011).
9. 'Comment: Saleem Shahzad, Al Qaeda and ISI by Khaled Ahmed', 18 June 2011, https://defenceforumindia.com/threads/saleem-shahzad-al-qaeda-and-isi.22747/.
10. Shahzad, *Inside Al-Qaeda and the Taliban*, p. 9. The quotes that follow in this section are from the same book.
11. Ibid. p. 83.
12. Ibid. p. 88.
13. Ibid. p. 92.
14. Ibid. p. 93.
15. Ibid. p. 200.
16. Ibid. p 95.
17. Ibid. p. 125.
18. 'Censors at Work', *Pakistan Today*, 29 December 2019, https://www.pakistantoday.com.pk/2019/12/29/censors-at-work/.
19. Khaled Ahmed, 'Shuja Nawaz's New Book Explores Differences between Pakistan Army and Radical Elements', *Indian Express*, 1 February 2020, https://indianexpress.com/article/opinion/

columns/khaled-ahmed-pakistan-military-us-india-relations-6244973/.

All quotations in this section are from this source.

20. Nawaz, *Battle for Pakistan.*

Chapter 6: Hekmatyar: The Bridegroom of Jihad

1. Michael Griffin, *Reaping the Whirlwind: The Taliban Movement in Afghanistan* (Pluto Press, 2001).
2. Jeffrey St. Clair, '"I Could Live With That": How the CIA Made Afghanistan Safe for the Opium Trade', Counterpunch, 10 July 2010, https://www.counterpunch.org/2020/07/10/i-could-live-with-that-how-the-cia-made-afghanistan-safe-for-the-opium-trade/.
3. Lawrence Wright, 'Postscript: Hamid Gul, 1936–2015', *New Yorker*, 18 August 2015, https://www.newyorker.com/news/news-desk/postscript-hamid-gul-1936-2015.
4. Tariq Khosa, 'Power of the State', *Dawn*, 3 October 2016, https://www.dawn.com/news/1287566.
5. Christophe Jaffrelot, *Pakistan at the Crossroads: Domestic Dynamics and External Pressures* (Vintage books, May 2016).
6. https://www.mei.edu/publications/post-soviet-pakistani-interference-afghanistan-how-and-why; https://thewire.in/external-affairs/pakistans-two-pronged-game-in-kabul.
7. *Hizb-i-Islami Gulbuddin* (HIG), Institute for the Study of War, undated document, quoted in https://www.ecoi.net/en/file/local/2006228/89892.pdf.
8. M.K. Bhadrakumar, 'India Loses Afghan Proxy War', Rediff.com, 16 July 2019, https://www.rediff.com/news/column/india-loses-afghan-proxy-war/20190716.htm.
9. Tahir Khan, 'Iran Destabilizing Afghanistan, Says Hekmatyar', Arab News, 28 June 2018, https://www.arabnews.com/node/1329536/world.
10. Syed Zafar Mehdi, 'Truth about Hekmatyar's Anti-Iran Tirade', *Tehran Times*, 10 December 2018, https://www.tehrantimes.com/news/430488/Truth-about-Hekmatyar-s-anti-Iran-tirade.

Chapter 7: A Debacle Difficult to Digest

1. Azfar-ul-Ashfaque, 'Shah's Tenure As CJ Saw Attack on Judiciary', *Dawn*, 8 March 2017, https://www.dawn.com/news/1319161; 'Bitter Memories of 1997 Contempt Case against Sharif', *News International*, 19 January 2012, https://www.thenews.com.pk/archive/print/619617-bitter-memories-of-1997-contempt-case-against-sharif.
2. Naziha Syed Ali, 'Dawn Investigations: Mystery Still Surrounds Gen Zia's Death, 30 Years On', *Dawn*, 12 March 2019, https://www.dawn.com/news/1427540.
3. Asad Durrani, *Pakistan Adrift: Navigating Troubled Waters* (London: Hurst & Co., 2018). Quotes in the following section are from the same book, unless stated otherwise.
4. M.A. Siddiqui, 'Hanging Up His Boots', *Friday Times*, 20 October 2017, https://www.thefridaytimes.com/hanging-up-his-boots/.
5. Asad Durrani, *Pakistan Adrift.* Quotes in the following section are from the same book, unless otherwise stated.

Chapter 8: The Sorrows of Identity

1. Francis Fukuyama, 'Letters to the Editor: E Pluribus Unum (Out of Many, One)', *Ceylon Today*, 28 August 2020, https://ceylontoday.lk/news/letters-to-the-editor-e-pluribus-unum-out-of-many-one.
2. Akbar Ahmed, *Journey into Europe: Islam, Immigration, and Identity* (Washington: Brookings Institution Press, 2018).
3. Ibid.
4. Marisa Iati, '"Perfectly Educated" Women Don't Have Big Families, Macron Said. Then the Moms Spoke Up', *Washington Post*, 19 October 2018, https://www.washingtonpost.com/religion/2018/10/19/perfectly-educated-women-dont-have-big-families-macron-said-then-moms-spoke-up/.
5. Hannah Arendt, *The Origins of Totalitarianism*, Vol. 244 of *A Harvest Book* (Harcourt Brace Jovanovich, 1973).

6. See: Khaled Ahmed, 'Hazards of Identity', *Indian Express*, 13 July 2019, https://indianexpress.com/article/opinion/columns/hazards-of-identity-globalisation-21st-century-identity-politics-5827089/?; Aman Memon, 'Dear India, Please Don't Turn into a Hindu Pakistan', *Madras Courier*, 8 November 2019, https://madrascourier.com/opinion/dear-india-please-dont-turn-into-a-hindu-pakistan/; Javid Husain, 'Hindutva: India's Descent into Bigotry', *Nation*, 18 February 2020.
7. 'Big Dominique and His Struggle against the Islamists', *The Economist*, 16 December 2004, https://www.economist.com/europe/2004/12/16/big-dominique-and-his-struggle-against-the-islamists.
8. Akbar Ahmed, *Journey into Europe: Islam, Immigration, and Identity* (Washington: Brookings Institution Press, 2018).
9. Ibid.

Chapter 9: Peace without Doves

1. Khurshid Mahmud Kasuri, *Neither a Hawk Nor a Dove: An Insider's Account of Pakistan's Foreign Relations including details of the Kashmiri Framework* (Karachi: Oxford University Press Pakistan, 2015).
2. 'Vajpayee Made Nawaz Sharif Speak with Dilip Kumar Over Kargil Conflict, Says Khurshid Kasuri's Book', *Economic Times*, 7 September 2015, https://economictimes.indiatimes.com/magazines/panache/vajpayee-made-nawaz-sharif-speak-with-dilip-kumar-over-kargil-conflict-says-khurshid-kasuris-book/articleshow/48856363.cms?from=mdr.
3. Kasuri, *Neither a Hawk Nor a Dove.*

Chapter 10: A Sad Surrender

1. Shamil Shams, '#DawnLeaks: Pakistani PM Sharif "Forces" Powerful Military to Back Off', DW, 11 May 2017, https://www.dw.com/en/dawnleaks-pakistani-pm-sharif-forces-powerful-military-to-back-off/a-38797365.

2. Khaled Ahmed, 'State's Surrender', *Newsweek Pakistan*, 3 December 2017, https://www.newsweekpakistan.com/states-surrender/.
3. 'Pakistan Blogger Aasim Saeed Says He Was Tortured', BBC, 24 October 2017, https://www.bbc.com/news/world-asia-41662595; Pamela Constable, 'Did Pakistani Security Agents Kidnap Bloggers to Make a Point?', *Washington Post*, 14 February 2017, https://www.washingtonpost.com/world/asia_pacific/did-pakistani-security-agents-kidnap-bloggers-to-make-a-point/2017/02/12/3f672d72-ed66-11e6-a100-fdaaf400369a_story.html.
4. 'The Barelvi Beast', *Newsweek Pakistan*, 17 November 2017, https://www.newsweekpakistan.com/the-barelvi-beast/.

Chapter 11: Sorting Out the State

1. Shuja Nawaz, 'Pakistan's Election May Further Fracture Its Polity', 24 July 2018, https://www.atlanticcouncil.org/blogs/new-atlanticist/pakistan-s-election-may-further-fracture-its-polity/.
2. Khaled Ahmed, 'Musings of the Marginalized', *Newsweek Pakistan*, 28 May 2019, https://www.newsweekpakistan.com/musings-of-the-marginalized/.

Chapter 12: The Begum We Bypassed

1. Khaled Ahmed, 'Pakistan's First Lady', *Indian Express*, 24 June 2019, https://indianexpress.com/article/opinion/columns/begum-raana-liaquat-ali-khan-pakistan-first-lady-namita-gokhale-book-pakistans-first-lady-5793889/.

   See also: Deepa Agarwal and Tahmina Aziz Ayub, *The Begum: A Portrait of Ra'ana Liaquat Ali Khan, Pakistan's Pioneering First Lady* (Oxford University Press, 2019).
2. 'Jinnah's Address', *Dawn*, 11 August 2017, https://www.dawn.com/news/1350847.
3. Hamid Khan, *Constitutional and Political History of Pakistan* (Karachi: Oxford University Press, 2001).

4. Deepa Agarwal, 'The Begum: A Portrait of Ra'ana Liaquat Ali Khan, Pakistan's Pioneering First Lady; From Almora to Pakistan', *National Herald*, 3 March 2019, https://www.nationalheraldindia.com/book-extract/the-begum-a-portrait-of-raana-liaquat-ali-khan-pakistans-pioneering-first-lady-from-almora-to-pakistan.
5. Khaled Ahmed, 'History: Liaquat's Resignation Letter to Jinnah', 28 June 2006, Watandost, http://watandost.blogspot.com/2006/06/history-liaquats-resignation-letter-to.html.
6. Muhammad Reza Kazimi, *Liaquat Ali Khan: His Life and Work* (Karachi: Oxford University Press Pakistan, 2003).
7. Afsheen Zubair, 'Corruption within the Ranks Was There Even When Jinnah Was Alive: Begun Ra'ana Liaquat Ali Khan', *Herald*, 14 July 2017, http://herald.dawn.com/news/1153802.

Chapter 13: In Marker's Memory

1. Jamsheed Marker, *Quiet Diplomacy: Memoirs of an Ambassador* (Oxford University Press, 2010). All quotations by Marker are from this book unless stated otherwise.
2. Jamsheed Marker, *East Timor: A Memoir of the Negotiations for Independence* (McFarland & Co., 2003).
3. Roedad Khan, *Pakistan: A Dream Gone Sour* (Oxford University Press, 1997).
4. Robert Pear, 'Washington Talk/Working Profile: Jamsheed K.A. Marker; Linchpin of U.S.-Pakistan Alliance', *New York Times*, 1 September 1988, https://www.nytimes.com/1988/09/01/us/washington-talk-working-profile-jamsheed-k-marker-linchpin-us-pakistan-alliance.html.

Chapter 14: Allama Iqbal: The Name Lives On

1. Khaled Ahmed, 'The Name, Not the Philosophy, Lives On', *Dawn*, 9 November 2019, https://www.dawn.com/news/1368130. This chapter, until the subhead 'Justice Javed Iqbal', appeared in this article.

2. Muhammad Iqbal (Allama Iqbal), *The Reconstruction of Religious Thought in Islam* (New Delhi: Kitab Bhavan, 2000 [1930]).
3. On the riba, see Farooq Aziz, Muhammad Mahmud and Emadul Karim, 'An Analytical Review of Different Concepts of Riba (Interest) in the Sub-Continent', Munich Personal RePEc Archive, 31 December 2018, https://mpra.ub.uni-muenchen.de/15455/1/MPRA_paper_15455.pdf.
4. Javed Iqbal, *Zindarood* (Lahore: Shaikh Ghulam Ali and Sons, 1989).
5. Rudrangshu Mukherjee (ed.), *The Great Speeches of Modern India* (Noida: Random House India, 2011).
6. Tanweer Fazal, *Nation-state and Minority Rights in India: Comparative Perspectives on Muslim and Sikh Identities* (New York: Routledge, 2015).
7. 'Jinnah's Address', *Dawn*, 11 August 2017, https://www.dawn.com/news/1350847.
8. Khaled Ahmed, 'The Wonderfully Disobedient Son', *Newsweek Pakistan*, 11 October 2015, https://www.newsweekpakistan.com/the-wonderfully-disobedient-son/. The rest of the chapter appeared in this article, unless stated otherwise.
9. Javed Iqbal, *Islam and Pakistan's Ideology* (Lahore: Iqbal Academy Pakistan; Vanguard book Depot, 2003).
10. Javed Iqbal, *Apna Gareeban Chaak* (My Torn Shirt-front) (2010).
11. Javed Iqbal, *Jahan-e-Javid*, Vol. 2 (Sang-e-Meel, 2010).
12. Muhammad Iqbal (Allama Iqbal), *The Reconstruction of Religious Thought in Islam*.
13. Khaled Ahmed, 'Javid Iqbal on Allama Iqbal', *Express Tribune*, 25 September 2010, https://tribune.com.pk/story/54527/javid-iqbal-on-allama-iqbal.

Chapter 15: Deeds of a Doomed State

1. Atif Mian, 7 September 2018, https://twitter.com/AtifRMian/status/1038058613372321792.
2. Jemima Goldsmith, 7 September 2018, https://twitter.com/jemima_khan/status/1038037991720198146?lang=en.

3. Khaled Ahmed, 'Ahmadi Embarrassment', *Indian Express*, 4 June 2016, https://indianexpress.com/article/opinion/columns/ahmadi-embarrassment-pakistan-constitution-muslim-identity-2833302/.
4. 'Pak May Launch Operation in Punjab against Militants: Malik', *Indian Express*, 31 May 2010, http://archive.indianexpress.com/news/pak-may-launch-operation-in-punjab-against-militants-malik/627171/0.
5. Robert M. Gates, 'Helping Others Defend Themselves', *Foreign Affairs*, May/June 2010, https://www.foreignaffairs.com/articles/2010-05-01/helping-others-defend-themselves.
6. Khaled Ahmed, 'Defined by Exclusion', *Indian Express*, 22 July 2015, https://indianexpress.com/article/opinion/columns/defined-by-exclusion/. The rest of this chapter appeared in this article, unless stated otherwise.
7. Arjun Appadurai, *The Fear of Small Numbers: An Essay on the Geography of Anger* (Duke University Press, 2006), p. 53.
8. Ali Usman Qasmi, *The Ahmadis and the Politics of Religious Exclusion in Pakistan* (London and New York: Anthem Press, 2015).
9. Ibid. p. 126.
10. Ibid. p. 149.
11. Ibid. p. 205.
12. Ibid. p. 214.
13. Vali Nasr, *The Shia Revival: How Conflicts within Islam Will Shape the Future* (New York: W.W. Norton &Co., 2006).

Chapter 16: UK Muslims: 'The Enemy Within?'

1. Sayeeda Warsi, *The Enemy Within: A Tale of Muslim Britain* (London: Penguin UK, 2018), Introduction.
2. Ibid.
3. Giles Kepel, *Allah in the West: Islamic Movements in America and Europe* (Polity Press, 1997).
4. Muhammad Anwar, 'The Participation of Ethnic Minorities in British Politics', *Journal of Ethnic and Migration Studies*, 27:3, 533-

549, DOI: 10.1080/13691830120026622O (2001); H.A. Hellyer, 'A British Pioneer in the Study of Ethnic Relations: Muhammad Anwar', *Maydan*, 16 July 2020, https://themaydan.com/2020/07/a-british-pioneer-in-the-study-of-ethnic-relations-muhammad-anwar/.

5. Samuel Earle, '"Rivers of Blood": The Legacy of a Speech That Divided Britain', *Atlantic*, 20 April 2020, https://www.theatlantic.com/international/archive/2018/04/enoch-powell-rivers-of-blood/558344/.

Chapter 17: Strongwomen of South Asia

1. Anna Suvorova, *Widows and Daughters: Gender, Kinship, and Power in South Asia* (Karachi: OUP Pakistan, 2019).
2. Ibid.
3. Soli J. Sorabjee, 'Babasaheb's Warning: In Politics, Hero-worship Is a Path to Degradation and Eventual Dictatorship', *Indian Express*, 15 October 2019, https://indianexpress.com/article/opinion/columns/constitution-babasaheb-ambedkar-warning-hero-worship-6069022/.
4. Suvorova, *Widows and Daughters.*
5. Composed by Bankim Chandra Chatterjee, a part of his book *Anandamath* (1882).
6. Liaqat H. Merchant, *Jinnah: A Judicial Verdict* (Karachi: East & West Publishing, 1990).
7. Suvorova, *Widows and Daughters.*
8. Abida Sultaan, *Memoirs of a Rebel Princess* (Karachi: OUP Pakistan, 2004).
9. Suvorova, *Widows and Daughters.*
10. Dina Wadia, Jinnah's Daughter, Is No More', *Mumbai Mirror*, 3 November 2017, https://mumbaimirror.indiatimes.com/mumbai/other/dina-wadia-jinnahs-daughter-is-no-more/articleshow/61475051.cms.
11. Barbara Crossette, 'Bhutto Is Dismissed in Pakistan After 20 Months', *New York Times*, 7 August 1990, https://www.nytimes.com/

1990/08/07/world/bhutto-is-dismissed-in-pakistan-after-20-months.html.
12. Suvorova, *Widows and Daughters*.
13. 'Dynasties Still Run the World', Conversation, 26 March 2019, https://theconversation.com/dynasties-still-run-the-world-113098.

Chapter 18: The Sheedi of Sindh

1. 'Africans in India', *Frontline*, 9 September 2005, https://frontline.thehindu.com/science-and-technology/article30206182.ece.
2. Manu S. Pillai, 'A Slave Who Defied the Mughals', *Mint*, 13 December 2019, https://www.livemint.com/mint-lounge/features/a-slave-who-defied-the-mughals-11576211733059.html.

Chapter 19: A Landscape of Alpha Male Leaders

1. Reema Omer, 'Suo Motu Action', *Dawn*, 27 May 2018, https://www.dawn.com/news/1410267.
2. Richard Haass, 'Europe in Disarray', Project Syndicate, 13 December 2018, https://www.project-syndicate.org/commentary/growing-threats-to-europe-democracy-security-by-richard-n--haass-2018-12?a_la=english&a_d=5c1291d978b6c74640d4d604&a_m=&a_a=click&a_s=&a_p=homepage&a_li=growing-threats-to-europe-democracy-security-by-richard-n--haass-2018-12&a_pa=curated&a_ps=&barrier=accesspaylog.

Chapter 20: Musings of the Marginalized

1. Bilal Zahroor and Raza Rumi (eds.), *Rethinking Pakistan: A 21st-century Perspective* (Folio books, 2019).
2. Raza Habib Raja, 'Terming Liberals As "Khoonis" Only Further Exposes Imran Khan's Taliban-Apologist Tendencies, Lack of Knowledge and Right-Wing Mindset', *Express Tribune*, 4 December 2017, https://tribune.com.pk/article/61061/terming-liberals-

as-khoonis-only-further-exposes-imran-khans-taliban-apologist-tendencies-lack-of-knowledge-and-right-wing-mindset.

3. Khaled Ahmed, 'Sorting Out the State', *Newsweek Pakistan*, 6 August 2018, https://www.newsweekpakistan.com/sorting-out-the-state/.
4. Khaled Ahmed, 'Musings of the Marginalized', *Newsweek Pakistan*, 28 May 2019, http://www.newsweekpakistan.com/musings-of-the-marginalized/?.
5. Tariq Rahman, *Interpretations of Jihad in South Asia: An Intellectual History* (Walter de Gruyter GmbH & Co KG, 2020), p. 235.
6. Tahir Kamran, 'Religious Modernism and Barelvi Creed', *News International*, 3 December 2017, https://www.thenews.com.pk/tns/detail/564499-barelvi-creed.
7. Nadeem Farooq Paracha, 'The Crisis of Muslim Nationalism in Pakistan', Naya Daur Media, 27 March 2018, https://medium.com/@nayadaurpk/the-crisis-of-muslim-nationalism-in-pakistan-a7998d5f0e4b.
8. Muhammad Abrahim Zaka, Fasi Zaka, 'From Figures of Speech to Fists of Fury: Unchecked Incitements to Violence', *Rethinking Pakistan*, Bilal Zahroor and Raza Rumi (eds.), p. 61.
9. Rubina Saigol, 'Curriculum and the Constitution', *Rethinking Pakistan*, p. 68.
10. Charles Amjad Ali, Karamat Ali, 'Labour Policies and Industrial Relations in Pakistan: A Critical Evaluation', *Rethinking Pakistan*, p. 75.
11. I.A. Rehman, 'Land Reforms: Key to Justice and Social Progress', *Rethinking Pakistan*, p. 89.
12. *Rethinking Pakistan*, p. 98.
13. Ibid. p. 131.
14. Ibid. p. 143.
15. Ibid.
16. Ibid.
17. Ibid. Also see 'Pakistan Activist Waqass Goraya: The State Tortured Me', BBC, 9 March 2017, https://www.bbc.com/news/world-asia-39219307.

18. Ibid.
19. Ibid
20. Ibid
21. Ibid
22. Ibid

Chapter 21: High or Hybrid?

1. Khaled Ahmed, 'High or Hybrid', *Newsweek Pakistan*, 21 February 2019, https://www.newsweekpakistan.com/high-or-hybrid/?.
2. Muneeza Shamsie, *Hybrid Tapestries: The Development of Pakistani Literature in English* (Oxford University Press, 2017).
3. Sujit Nath, 'Amit Shah on Why Congress "Used Only Two Stanzas" of Vande Mataram During Freedom Struggle', News18, 27 June 2018, https://www.news18.com/news/politics/amit-shah-on-why-congress-used-only-two-stanzas-of-vande-mataram-during-freedom-struggle-1793031.html.
4. Atiya Begum Fyzee-Rahamin, Illustrated by S. Fyzee Rahamin, *Indian Music* (W. Marchant & Company, 1914).
5. Samuel Fyzee-Rahamin, *Gilded India* (London: Herbert Joseph, 1938).
6. Atiya Begum Fyzee-Rahamin, *Iqbal* (Oxford University Press, 2011).
7. Shahid Hosain, *First Voices: Six Poets from Pakistan: Ahmed Ali, Zulfikar Ghose, Shahid Hosain, Riaz Qadir, Taufiq Rafar, Shahid Suhrawardy* (Oxford University Press, 1965).
8. Shahid Suhrawardy, Naz Ikramullah Ashraf, *The Art of the Mussulmans in Spain* (Oxford University Press, 2005).
9. Tariq Ali, *The Clash of Fundamentalism: Crusades, Jihads, and Modernity* (Verso, 2003).

Chapter 22: Syed Babar Ali: Batting till the Last Ball

1. Syed Babar Ali, *Learning from Others: The Autobiography of Syed Babar Ali* (2015).

2. Khaled Ahmed, 'Syed Babar Ali: A Non-confrontational Winner', *Indian Express*, 9 January 2016, https://indianexpress.com/article/opinion/columns/syed-babar-ali-a-non-confrontational-winner/.
3. Syed Babar Ali, *Learning from Others*. All quotes in this chapter are from this volume, unless stated otherwise.
4. David A. Andelman, 'A Pakistani Capitalist Runs a Nationalized Industry', *New York Times*, 31 July 1977, https://www.nytimes.com/1977/07/31/archives/a-pakistani-capitalist-runs-a-nationalized-industry.html.
5. Khaled Ahmed, 'Batting to the Last Ball', *Friday Times*, 1 May 2020, https://www.thefridaytimes.com/batting-to-the-last-ball/.

Chapter 23: A Life in Watercolours

1. Khaled Ahmed, 'A Life in Watercolors', *Newsweek Pakistan*, 17 January 2019, https://www.newsweekpakistan.com/a-life-in-watercolors/.
2. Fakir Syed Aijazuddin, *Sketches from a Howdah: Charlotte, Lady Canning's Tours: 1858 – 1861* (Harewood, 2018). All the quotes in this chapter are from the same book unless stated otherwise.
3. Ahmed, 'A Life in Watercolors'.

Chapter 25: NAB: The Wrong Road Taken

1. Ahmed, 'An Epitaph for NAB', *Newsweek Pakistan*, 22 July 2020, https://www.newsweekpakistan.com/an-epitaph-for-nab/.
2. Asim Yasin, 'Fake Accounts Case: NAB Arrests Iqbal Z Ahmed', *News International*, 5 September 2019, https://www.thenews.com.pk/print/522516-fake-accounts-case-nab-arrests-iqbal-z-ahmed.
3. Sabir Shah, 'Steps against Corruption Remained Futile in Pakistan's History', *News International*, 20 April 2016, https://www.thenews.com.pk/print/114035-Steps-against-corruption-remainedfutile-in-Pakistans-history.
4. 'Energy Entrepreneur Iqbal Z Ahmed Seeks Fairness and Transparency', *Profit*, 7 November 2019, https://profit.pakistantoday.com.pk/

2019/11/07/energy-entrepreneur-iqbal-z-ahmed-seeks-fairness-and-transparency/.

5. Zafar Bhutta, 'NAB Probe Deters Investment in LNG Market', *Express Tribune*, 10 September 2019, https://tribune.com.pk/story/2053194/nab-probe-deters-investment-lng-market.
6. Imtiaz Ali, 'NAB Has "Perfected" Procedures to Yield Excellent Results in Graft Cases, Says Chairman', *Dawn*, 24 October 2019, https://www.dawn.com/news/1512485.
7. Maryam Malik, 'National Accountability Bureau: Accountable to Nobody', *Express Tribune*, 17 September 2016, https://tribune.com.pk/article/40498/national-accountability-bureau-accountable-to-nobody; Asim Khan, 'NAB's Crusade against Corruption', *Express Tribune*, 1 September 2016, https://tribune.com.pk/story/1174352/nabs-crusade-corruption.
8. 'Court Gives NAB Until Aug 6 to File Final Reference against Abbasi in LNG Case', *Express Tribune*, 3 July 2020, https://tribune.com.pk/story/2253109/court-gives-nab-until-aug-6-to-file-final-reference-against-abbasi-in-lng-case; 'SHC Extends Bail of Shahid Abbasi in PSO Appointment Case', *Nation*, 31 August 2020, https://nation.com.pk/31-Aug-2020/shc-extends-bail-of-shahid-abbasi-in-pso-appointment-case.
9. "57 Billionaires Control 70% of India's Wealth . . . India Is Second Most Unequal Economy after Russia', *Times of India*, 27 January 2017, https://timesofindia.indiatimes.com/blogs/the-interviews-blog/57-billionaires-control-70-of-indias-wealth-india-is-second-most-unequal-economy-after-russia/.
10. Ghulam Abbas, 'Business Tycoons Call on Gen Bajwa As Economy Nosedives', *Pakistan Today*, 3 October 2019, https://www.pakistantoday.com.pk/2019/10/02/business-tycoons-call-on-gen-bajwa-as-economy-nosedives/.
11. I.A. Rehman, 'A Bureaucracy Paralysed', *Dawn*, 31 October 2019, https://epaper.dawn.com/DetailImage.php?StoryImage=31_10_2019_008_005.
12. Khaled Ahmed, 'Bureaucrats" Beef', *Newsweek Pakistan*, 31 December 2019, https://www.newsweekpakistan.com/bureaucrats-beef/.

13. 'Ease of Doing Business in Pakistan 2008–2019 Data', Trading Economics, https://tradingeconomics.com/pakistan/ease-of-doing-business.
14. Ahmed, 'Bureaucrats" Beef'.
15. Ahmed Bilal Mehboob, 'Credibility of Accountability', *Dawn*, 11 November 2019, https://www.dawn.com/news/1515959.
16. Ansar Abbasi, 'Bail Chances for Bureaucrats Brighten after Judiciary's Decisions against NAB', *News International*, 15 December 2019, https://www.thenews.com.pk/print/583746-bail-chances-for-bureaucrats-brighten-after-judiciary-s-decisions-against-nab.
17. Ibid.
18. Ibid.
19. Ibid.
20. 'Khursheed Shah Released from NAB Detention in Assets Case', ARY News, 18 December 2019, https://arynews.tv/en/khursheed-shah-released-from-nab-detention/.
21. Mehboob, 'Credibility of Accountability'.
22. Ibid.
23. Abbasi, 'Bail Chances for Bureaucrats Brighten after Judiciary's Decisions against NAB'.
24. 'An Eye on Excellent Performance of NAB', *News International*, 2 June 2019, https://www.thenews.com.pk/print/488611-an-eye-on-excellent-performance-of-nab.

Chapter 26: Was Jinnah Shia or Sunni, or Descended from Ram?

1. Liaqat H. Merchant, *Jinnah: A Judicial Verdict* (East-West Publishing Company Karachi, 1990).
2. Ibid. See the Introduction.

Epilogue: The Future of Follies

1. F.S. Aijazuddin, 'G-20, or G-2?', *Dawn*, 10 September 2020, https://www.dawn.com/news/1578908

2. Nadeem F. Paracha, 'Smoker's Corner: The Order of Words', *Dawn*, 8 October 2017, https://www.dawn.com/news/1362296
3. Shafqat Mahmood, 'Debating the SNC', 8 September 2020, *News International*, https://www.thenews.com.pk/print/711437-debating-the-snc.
4. Farhat ullah Babar, 'Why a Single National Curriculum Is Dangerous', 17 August 2020, https://pakistan.shafaqna.com/EN/106723.
5. Shaheen Sardar Ali, Javaid Rehman, *Indigenous Peoples and Ethnic Minorities of Pakistan: Constitutional and Legal Perspectives*, (Curzon Press, 2001).
6. A.H. Nayyar, 'Dissecting the Single National Curriculum', *Dawn*, 9 August 2020, https://www.dawn.com/news/1572130.
7. Pervez Hoodbhoy, 'Is It Science or Theology?', *Dawn*, 3 December 2016, https://www.dawn.com/news/1256797.